# *Some* MANCHESTER DOCTORS

*A biographical collection to mark
the 150th anniversary of the*
MANCHESTER MEDICAL SOCIETY
*1834-1984*

# *Some* MANCHESTER DOCTORS

A biographical collection to mark
the 150th anniversary of the
MANCHESTER MEDICAL SOCIETY
*1834-1984*

edited by
## Willis J. Elwood
and
## A. Félicité Tuxford

*Published for the*
**MANCHESTER MEDICAL SOCIETY**
*by*
**MANCHESTER UNIVERSITY PRESS**

Copyright (c) The Manchester Medical Society 1984

Published by Manchester University Press
Oxford Road, Manchester M13 9PL, UK
and 51 Washington Street, Dover,
New Hampshire 03820, USA


British Library Cataloguing in Publication Data

Some Manchester doctors: a biographical
  collection to mark the 150th anniversary of
  the Manchester Medical Society.
  1. Physicians - England - Manchester (Greater
  Manchester) - Biography
  I. Elwood, Willis J.   II. Tuxford, A. Félicité
  610'.92'2    R489.A1
  ISBN 0-7190-1754-8


Library of Congress Cataloguing in Publication Data

Some Manchester doctors.

  "Printed for the Manchester Medical Society."
  Bibliography: p.216
  Includes index.
  1. Physicians - England - Manchester (Greater
  Manchester) - Biography - Addresses, essays, lectures.
  2. Medicine - England - Manchester (Greater Manchester) -
  History - Addresses, essays, lectures.  3. Manchester
  (Greater Manchester) - Biography - Addresses, essays,
  lectures.  4. Manchester Medical Society - History.
  I. Elwood, Willis J.   II. Tuxford, A. Félicité (Ann
  Félicité)   III. Manchester Medical Society.
  R489.A1S6   1984      610'.92'2 [B]        84-20093
  ISBN 0-7190-1754-8


Printed by Unwin Brothers Ltd
The Gresham Press
Old Woking
Surrey

CONTENTS

FOREWORD

by

Professor S W Stanbury, MD, FRCP

Professor of Medicine, University of Manchester

This is the story of the medical men and women of a great city, encapsulated in the history of the first 150 years of one of the country's oldest medical societies. It is also a part of the history of that city - or rather of two great cities, since Manchester and Salford merge inextricably together and with much of Lancashire and Cheshire in the evolution of the story. It tells of some who were largely responsible for the foundation of their disciplines - in cardiology, neurosurgery, radiology and prosthetic surgery of the hip; and others who contributed greatly to the health and welfare of their native or adopted city; or reached fame in the universities and the Royal Colleges. There are detailed biographies of doctors who achieved eminence in their several fields and contributed to the stature of the Manchester School of Medicine. We read of pioneers in public health, and in the care of the mentally ill and of those in childbirth; of a great environmentalist, an internationally renowned bibliophile, a medical architect of hospital design. Brief biographical notes on many others are appetitive and a tribute to the Editors' skill in selecting the representative few for more comprehensive description.

In this epitome of local medical history there is much of which any Mancunian can be proud, be he a medical man, a citizen of Greater Manchester or a member of its universities. The contemporary doctor and the medical student should take heart from the story. At a time of dismay and potential disillusionment in the profession with the threat to this country's greatest ever medical achievement - the National Health Service - it reminds us that the strength of a caring profession lies now, as always, in the quality of its individual members. Fellows of the Manchester Medical Society might be reminded too that its original Articles of Agreement aimed at preventing dissolution of the Society before the term of 999 years. With them is the responsibility of ensuring that apathy does not convert this splendid epitome into the Society's epitaph!

S W STANBURY

Department of Medicine
University of Manchester
The Royal Infirmary
Manchester M13 9WL

## ACKNOWLEDGEMENTS

A glance at the list of contributors which follows is sufficient to indicate that this commemorative volume is the work of many hands. Our thanks are due to them all – both to those who were able to write of individuals and events they could remember, and to those who required to search the literature in order to bring to life people and happenings before their time. We are indebted to the late Dr William Brockbank both for what he has written specially for this book, and also to him and to the Manchester University Press for permission to republish his essay on Sir Geoffrey Jefferson.

Advice and help has been freely given from many sources – from the staff of the John Rylands University Library of Manchester (University Librarian: Dr M A Pegg) particularly Mr David F Cook (now retired) and Mrs Jackie Sen; from Mr John V Pickstone of the University of Manchester Institute of Science and Technology Department of History of Science & Technology; from other bodies such as the Libraries of the Royal Colleges both in England and in Edinburgh and the Master of the Worshipful Society of Apothecaries of London; from Mrs Charlotte Beswick; from Miss Georgina Miller; and from Miss P M Leech, daughter of the Society's centenary president.

The work would have required for its accomplishment far more labour than it did if the 'Manchester collection' had not been in existence. This remarkable collection, initiated by Dr E Bosdin Leech (1875–1950), comprises biographical details of thousands of medical men and women who worked in the area of which Manchester is the centre. It is housed (not on open access) in the John Rylands University Library of Manchester.

For the production of the book our thanks are due to the Manchester University Press; to the excellent word-processing support made available to us by Miss Brenda High through Mr T Graham H Davies of the Manchester Oral Research Unit of the Colgate-Palmolive Company, and to the Photographic Department of the John Rylands University Library under the direction of Mr J Witterance.

WILLIS J ELWOOD

A FELICITE TUXFORD

Manchester Medical Society
John Rylands University Library
Oxford Road
Manchester M13 9PP

LIST OF CONTRIBUTORS

AFT    = Dr Ann Félicité Tuxford, MD
         Lecturer in bacteriology
         University of Manchester

AMH    = Dr Anne M Holmes, MB, ChB, BSc, FRCP
         Consultant physician, Salford

ARH    = Professor A R Hunter, MSc, MD, FRCS, FFA RCS, DA
         Emeritus Professor of anaesthetics
         University of Manchester

BW     = Dr B Wolman, MD, FRCP, DCH
         Consultant paediatrician, Manchester

DAKB   = Sir Douglas A K Black, MD, FRCP
         Emeritus Professor of medicine
         University of Manchester

ECE    = Professor E C Easson (1915-1983), CBE, MD, MSc, FRCP, DMRT,
         FRCR
         Emeritus Professor of radiotherapy
         University of Manchester

EGW    = Dr E Geoffrey Wade, BSc, MD, FRCP
         Consultant physician, Manchester

FAL    = Professor F A Langley, MSc, MD, FRCOG, FRCPath
         Emeritus Professor of obstetrical & gynaecological pathology
         University of Manchester

FBB    = Dr F B Beswick, MB, ChB
         Bursar, University of Manchester

GAGM   = Professor G A G Mitchell, OBE, TD, MB, ChM, DSc, FRCS
         Emeritus Professor of anatomy
         University of Manchester

HLF    = Dr H L Freeman, MSc, MA, BM, BCh, FRCPsych, DPM
         Consultant psychiatrist, Salford

HP     = Sir Harry Platt Bt, LLD, MD, MS, FRCS
         Emeritus Professor of orthopaedic surgery, University of
         Manchester
         Honorary president,
         International Federation of Surgical Colleges

HWA    = Dr H W Ashworth, BSc, MD, FRCGP
         General practitioner, Manchester

II     = Professor Ian Isherwood, MB, ChB, DMRD, MRCP, FFRRCSI (Hon),
         FRCR
         Professor of diagnostic radiology
         University of Manchester

JD       = Dr James Davson, MB, BS, FRCPath
           Curator of the Museum
           Department of Pathology and Pathological Anatomy
           University of Manchester

JEH      = Dr J E Horrocks, JP, MB, ChB, FRCPath
           Consultant pathologist (retired)

JHJ      = Professor J Harold Jones, MD, MSc, FFDRCSI, FRCPath
           Professor of oral medicine and Dean of the Turner Dental
           School, University of Manchester

JKH      = Mr J K Holt, MSc, FDS RCS, DDS
           Forensic odontologist and consultant dental surgeon
           Manchester

JLB      = Dr J L Burn, MB, ChB, FRCP, DCH
           Consultant paediatrician, Bolton

JM       = Mrs Joan Mottram, BA
           Department of History of Science and Technology
           University of Manchester Institute of Science and Technology

KH       = Mr K Harrison, MD, FRCS, DLO
           Consultant ear, nose and throat surgeon, Manchester

KW       = Mrs Katherine Webb, BA, Dip.Archiv.
           Department of History of Science and Technology
           University of Manchester Institute of Science and Technology

LD       = Dr Leslie Doyle, FRCPI, DCH
           Consultant physician, Manchester

LT       = Mr Leslie Turner, MD, FRCS
           Consultant surgeon, Manchester

NFK      = Mr N F Kirkman, MD, FRCS
           Consultant surgeon (retired)

NJdeVM = Dr N J de V Mather, MA, MB, ChB, FRCPsych, DPM
           Consultant psychiatrist (retired)

RIM      = Dr R I Mackay, BSc, MB, ChB, FRCP, DCH
           Consultant paediatrician (retired)

RMS      = Dr R M Stirland, MD, MA, FRCPath
           Consultant bacteriologist, Manchester

RWB      = Dr R W Burslem, MD, FRCOG
           Consultant obstetrician and gynaecologist, Manchester

SO       = Dr S Oleesky, MSc, MD, FRCP
           Consultant physician, Manchester

TM       = Mr Thomas Moore, MD, MS, FRCS
           Honorary consultant urologist, Manchester

WB      = Dr William Brockbank (1900-1984), TD, MSc (Hon), MA, MD, FRCP
          Consultant physician (retired)

WJE     = Dr Willis J Elwood, MB, BCh, BAO, FFCM, DPH
          Honorary Secretary, Manchester Medical Society
          Specialist in community medicine, Salford

WME     = Dr W M Elder, O St J, TD, QHP, MB, ChB, MFOM
          Regional medical officer,
          Central Electricity Generating Board

WPP     = Dr W P Povey, MSc, MRCS, LRCP, FFCM, DPH, D Obst RCOG
          District medical officer, Central Manchester Health Authority

WWW     = Mr W Weatherston Wilson, ChM, FRCS
          Surgeon emeritus, Wigan

## EDITORS' ADDENDUM

Dr William Brockbank died on 12 March 1984 while this book was in press. The Medical Society owes a great deal to him: he was mainly responsible for the amalgamation of the five societies in 1950 which is described in chapter 3; since 1930 he served as a member of Council, as Honorary Secretary, as President of the Section of Medicine and as President of the Society; and he was made an Honorary Fellow in 1973.

Born in Manchester in 1900, and trained in Cambridge and Manchester, he was, like his father Edward Mansfield Brockbank (1866-1959) an honorary physician to the Manchester Royal Infirmary. Besides his publications on his main clinical interest - chest disease - he will be remembered for his book *Portrait of a hospital, 1752-1948* (Heinemann, 1952) which was written to commemorate the bi-centenary of the Manchester Royal Infirmary, for *The Honorary Medical Staff of the Manchester Royal Infirmary, 1830-1948* (Manchester University Press, 1965) and for many shorter papers of historical interest.

Long after his official retirement from clinical work he died in harness as honorary archivist and keeper to the John Rylands University Library after three months in hospital following a fall.

WJE/AFT

LIST OF ILLUSTRATIONS

ChAPTER 1

THE MANCHESTER MEDICAL SOCIETY, 1834-1950

## Beginnings

There was no Medical Society in Manchester a hundred and fifty years ago. The nearest thing was the Literary and Philosophical Society which had been started in 1781 by two members of the Infirmary staff, Doctors Thomas Percival and Thomas Henry, together with the Minister of the Unitarian Cross Street Chapel, the Reverend Thomas Barnes. Thirteen of the Society's twenty-four founders were medical men and one of them, Dr Peter Mainwaring, then eighty-five years old, was elected one of the two Joint Presidents for its first year with James Massey, Treasurer of the Infirmary, as the other. Dr Percival became the sole President after a year and held the post for thirty-three years. Many of the Vice-Presidents were members of the Faculty, as the medical profession was then called, and it was much the same with the two secretaries. The first four communications to the Society were given by medical men on general subjects and sixteen of the first twenty-eight. Gradually with the advent of Dalton and Joule, science took over from medicine.

In spite of the need for a purely medical society it was not until fifty years after the foundation of the 'Lit. and Phil.' that any move was made. Then, at a public meeting in the York Hotel on 29 January 1834, with Dr Hull, an obstetrician, in the Chair, it was agreed to form an association of members of the medical profession residing in the North of England and also to provide a medical library and reading room. It was agreed that a canvass be undertaken of the whole profession living in and around Manchester. Things moved slowly until

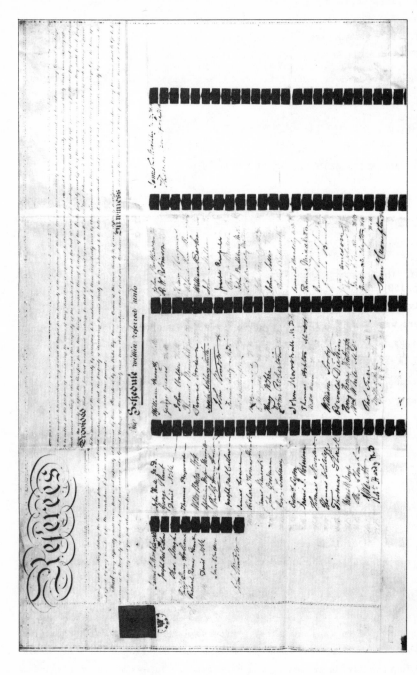

1. This photograph shows just the concluding sentences, the seals and the signatures of those who put their name to a formidable document – the Articles of Agreement of the Manchester Medical Society – in 1835. See chapter 1.

Joseph Peel Catlow, a general practitioner, and John Walker, a surgeon in the Eye Hospital, finally determined to do the job. Accordingly the following document was drawn up for signature:

> The necessity of a Medical Library, Reading Room, and Society having been acknowledged at a public meeting ... we the undersigned agree to support such a Library, Reading Room and Society for the use of the members of the medical profession resident in Manchester and its vicinity.

The main conditions of agreement were that the payment of a premium of a guinea entrance and an annual subscription of one guinea constitute an ordinary member and ten guineas a life member. For double the annual subscription and life membership fee there was to be the privilege of taking out at one time a double allowance of books.

Dr Catlow and Dr Walker actually paid 230 calls within a fortnight, those men being away, or ill, being called on two or three times. The results of this canvass are set forth in detail in the *Journal of the Proceedings of the Medical Society* with the names of all the doctors, over 150 in number, and their answers to the canvass are recorded individually and faithfully. Many declined to support the proposal. Others were half-hearted. Much credit must be given to the canvassers. If they had failed the scheme would probably have fallen through. There was sufficient support to call a meeting of those favourable and at it the first Council was elected with John Hull as President. A small council was appointed to find a suitable room for a Library. They made an arrangement with Mr Boond to rent a room for £30 a year at 40 Faulkner Street close to the back of the Royal Infirmary, which was then on the site now occupied by the Piccadilly Gardens. The room was opened at 9 a.m. on 1 October 1834. Mrs Boond was appointed Librarian at a yearly salary of £5. The first meeting was held there on that date but Dr Hull was prevented from giving his introductory address until 15 October. Unfortunately we do not know his subject for the papers are lost. Ninety-one members' names appear in the first list published in 1835. In that year very elaborate Articles of Agreement were drawn up. The object as stated in them was to prevent the Society from being dissolved before the term of 999 years unless such dissolution was decided on by two extraordinary general meetings of members called for the purpose and at an interval of one month. (This requirement was never mentioned in 1947 when an unsuccessful attempt to dissolve the Society was made.)

## The first hundred years

Memories of former public medical disputes may have led to a resolution being passed at an early meeting of the Society to the effect that 'no reporters from the daily press should attend the meetings and that no papers or proceedings should be published without the consent of the Society'. After a year Mr Boond was given notice to quit his tenancy and although this did not happen the question of finding permanent quarters owned by the Society was gone into carefully and fully. This proved impracticable and arrangements were made to secure the use of two rooms in 1845 at an annual rental of £35 in the Royal Institution in Moseley Street, now the Art Gallery, then the home of several societies. The larger room was for meetings, the smaller for the Library.

For some reason not stated it was decided to discontinue the office of President. The Treasurer, John Windsor, a successful general practitioner, took the chair from 1850 to 1859 when the office of President was restored and Dr Windsor appointed to it. In 1856 the Society was at its lowest ebb, the income for the year being less than £27. Not a single book was bought. One fourth of the books needed rebinding. The reading room was uncomfortable and only six or nine members attended the Society's meetings. Dr Samuel Crompton, a physician at Salford Royal Hospital, then became Secretary from 1856 to 1858 and by his energy raised £55 in subscriptions to clear off a debt and the income rose to £112 in 1858 and from this time the affairs of the Society took a turn for the better. The cost of the Library was causing concern and an appeal for help was addressed to the general public in 1859;

> but not one poor little duodecimo was received in response. Yet it is obvious that the existence of such an important reference library of medical literature is a matter of personal interest to every citizen as a means of enabling the professional advisors of the community to acquaint themselves with the advances made from time to time in the science and practice of medicine. Everything that tends to raise the scientific character of the medical profession is, in the long run, an indisputable gain to the public at large.

So Dr Charles Cullingworth recalled, writing in 1876.

With improved fortunes the Library grew rapidly in size, the number of volumes in 1866 being 7,890 and double this in 1875. By then the accommodation at the Royal Institution had become too limited for comfort. An opportunity for a change arose in 1872 when the Manchester Royal School of Medicine and Surgery in Pine Street, close to the Infirmary, amalgamated with Owens College about the time of its removal to its present site on Oxford Road with the intention of building a Medical School. It was seen that it would be a great advantage to the Society if it could find suitable accommodation there. Negotiations were therefore entered into, chiefly through the initiative of Thomas Windsor, John's son, who saw the great advantage which a close association with a school of medicine would be to the Society and its members. The College offering suitable terms and accommodation, an amalgamation of interests between it and the Society was satisfactorily arranged. Windsor superintended the removal of the books to their new quarters and on completion of the whole transaction received a special vote of thanks for his services in the matter. He should have received another as will be seen shortly, but did not do so.

## The Society at Owens College

The Medical School at Owens College was fortunate to begin life with a top class medical library even if it was on loan. In the Deed of Agreement the Council of the College undertook to provide accommodation for the Society's Library and a reading room and lecture theatre for its meetings. It also agreed to contribute an annual sum of £100 to the funds of the Society which was to manage the library and pay all other expenses of maintenance. Its members were to have free access to and use of the medical museum and its contents. On the other hand the members of the Council, the professors, lecturers and medical students were to have the right of access to and use of the library but to have none of the other privileges of membership of the Society. An important clause was that if the Society were to be dissolved at any time the library was to be retained by the College, in trust for use of the members of the medical profession residing in or near Manchester provided always that under no circumstances was the library to be dissolved or parted or the books sold separately.

While the Society was evidently pleased with the accommodation at the College for its Library, some disappointment was felt with that

provided for the reading room. It was too small and eventually became
the Librarian's room. Moreover many members, especially those living
in the north of the town, missed the convenience of the Moseley Street
quarters. There were no motor cars in those days and the buses were
drawn by horses. Some meetings were held in the centre of the town but
they were not successful enough to be worth the cost of hiring the
rooms. The 1881 report stated that plans for a new reading room to
hold seventy members and one for the students were being prepared, but
it was two years before they were ready for use as we knew them before
the new Medical School was built. They were opened on 6 November 1883
in the Jubilee year of the Society's existence during the Presidency
of Dr D J Leech. The important event was celebrated by a soirée to
which 800 guests were invited. The Committee's report for the year
states that 'if the execution of the promise made in 1875 in the Deed
of Agreement had been somewhat tardy, it had finally been accomplished
on a magnificent scale and with a liberality that is beyond praise'.

In spite of this view dissatisfaction persisted on and off for many
years and the idea was mooted of building a place for the Society or
finding a room in the centre of the town in telephonic communication
with the College so that books could be sent down on request from the
Library. The latter plan was tried but was only used by eight town and
four country members. In the 1880s a central medical institute in
which the library should be located would have cost £10,000 to build
and an extra £300 annually to run. This was impracticable. In 1889 the
upkeep of the Library, which contained 31,736 volumes, cost £352 and
the income, excluding the £100 grant from the College, was only £347.
Time had shown the move to Owens College was indeed a beneficial one
for both parties to it and for the promotion of medical knowledge.

In 1883 the Society unfortunately lost the services and help of
Thomas Windsor. A top-class eye surgeon, his immortal fame rests on
his hobby of collecting old medical and scientific books. He was
honorary librarian to the Society from 1858 for twenty-five years.
Under his supervision the number of volumes and pamphlets rose from
2,558 in 1858 to 12,954 five years later. He had conceived the idea of
transferring the library to Owens College and superintended its
removal. But differences of opinion arose between him and the library
committee culminating in his resignation in 1883. He had, for years,
had a free hand in the purchase of old medical books and often

returned from his annual holiday abroad with a sackful for which he had paid five pounds. It is unlikely that in any other library had such valuable purchases been made at so little cost and the credit was entirely due to Thomas Windsor. During eight years he had added over ten thousand volumes to the library at an average cost of 2s 2½d (eleven pence) a volume. Many of these volumes are now worth three and four figures and are the glory and strength of our library. The library Committee objected to this waste of money on old books. They wanted contemporary ones. So he resigned and collected for the great library at Washington where he is regarded as one of their greatest benefactors. (Manchester's loss was Washington's great gain.)

In January 1900 the Owens College authorities gave notice to terminate the existing agreement probably because the Society's funds had passed from a debit balance of £21 in 1893 to a credit balance of £385 in 1899 in spite of having spent in the four previous years 70 per cent of its income on the library alone. It should be noted that the £100 paid by the College had gone into the general account of the Society and any books and periodicals purchased with it became the property of the Society. After negotiations it was agreed that the College should pay £50 for 1900 and £50 for 1901 and after that give no monetary payment. The other clauses of the agreement were to remain as before. In 1902 the condition of the books was examined and large numbers were found to be in need of rebinding, the cost of which would have wiped out the credit balance. A considerable sum was, however, spent on rebinding and the credit balance fell in 1904 to £99. In that year the College was raised to the status of a university and became the University of Manchester.

In 1905 with the surgeon, Mr (later Sir William) Thorburn President, a better arrangement was made with the Council of the University which then saw more clearly the importance to the Medical School and to research workers of an efficient reference library of medical literature. By it £200 was allowed for the purchase of books and periodicals which were to become the property of the University. In this way, the medical library of the University began its existence. The Society undertook to spend not less than 70 per cent of its own income on the library and continued to do so until the constantly increasing number and cost of books and periodicals (most of which were chiefly valuable for research purposes) and the need for increased library staff threw much too heavy a financial burden on it. The Council of the University in 1920 recognising these facts increased its grant to £500 but it wasn't enough.

Matters were brought to a crisis when in 1927 the library sub-committee asked for increased accommodation for the books. The Council for the University replied with a request for definite information about the prospect of the books belonging to the Society being at some future date removed to a medical institute in town. The matter was carefully considered for two years and it was decided that a move was impossible. It was also felt that the best place for such a valuable collection of medical literature - the most valuable outside London - was at the University where it was in daily use by research workers. Such being the case and because of financial considerations it was finally decided to offer to present the library to the University. The conditions of the offer were that the Society should have the permanent use of suitable rooms at the University, that its members should continue to have the right of access to and use of the library as they had always had, that it should pay 70 per cent of its income from subscriptions towards the cost of maintenance of the library so long as the Society made its headquarters in the Medical School and that the University should be responsible for the remaining cost of the library. If the Society ever moved its headquarters it was to pay ten per cent of its subscription income for the continued privilege of access to the library. The University expressed its willingness to accept the offer on terms very favourable to members of the Society including the right of access to the Christie Library. They were mutually agreed upon. Legal opinion was taken on the right of the Society to dispose of its property in such a manner. It was quite within its power to do so. The formal transfer of the library took place on 24 October 1930, at a meeting of the Society with representatives of the University Council including the Chancellor, Vice-Chancellor and Chairman of Council. The President of the Society, Mr Howson Ray, FRCS offered the library to the University. A brief account of its contents was given. The Chancellor in accepting the offer thanked the Society for the handsome gift, the value of which the University fully appreciated and he expressed the determination of the Council to maintain the library in its very worthy condition.

The terms which had been agreed were written into a formal

2. The Presidential chair of the Manchester Medical Society – a fine piece of craftsmanship, which was provided from the bequest to the Society of Dr Richard Walter Marsden who had been President in the session 1928–29.

agreement between the Victoria University of Manchester and the Manchester Medical Society which was dated 13 November 1930. This also provided that 'the Library shall be managed by a Committee to consist of five representatives nominated by the University and three representatives nominated by the Society'. One might note that, so far as the medical section of the University Library is concerned, this management arrangement has continued for over fifty years: further comment will be reserved for Chapter 6.

## The centenary

As the centenary year of the Society approached a small committee was appointed on 17 January 1933 to make the necessary arrangements. It consisted of Professors Stopford and Telford, Dr Bosdin Leech (President Elect) and Mr Wilson, the Librarian. They held many meetings, asked E M Brockbank and his son, and others, to join them and in the end they produced the following programme.

The Centenary meeting was to be held on Wednesday afternoon 3 October 1934 in the Physiology Theatre almost exactly on the same date as the first meeting a hundred years earlier. There were to be a good number of guests who would be made honorary members of the Society. Then the President would give his address on some local medical history.

A dinner with many guests would be held in the Midland Hotel. There would be a Centenary Service in the Cathedral the following Sunday. It was thought the cost would be between £100 and £150. Each Member of the Society would be asked to pay ten shillings and the Society could contribute up to £100 if necessary. A distinguished guest would be asked to speak on a medical subject. Eventually the choice fell on Dr Nixon of Bristol who addressed the Society in November on medical service in the Mercantile Fleet in olden times.

There were two other decisions: 1) to hold an exhibition of books and paintings in the Exhibition Hall in the recently opened Manchester Central Reference Library, and 2) Dr E M Brockbank was asked to write a book on the history of the Society. Almost at the last moment the BBC agreed to broadcast the two main speeches at the dinner from 9.15 to 9.45 p.m. prompt. This was to cause much anxiety to the writer who had been made responsible for the dinner.

## The centenary meeting

This was to start at 4.15 p.m. with the election of the six Honorary Members. The principal one was the University's Chancellor, the Earl of Crawford and Balcarres who made an unexpected and rather long witty speech of thanks, more like an after-dinner speech. This upset the vital time schedule right at the start. When he rose, Dr Bosdin Leech, the Centenary President, said that he intended to present to the Society his collection of books by, and papers concerning, Manchester doctors. He then proceeded to give his Presidential Address on 'Some picturesque episodes of Manchester medical history' dealing mainly with the Prince Charlie affair of 1745. This was Bosdin Leech at his best. The meeting ended rather late and it was a rush to get home, change into evening dress with decorations and reach the Midland Hotel by 7.15 for 7.30 but it was managed.

## The dinner

Tickets were fifteen shillings (75 pence of modern money). Two hundred and thirty-three members and guests were present and it was a worthy menu:

Huitres Whitstable
Hors d'Oeuvre Riche
**
Consommé Royal
Creme Parisienne
**
Zéphyr de Sole Waleska
**
Noisette d'Agneau Périgourdine
Pommes Croquettes
Timbale de Petits Pois Rodel
**
Faisan Roti à la Broche
Salade Suzette
**
Pêches Glacées Mignon
Petits Fours
**
Moka

The hotel management knew the broadcast had to start at 9.15 sharp and they played their part nobly. The writer had chosen to sit at the end of one of the tables next to the BBC representative where he could be 'got at' if anything went wrong.  It did.  Praise be, Lord Crawford rose promptly at 9.15 to propose the toast of the Manchester Medical Society. He had been allowed fifteen minutes but he sat down after two. Presumably he reckoned he had made his speech in the afternoon. I thought the BBC man was going to black out. He said the third speaker would have to go on the air. This was Professor Ramsbottom proposing the toast of 'Our Guests'. I raced round the tables to warn him while Leech was speaking. He jibbed for a moment. I said there was no alternative and, being the person he was, he agreed and did the job splendidly.

## The service

By invitation of the Dean this took place at 3.30 p.m. on Sunday, 7 October 1934. The preacher was the Right Reverend Cecil Wilson, Lord Bishop of Middleton. There was a good congregation.

## The exhibition

This was a great success, visited daily by hundreds of the general public for whom it was really intended. There were portraits of distinguished local doctors borrowed from the Art Gallery and various hospitals with a short biographical note about each. There was a series of pictures showing the growth of the Royal Infirmary. There was an exhibition of books and pamphlets concerning the great vaccination controversy and the ravages of smallpox. Many of the old and now valuable books bought by Thomas Windsor, the glory of the Medical Library, were shown, also Braid's book on hypnotism and Blackley's on hay fever. They were local general practitioners. The exhibition was opened in the afternoon of 1 October by Walter Cobbett, Chairman of the Board of Management of the Royal Infirmary. It remained on view for three weeks.

## The history of the Society

Dr E M Brockbank's book was published in 1934 under the title *A centenary history of the Manchester Medical Society with biographical notices of its first President, Secretaries and Honorary Librarian*. It has supplied the information used in the early part of this chapter.

Afterwards

The Centenary brought important changes to the Library and the Society. Two showcases were bought for the former. One, to house the book of the month, was made so that it could show the Library's largest book, *Albinus's Anatomy*, fully opened. The other case was longer and was intended to show a group of books and pictures. The contents of the cases were changed once a month thereafter.

Unlike most kindred societies ours had no motto, no emblem and no presidential badge to be worn at its meetings or on official visits to other Societies, or public receptions. During the celebrations when there were many decorated visitors this want of a distinguishing mark of honour for its President was especially conspicuous and the committee decided to put this right. A letter was sent to The Observer headed 'Wanted a Motto'. It read:

> Can any of your readers suggest a suitable short motto in Latin or English for a Medical Society? This Society was founded a hundred years ago to patch up the quarrels prevalent among the doctors of the period. It created and built up an important medical library and holds scientific meetings once a month. Any suggestions will be most welcome.

They came in, and the committee chose 'Fovet Medicinam Concordia'. Various designs were submitted for the emblem. The committee chose a crest which tradition says was granted with a Coat of Arms by Edward III to John the Leche, a doctor to the Black Prince. It had a medical origin very much in tune with the Leech family, for Daniel John had been President in the Society's fiftieth year and Ernest Bosdin had been its Centenary President.

The adoption of an emblem and motto of such a nature having been decided on by the committee, Dr Leech expressed a wish on behalf of himself and his wife to present a presidential badge to the Society – a very generous offer which was gratefully accepted. On completion of the handsome and impressive design embodying both emblem and motto in gold and enamel, the badge was presented by Mrs Leech to Mr Garnett Wright, President of the Society and worn by him at the Annual Meeting of 5 May 1937.

WB

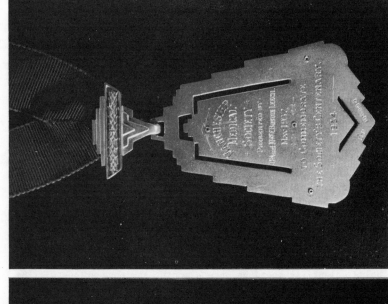

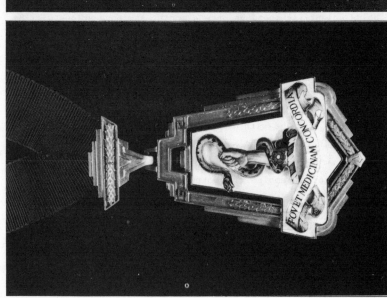

3 and 4. The obverse and reverse of the beautiful presidential medallion which was presented to the Manchester Medical Society by Dr and Mrs E Bosdin Leech to mark the centenary of the Society in 1934 and first worn by Mr Garnett Wright at the Annual General Meeting on 5 May 1937. See chapter 1.

CHAPTER 2

THE SOCIETIES WHICH MERGED WITH THE MANCHESTER MEDICAL SOCIETY IN 1950

It is necessary now to give some information about four independent societies which for varying lengths of time had co-existed with the Manchester Medical Society and which - as will be related in chapter 3 - merged with it in 1950. These were: the Manchester Surgical Society, founded in 1922; the Pathological Society of Manchester, founded (as an off-shoot of the Manchester Medical Society) in 1885; the Manchester & District Society of Anaesthetists, founded in 1946; and the Manchester Odontological Society, founded in 1885.

## The Manchester Surgical Society, 1922-50[1,2]

Surgical conditions naturally formed part of the regular proceedings of the Manchester Medical Society before 1922. Sir Harry Platt, for example, has recalled a meeting on acute appendicitis which was held before he graduated in 1909.

The formation of the Manchester Surgical Society was not a new conception, but the maturing to independence of one speciality. Sir Harry Platt has written of ill feeling after the first World War between the staffs of the Manchester Royal Infirmary and those of the non-teaching hospitals. As many had served together in the second North Western General Hospital locally or abroad, this was surprising. It had however been the practice for many years at the Manchester Royal Infirmary that only those who had held certain junior surgical appointments in the hospital were eventually elected to the honorary consultant staff. None of the surgical members of the staffs of Salford Royal Hospital and Ancoats Hospital had held the necessary appointments and were, therefore, unlikely eventually to succeed to the teaching hospital staff. At that time members of the staff of both the non-teaching hospitals were holding teaching classes for FRCS candidates with considerable success and had applied to the University for recognition as teachers of surgery.

It was against this background that local surgeons from teaching and non-teaching hospitals met at the Manchester Royal Infirmary on 24 April 1922 to discuss the formation of a Surgical Society. The idea was well received. A small executive committee was formed to draft a constitution and by-laws. No time was lost. On 18 May 1922, the executive committee met at the consulting rooms of Mr A H Burgess. A draft of the constitution and by-laws was presented by Mr H Platt and approved with minor alterations.

A full meeting was held at the Manchester Royal Infirmary on the 29 May 1922. Mr A H Burgess explained from the Chair the proposed constitution and by-laws which were accepted. He then proposed the following resolution:

> That this meeting declares that a Society to be called the 'Manchester Surgical Society' is hereby constituted and that the following surgeons will be the original members thereof:-  A.H. Burgess; H. Buck; J.B. Buckley; W.R. Douglas; J. Gow; E.E. Hughes; W.H. Hey; G. Jefferson; R.R. Kerr; J. Morley; J.B. MacAlpine; R. Ollerenshaw; H. Platt; H.H. Rayner; C. Roberts; J.H. Ray; J.W. Smith; A.H. Southam; E.D. Telford; G. Wright; P.R. Wrigley; and G.B. Warburton.

It was a total of 22. Mr A H Burgess was elected President; G B Warburton, Treasurer; H Platt, Honorary Secretary and H H Rayner and G Wright, Committee Members.

It was also agreed that not more than one member from each special branch of surgery in the Manchester Hospitals should be invited to join the Society. Those to be invited were:-

| | |
|---|---|
| Manchester Royal Infirmary | Sir William Milligan - E.N.T. |
| | W.E. Fothergill - |
| | Obstetrics and Gynaecology. |
| Salford Royal Hospital | H. Clifford - |
| | Obstetrics and Gynaecology. |
| | A.A. Smalley - E.N.T. |
| Ancoats Hospital | F.H. Diggle - E.N.T. |
| Manchester Children's Hospital | J.A. Jones - E.N.T. |
| St Mary's Hospital | W.F. Shaw - |
| | Obstetrics and Gynaecology. |
| Manchester Ear Hospital | D.L. Sewell - E.N.T. |
| Northern Hospital | G.W. Fitzgerald - |
| | Obstetrics and Gynaecology. |

One member of the staff of each of the following Hospitals was also
to be invited:

| | | |
|---|---|---|
| Ashton-under-Lyne | - M. Mamourian | A G.P. and a surgeon. |
| Blackburn | - R.G. Aitken | Former G.P. afterwards consultant surgeon. |
| Burnley | - J.H. Watson | Former G.P. afterwards consultant surgeon. |
| Rochdale | - J.C. Jefferson | Former G.P. afterwards consultant surgeon. |
| Southport | - G.R. Anderson | A G.P. who was very much involved in local politics. |
| Altrincham | - P.R. Cooper | G.P. |
| Bolton | - R.D. Mothersole | G.P. |
| Macclesfield | - J.H. Marsh | G.P. |
| Preston | - F.W. Collinson | Consultant in medicine and surgery, but very much involved in public life. |

Mr F A Southam, Sir William Thorburn and Professor A Donald were to be
elected honorary members. All the invitees accepted but Dr G R
Anderson, Southport, soon opted out because of heavy local
commitments. The Society therefore had an initial membership of
thirty-nine.

By 1928 the membership had risen to 74 including 34 active, 7
honorary and 28 associate members, demonstrating the enthusiasm and
wise counsels of the elected officers and committees, but particularly
of the secretary, H Platt. Undoubtedly the prime stimulant in the
formation of the Manchester Surgical Society in 1922, he had been able
to draw on his previous experience in the formation of the British
Orthopaedic Association in 1918 to frame a draft constitution which
was readily accepted by the elected temporary executive committee, and
the subsequent full formal meeting of the Society. It was also decided
to protect the future standard of members by instituting a category of
Associate Member to accommodate those more junior surgeons who were of
the right calibre and likely eventually to become full members. The
first to be elected were: P McEvedy of Ancoats Hospital as a full
member; and W Briggs of Blackburn Royal Infirmary and S R Wilson,
Anaesthetist at Manchester Royal Infirmary, as associate members.

A general pattern of an annual programme of meetings with papers,
discussions, one or two clinical meetings, the occasional operation
meeting and visits to fellow Societies in Liverpool or Leeds was soon
established. Mr Harry Platt, the Honorary Secretary of the Society
from 1922-30, was undoubtedly the architect of its foundation and

success. He arranged the programmes so that all branches of surgery were represented and those with special interests were kept informed by attending meetings. In the improved general atmosphere between the groups previously apart, all members realised that there was much to learn from private discussion with colleagues and the good-natured banter in the discussions, whereby lessons were learned by contemporaries and seniors alike.

The following examples may be taken as typical of the meetings held during the years of activity of the Society:

| | | | |
|---|---|---|---|
| 24 October | 1922 | Mr A.H. Burgess | Presidential address – some remarks on exploratory laparotomy. |
| 12 December | 1922 | Mr M. Mamourian | Massive excision of diseased bone, followed by early bone grafting. |
| | | Mr H.H. Rayner | After results of gastrectomy for ulcer. |
| 23 January | 1923 | The first of the | Society's 'Operations at home' meetings, at which all the operating theatres at Manchester Royal Infirmary were used. |
| 17 April | 1923 | Mr F.H. Diggle | Laryngo-fissure for carcinoma of the larynx. |
| | | Mr J. Morley | Relation of gastric ulcer to gastric carcinoma. |
| | | Mr J.B. Buckley | Causation and treatment of femoral hernia. |
| 23 October | 1923 | Mr E.D. Telford | Presidential address – The surgeon and the physiologist. |

At the meeting on 18 October 1938 Mr (later Sir) Geoffrey Jefferson gave his presidential address on 'Neurosurgery as a speciality'. The final meeting of the 1938-9 session was held on the 21 March 1939. Because of the second world war, meetings were not resumed until 13 November 1945. On that occasion Mr H T Cox, a surgeon on the staff of Withington Hospital read a paper on 'The Treatment of Carcinoma of the Prostate by Transurethral Resection and Stilboestrol'. To the writer, as one who had been for some years away from civilian surgery, the results were a revelation, almost magic. Of 26 cases with retention of urine, all were relieved – Mr Cox being an expert in the technique. Three patients who had been bedridden for up to three months with severe pain and one who had paraplegia due to spinal metastases were relieved within three to seven days by the endocrine treatment, and the paraplegic patient was eventually able to walk, to return to work

and live for two and a half years. The great advances in the treatment
of the disease during the war years were astonishing.

Another memorable meeting was  held on the 14 February 1950. The
subject was 'Tumours of the Bladder' and the speakers were Dr D S
Poole Wilson, consultant urologist, Dr Helen Russell, consultant
pathologist, Dr J M Gibson and J L Millin, consultant radiotherapists,
all of the Christie Hospital and Holt Radium Institute. It was a very
good meeting at which the results of treatment by radiotherapy were
presented and a very full discussion followed.

The Manchester Surgical Society played a very important role in
bringing all North Western surgeons together and initiating
improvements in practice, social, administrative and technical. Annual
contributions were regularly made to the Medical Benevolent Fund and
to the Medical Library for the purchase of books. In 1928, through the
initiative and persistence of Dr E Bosdin Leech (later to become the
centenary president of the Manchester Medical Society) certain relics
of the great surgeon John Hunter (1728-93) were acquired by the
Manchester Surgical Society. These were his grandfather clock, the
silver seal of his diploma of the fellowship of the Royal College of
Surgeons of Ireland and his dinner bell. At a ceremony on Founder's
Day, 15 May 1929 these relics were presented to the University of
Manchester by Colonel F H Westmacott on behalf of the Manchester
Surgical Society, Dr E Bosdin Leech and Mr Harry Platt. A stipulation
which had been made by the Society and accepted by the University was
that 'in the event of the ... Society removing ... to suitable
accommodation for the proper housing and care of the relics,
favourable consideration will be given by the University, under
certain conditions, for the removal of the property to such
Institution'. These relics were for many years on view in the reading
room used by the Manchester Medical Society in the old Medical School
and are now in the care of the Manchester Medical Society.

In 1927, the Society had its first distinguished speaker from
outside the Society. Sir John Thompson-Walker, well known London
surgeon, spoke on 'Enlargement of the Prostate and Prostatectomy'. It
became the practice in each session for the President to invite some
distinguished speaker to address the Society. Subsequent speakers
included Mr T P Dunhill, Mr Walter Rowley Bristol, Lord Moynihan,
Professor George Grey Turner, Sir Alfred Webb Johnson, Mr W B Gabriel,

Professor Beckwith Whitehouse, Mr Lawrence Abel and Professor Hugh
Cairns. After the break for the second World War, Professor Charles
Illingworth, Dr Alfred Barclay, Professor Charles Wells, Mr T
Twistington Higgins, Mr Philip Allison and Sir Thomas Holmes-Sellars
addressed the Society.

The annual lecture by some distinguished surgeon, usually at the
December meeting, became the highlight of every session, and this
tradition has been continued after 1950 under the aegis of the Section
of Surgery of the Manchester Medical Society. Afterwards at the annual
dinner at which the visitor is the main guest, more friendly
discussion ensues. Such contacts serve to enhance the reputation of
the Manchester Surgical School. Long may these continue.

TM

## The Pathological Society of Manchester, 1885-1950[3]

When in June 1846 the Editor of the London Medical Gazette wrote 'we
find pathological societies springing up in many parts of the country'
he will have had in mind, amongst others, one that had been
inaugurated as the Manchester Pathological Society in April of that
year - some four decades before the Pathological Society of Manchester
was to be founded in 1885. The stated aims of the earlier society were

> to hold meetings for the purpose of exhibiting the products of
> disease, of making a statement of facts and opinions upon them, of
> publishing the most noteworthy specimens, and of forming a museum.

Within two months of the inaugural meeting the first batch of
descriptions of specimens appeared in the London Medical Gazette (a
promptness that would be remarkable to-day!) and these publications
continued to appear in the Gazette until 1849, after which it seems
the Society itself became defunct.

The Manchester Medical Society, founded in 1834, continued to
flourish, however, and in 1875 the Microscopical Section was formed
within it; its objectives included ... 'the exhibition of morbid
specimens illustrated by microscopical sections, the reading of
papers' (an advance on the 1846 society), 'and the discussion of
subjects relating to microscopical science'. It is reasonably certain
that Julius Dreschfeld (1845-1907) was the driving force behind the
formation of the Microscopical Section; an Owens College graduate, he

undertook post-graduate studies in Würzburg, where he was taught by the great Rudolf Virchow, obtaining an MD there and returning to Manchester to become assistant physician at the Royal Infirmary and lecturer in pathology at Owens College - posts which he held in 1875 when the Microscopical Section was formed.

One decade later, in 1885, with Dreschfeld as president, the secretary of the Microscopical Section Professor A H Young (professor of anatomy and honorary surgeon at the Salford Royal Hospital) addressed the following letter to the secretary of the Manchester Medical Society:

Dear Sir,
For some time the Microscopical Section of the Medical Society has found its field of work materially curtailed in consequence of a regulation which precludes any but members of the Medical Society from becoming members of the section; whilst, further, the strict limitation of preparations exhibited to those of microscopical sections has been found detrimental to the progress of the section. The Members of the Section decided it was desirable to give to the Microscopic Section a more independent position affording it greater scope. To this end a committee was appointed to confer with the committee of the Medical Society with a view to the re-arrangement of the relationship now existing between the Section and the Society.
I have to ask you to be kind enough to bring the matter under the notice of the Medical Society on an early occasion and in the manner you consider best.
Yours faithfully,
A.H. Young
Hon. Sec. of the microscopical section.

One cannot but admire the firm mannerly tone; obviously a letter between equals. The resultant negotiations were speedily concluded and a few weeks later, on 24 March 1885, the first meeting of the new Pathological Society of Manchester took place in the Anatomy theatre of Owens College under the presidency of Dr H Ashby (1846-1908), physician to the Manchester General Hospital for Children; the Vice-President being Julius Dreschfeld, Professor of Pathology, and the secretary A H Young; thus effectively preserving continuity with the now defunct Microscopical Section.

The Pathological Society quickly asserted itself as an independent entity in the provincial medical world by inviting the president and council of the Liverpool Medical Institute to attend a meeting in Manchester in November 1885: in his letter of acceptance the president commented that 'such reunions were very favourable to the furtherance of medical science and in every way to be commended'.

The Society's meetings were held in the evenings at 7.30 p.m. in the pathology laboratory at Owens College; this laboratory had been designed by Dreschfeld and completed in 1876 when he was lecturer in pathology, and it is not difficult to see how the development of academic pathology in Owens College and the final emergence of the Pathological Society were both masterminded by Dreschfeld.

The Society's rules were revised in 1891 and one decision then made was to publish the Society's transactions. The first volume (and, sadly, the only volume) was published in 1893. Among the transactions we find the description, with histology, of four cases of 'Epithelioma adenoides cysticum' by H A Brooke (1854-1919), a founder member of the Society and physician to the Manchester and Salford Hospital for diseases of the skin. Since then this benign skin lesion has been known world-wide as 'Brooke's tumour'. A second paper in the transactions is entitled 'The reflexes in spinal injuries' by the treasurer of the Society, William Thorburn (1861-1923), later Professor of Clinical Surgery 1910-21 and world famous pioneer of the surgery of the spinal cord; some of his beautifully dissected specimens of cervical spine fractures can still be seen in the Pathology museum in the Manchester Medical School. A third paper recorded in the transactions of 1891-92 was read by Dr H Ashby and entitled 'Loeffler's Diphtheria Bacillus'. The causal organism of diphtheria had been discovered a few years previously and one can imagine the intense interest the lecture would have aroused in that grave and responsible audience of medical men, almost every one of whom would have had clinical experience of the dreaded infection and its youthful victims. The editorial sub-committee met in November 1893 for the last time, however, having decided for financial reasons to discontinue the publication of the transactions. They may have been influenced also by the fact that the *Journal of Pathology and Bacteriology* had already commenced publication in 1892.

Sheridan Delépine (1855-1921) was now Professor of Public Health and Bacteriology, occupying a new chair created when Julius Dreschfeld became Professor of Medicine in 1891. Delépine joined the society as an ordinary member in 1893 and became President in 1894. The first laboratory meeting of the Society when all members were invited to demonstrate specimens took place at the annual meeting in 1903. Since then the laboratory meeting, always successful, has continued to be held on the day of the Society's annual meeting in April. In this year one notes that A H Burgess (1874-1948), later Professor of Surgery and a pillar of the medical establishment in Manchester, had been elected a member of the Committee, and in this year also German Sims Woodhead, professor of Pathology at Cambridge, was elected an honorary member; Woodhead had founded the *Journal of Pathology and Bacteriology* in 1892 and edited it single-handed for 13 years. The Journal remains today pre-eminent among such publications.

In the following year, 1904, Lorrain Smith (1862-1931) newly appointed to the chair in Pathology and Pathological Anatomy, was elected a member of the Society; addressing the Manchester Medical School in October 1904 he said

> the work which I have to take up has been handed over to me by my distinguished colleague Professor Delépine. To him and his predecessor in the department of Pathology, Professor Dreschfeld, the development of the teaching of pathology in the school has been directly due ... and now the University in founding and organising two departments, one of Bacteriology and another in General Pathology has given the teaching of the subject a position it holds *in no other school in the United Kingdom.*

Thus it came about that the active membership of the Pathological Society of Manchester contained a powerful nidus composed of an ex-professor of Pathology (Julius Dreschfeld), a professor of Pathology (Lorrain Smith) and a professor of Bacteriology (Sheridan Delépine). In 1905 Louis Savatard was elected member (later to be Vice-President in 1931); a true 'savant' of dermatological histology – the present writer recalls listening to one of his brilliant, 'off the cuff', tutorials on mycosis fungoides type d'emblée.

In 1906 the Pathological Society of Manchester played a significant part in the formation of the Pathological Society of Great Britain and Ireland. Almost certainly at the suggestion of Lorrain Smith, and supported by fellow members Dreschfeld and Delépine, the inaugural meeting of the new society was held, on 14 July 1906, in the Physiology Theatre of Owens College, and all three became founder members. The first dinner of the Pathological Society of Great Britain and Ireland was held in the Queen's Hotel in Manchester with Julius Dreschfeld presiding, and among the speakers of that evening we find Sir William Thorburn, one time treasurer of the Pathological Society of Manchester. One vivid sentence from his speech has been recorded[4] 'You have to-day lighted a candle, which will bear marvellous fruit'.

In 1914 World War I led to a cessation of the Society's meetings; in 1919 the question of the Society's amalgamation with the Manchester Medical Society was discussed, but nothing came of this and the Society resumed its normal meetings. The presidents were usually clinicians but in 1932 the Professor of Bacteriology, H B Maitland became president; it is perhaps timely to remember that the modern practice of prevention of whooping cough by vaccine is based on Maitland & Evans' work on pertussis toxins in 1937-9.[5]

In 1939, with the arrival of World War II, the Society's activities again virtually ceased. Of considerable historical interest was the symposium, held just after the war on 9 October 1946, on the successful treatment in Manchester of cases of bacterial endocarditis (hitherto always fatal) with penicillin - the contributors being Dr A Morgan Jones, Dr F A Langley and Dr R Herring.

In 1946, under the presidency of Sir Geoffrey Jefferson (1886-1961), renewed discussion took place of a proposal to amalgamate the Society with the Medical and other Societies such as the Manchester Surgical Society.

In 1947, under the presidency of Dr J Crighton Bramwell (1889-1976), the cardiologist, the Society moved a step nearer amalgamation with the Medical Society by taking legal advice, and found that it could not legally transfer its assets to another society until it had become 'incorporated'; eventually this manoeuvre was accomplished, and in 1949, under the presidency of F C Wilkinson, Professor of Dental Surgery, the process of amalgamation got under way and in 1950 the Pathological Society of Manchester of 1885 became the Section of Pathology of the reorganised Manchester Medical Society.

The first president of the Section of Pathology was Dr G J Crawford, consultant pathologist at Hope Hospital, Salford; and with this election clinical pathology can be seen to have received its overdue accolade.

JD

## The Manchester and District Society of Anaesthetists, 1946-50[6]

The Section of Anaesthetics of the Manchester Medical Society is the lineal descendant of the Manchester and District Society of Anaesthetists. This came into being in 1945. By this time there were a

number of doctors in full-time practice of anaesthesia in the
Manchester area and there were others in the Lancashire towns who were
partly in general practice and partly in anaesthetic practice.
Informal discussions took place among the Manchester-based
anaesthetists and as a result the following letter was sent to all who
might potentially be interested.

Dear Dr.
Many of us here in the Manchester area think that the time is ripe
for the formation of a local Society of Anaesthetists. You are
therefore cordially invited to attend a meeting of anaesthetists to
be held in the Board Room of the Manchester Royal Infirmary on
Thursday, November 29th, at 5.30 p.m. Dr. E. Falkner Hill, Senior
Anaesthetist to the Infirmary has kindly consented to take the
chair.
At the meeting you will be asked to consider the following:-
1. The desirability of the formation of a Manchester and district
Anaesthetic Society
2. If agreed on, to proceed to elect officers and committee for
such a society
3. To discuss the relations of such a society to existing
organisations
If you are unable to attend we should be very glad to receive
your observations, in order that they may be presented to the
meeting.
Yours faithfully,
E.A. Marson
A.R. Hunter

The meeting thus called, which took place on 29 November 1945 was
attended by 32 anaesthetists under the chairmanship of Dr Falkner
Hill. It was unanimously agreed that a society be formed. Dr Hill was
elected President, Dr Marson Secretary and Dr (now Professor) Hunter
Treasurer. It quickly became apparent that considerable support for
the Society was forthcoming from those who would have to travel some
distance, from peripheral Lancashire in particular, to the meetings.
Accordingly a pattern of arrangements was established in which the
Society met initially for a meal with the scientific business
following. This not only helped those who lived in the immediate
Manchester vicinity whose lists might run late to come to meetings. It
also made it possible for members of the Society from as far away as
Stoke-on-Trent, Chesterfield and Huddersfield to attend. Initially
meetings were held in the dining rooms of convenient hotels.
Subsequently the facilities of the Staff House of the University of
Manchester became available to the Society. Later, when the University
catering premises were rebuilt the meal was organised in the Refectory

by the Manchester and District Anaesthetists' Club, timed to precede the scientific part of the activities which took place in the new Medical School.

In 1948, not long after its formation, the Manchester and District Society of Anaesthetists was approached by the Liverpool Society of Anaesthetists and a joint meeting arranged. A similar meeting has taken place every year without interruption since that date, alternately in Liverpool and Manchester. Today members of the Societies make their way to and fro by car: in the early days of such joint meetings however petrol was rationed, and on at least one occasion the members of the Liverpool Society travelled to Manchester in a hired omnibus. It is understood that on this occasion the return journey was a very cheerful occasion. The Liverpool Society of Anaesthetists had been in existence from before the First World War. The Manchester and District Society was the first of the post-war societies to be formed. Shortly afterwards societies of anaesthetists were established in Sheffield and in Leeds, and as a result close relationships have developed between anaesthetists on both sides of the Pennines.

The Manchester and District Society of Anaesthetists was in existence as an independent body until the amalgamation of the Manchester area medical societies in 1950. During each year of its existence the Society held some four meetings in addition to the joint meeting with the Liverpool, and subjects of current topical interest were discussed, including the agents which were then popular such as cyclopropane and thiopentone, not to mention the muscle relaxants which were of special topical interest at that time.

It was a matter of great regret that Dr Marson's health deteriorated and he was unable to continue in office so that the Society was deprived of what had promised to be most valuable leadership.

Dr Falkner Hill was succeeded as President of the Manchester and District Society of Anaesthetists by Dr H J Brennan who continued in this capacity until the amalgamation of the Manchester medical societies in 1950.

Though it is not possible for the Section of Anaesthetics of the Manchester Medical Society to become involved in political activity the Manchester and District Society of Anaesthetists was able to do so and when it became necessary to mobilise provincial anaesthetists' opinion in relation to the composition of the Board of the Faculty of Anaesthetists of the Royal College of Surgeons of England, the Manchester Society initiated the setting up of the liaison committee which linked together all provincial Societies of Anaesthetists in Britain. This body also made arrangements whereby distinguished speakers from abroad might visit a number of provincial centres whenever they came to the United Kingdom. Some of the functions of this committee in more recent years have been taken over by the Association of Anaesthetists of Great Britain and Ireland.

The Manchester and District Society of Anaesthetists also was influential in persuading the Manchester Regional Board of the day of the importance of the specialty of anaesthesia and of the need to establish a regional advisory committee on matters relating to the practice of the specialty. This organisation remains in existence to this day and indeed has grown greatly in its influence of later years under the title of the Anaesthesia Subcommittee of the Regional Medical Committee.

ARH

## The Manchester Odontological Society, 1885-1920[7] and 1946-50

The earliest dental associations in Manchester date from the late 19th century. Dr G W Smith had been appointed the first honorary dental surgeon to the Manchester Royal Infirmary in 1873, and in 1885 he became the first president of the Manchester Odontological Society. This Society had for its objects[8] 'the diffusion of knowledge and the promotion of intercourse among Dentists, and the advancement of the general interests of the Dental Profession'. Five years after its foundation it was claimed that[9] '... it includes amongst its members nearly all the leading dentists in Manchester and its neighbourhood, and that it is able annually to publish a volume of valuable transactions ...'. Some notes on 'the leading dentists' of the period, and of the development of the Dental Hospital and the Turner School of Dentistry with which some of them were associated will be of general interest.

The first dental hospital in Manchester was opened on 21 June 1883 at 98 Grosvenor Street, and in the following year it was renamed the

Victoria Dental Hospital of Manchester in recognition of the need for a dental school and hospital to be associated with Owens College Medical School. It thus happens that the University Dental Hospital of Manchester celebrates its centenary at the same time as the Manchester Medical Society marks its 150th Anniversary. The School and Hospital were recognised for dental training by the Royal College of Surgeons in London in 1885. Dr Parsons Shaw was the first warden and from the beginning he encouraged invention and innovation, himself developing early dental units and advocating new methods of treatment including systematic extraction of the first permanent molar tooth.

The first student to qualify in 1887, Percy Allison Linnell, became a house surgeon in 1888. The title 'Warden' was changed to 'Dean' in 1887 and the School and Hospital moved to Devonshire Street in 1892. In the same year Dr G C Campion was appointed Dean and his seven years as Dean marked a period of consolidation and improvement as main core dental courses were formally established. He lectured on diagnosis and extractions. Campion also served as President of the British Dental Association and his son Denis became a dentist – setting a pattern which was to be followed in several Manchester families as sons followed their fathers in serving the same profession.

The subsequent Deanship of Mr William Simms saw the establishment of a degree course and a move to a new building on the Oxford Road close to the main University buildings. Simms, like Campion, initiated a family tradition in dentistry; his son Harold, also a dentist, being one of the first dental graduates to proceed to the MD degree. Early graduates from Manchester made important contributions to dental education nationally. A C W Hutchinson who graduated in 1911 later became Dean in Edinburgh and Messrs E W Fish (later Sir Wilfred) and H H Stones qualified additionally in medicine and made contributions recognised internationally to dental education, science and practice. Another family who contributed much to standards of clinical excellence in operative dentistry in the Manchester School was the Houghton family; Edwin being followed by his son Edgar who entered the School in 1903 and subsequently so influenced Sir Samuel Turner that he endowed the major part of the present Hospital at the corner of Bridgeford and Upper Cambridge Streets.

Turner had also assisted in establishing the first Chair in Dentistry in Manchester by which means F C Wilkinson came to

Manchester from Melbourne. Wilkinson was a man of wide vision and energy and he initiated a period of rapid development and expansion. He insisted on a firm biological foundation in dentistry and he gathered a group of bright young men around him who were sent from Manchester to gain experience in international dentistry. From Manchester men went as Professors and Deans to other schools; Arthur Prophet to University College Hospital, London, John Miller to Cardiff, Harry Allred to the London Hospital Dental School, Ralph Cocker to King's College Hospital, H F Atkinson to the Dental School in Melbourne, and others. In Manchester, a notable tradition in dental materials science and the clinical applications of these materials was encouraged by Ernest Matthews and D C Smith. Edgar Manley maintained the biological tradition and Leslie Hardwick developed studies in preventive dentistry which have contributed to the declining caries rate of today. Standards of clinical excellence were maintained and several graduates of the 1930s and early 1940s served the School from the immediate post-war years through to the present.

A tradition in oral surgery was fostered by Professor J R Moore who was also sometime Dean of the Faculty of Medicine, Pro-Vice-Chancellor of the University and President of the Manchester Medical Society.

The original Manchester Odontological Society lost its separate identity in 1920 when it became merged in the East Lancashire and East Cheshire Branch of the British Dental Association. In 1946 however when the restructuring of the Manchester Medical Society was being mooted a group of dental surgeons comprising members of the Dental School and Hospital staff together with general dental practitioners met to re-establish the Manchester Odontological Society. The new society thus revived was incorporated into the Manchester Medical Society as its Section of Odontology. Members of the founding committee, conscious of the part played by the original society in the past and by the British Dental Association in the contemporary scene, anticipated a greater contribution to the dental professional life of the community being made by this development. It was considered that a Section of Odontology, in addition to providing a forum for debate on dental scientific, clinical and educational topics, would also help to consolidate the mutual respect which had developed between medical and dental practitioners during the war years.

JHJ

CHAPTER 3

THE RE-FORMATION OF THE SOCIETY IN 1950

The Society and Library escaped damage during the war. Meetings were held but less frequently. The President elected at the start remained in office for four years and in 1943 was succeeded by the distinguished paediatrician Catherine Chisholm CBE - the only occasion when a woman has held that office.

In April 1946 the surgeon, Wilson Hey, then President, proposed that the Medical, Surgical, and Pathological Societies and the Society of Anaesthetists should amalgamate under the title of 'The Society of Medicine of Manchester' ultimately with the Royal Accolade. This was referred to the four societies. On the 28 April 1947 an extraordinary meeting of the Medical Society was held in the packed Large Anatomy Theatre. Members of all four Societies were present. Wilson Hey explained the history of the amalgamation and proposed the necessary resolution. Dr Bosdin Leech seconded and explained that it would mean the end of the Medical Society. At once William Brockbank took him to task. He was astonished that as he had been Centenary President, and his uncle, Daniel John Leech, had been President in the 50th year Dr Leech should now be proposing the Society's demise. Dr Brockbank was all in favour of the amalgamation of the Societies but did not see why this could not be done by altering the By-Laws to conform with those of the Royal Society of Medicine with sections of medicine, surgery, pathology, anaesthesia and odontology, as the Manchester Odontological Society was anxious to join and they could be included. After all, many members of the other four Societies were also members of the Medical Society which was by far the oldest of the lot. He was sure amalgamation could be easily arranged within the Medical Society. He

proposed that the union should be made of the principal medical
societies under the aegis and title of the Manchester Medical Society
and that three delegates of each of the five Societies should be
elected by those societies to carry this amalgamation into effect and
create a new constitution and By-Laws. This resolution was carried
almost unanimously. The first meeting of the Committee was held on the
18 December 1947 when Dr Brockbank was elected Chairman. It was noted
that there were 1009 members of the Medical Society, 60 of the
Pathological, 106 of the Surgical, 77 of the Anaesthetic and 84 of the
Odontological Societies.

It was realised that the essential thing was to write to the
Secretary of the Royal Society of Medicine to see if he could help and
advise us. We would have to rewrite the By-Laws. The subscription
would have to be raised and this would mean consulting the
Vice-Chancellor about how much we would have to pay for the Library
and the use of a lecture theatre for our meetings and what would
happen if we decided to hold our meetings outside the University. This
still remained a possibility. There was also the problem of where the
Life Fellows of the old Society stood. We were in for a busy time. But
first things first. We wrote to the Secretary of the Royal Society of
Medicine and found him most helpful. It is well worth quoting the help
and advice Mr Geoffrey R Edwards gave us:

> Sections need not be anything but a benefit. It is essential they
> should not overlap. Secretaries should get together and make sure
> they were not going to boil the same cabbages twice. Joint meetings
> between Sections should be encouraged also joint meetings with
> outside bodies. All Fellows could attend and speak at sectional
> meetings unless they were laying on a special stunt.
>
> Sections should be created in order to satisfy the natural desire
> to preserve their traditions. They should have a life of their own
> within the body corporate and their own regulations, so long as
> they did not conflict with those of the Society. Each Section
> should be entitled to invite one visitor annually and have his
> expenses paid. If a section did not use this privilege in any one
> year, it could not carry the privilege forward to the next year.
> This would upset the finances of the Society. Do not form Sections
> unless you really need them.
>
> The Council should be satisfied that the formation of the
> proposed Section will add to the efficiency of the scientific work
> of the Society. This is an essential touch-stone by which the
> foundations of the Sections should be decided upon or against. Once
> a Section is formed the Council has no power to destroy it. The
> Section itself dies only by committing hara-kiri.
>
> Subsections are absolutely no good in practice. The parent body
> is apt to sit on it and it is not represented on the Council of the
> Society. Therefore avoid subsections as you would the pest.

> The Society should be founded on bureaucratic principles allowing
> democraticism and change. This is most important and it is also
> important that people who want changes should be able to express
> their wishes effectively after mature consideration. It should be
> made difficult for the cantankerous, ill disposed or 'sea lawyers'
> to upset the running of an affair which is running to the complete
> satisfaction of the more normal members.
> The Bye-Laws should be vetted by a really good lawyer.

Splendid stuff. The Committee were most grateful and thanked him
profusely.

While this correspondence was going on it was decided that the
subscription for Fellows would be two guineas, members of sections
would pay one guinea and associate members, half a guinea. In the past
the Medical Society paid 70 per cent of its income to the University.
This varied from £272 to £714. The Vice Chancellor, Professor Sir John
Stopford, was approached and suggested the Society should pay a fixed
round sum of £500 annually. The University Council agreed. The Society
has always thought this was a most generous figure, for the Library
was bound to grow and as the Society itself expanded it has regularly
paid the University a greatly increased amount. The problems of Life
and Honorary members of the three Societies were discussed. It was
agreed Life members of the Medical Society should remain Life Fellows
if they so desired, that Life Members of the other Societies should
become Honorary Members of their respective Sections and that Honorary
Members should retain that title in the new sections. Looking ahead it
was hoped that the final acceptance by the Medical Society should be
during May 1949. The programme for the year should be completed by
March 1950 and the 'Grand Kickoff' should be in October 1950. These
target dates were successfully achieved.

Meanwhile, the By-Laws were being slowly and carefully drafted as a
mixture of those of the Royal Society of Medicine and those of the
Medical Society. By May 30 it was possible to ask the Professor of Law
(R A Eastwood) if he would be able to read the new By-Laws critically.
He was sent copies of the By-Laws of both the Royal Society of
Medicine and of the Society. His reply was highly complimentary but he
made some critical suggestions which were accepted and he became the
Society's Legal Adviser. It was now possible to send a typescript copy
of the new By-Laws to each Sectional Secretary and ask him to draw up
the Section's regulations. These were quickly done and vetted. All
were in order and the By-Laws remained unchanged for many years

in spite of the addition of new Sections. The Committee's work was completed. It had been very interesting. There had never been the slightest trouble. Everyone wanted to bring the much altered Society into perfect working order. Two things remained to be done. The first was the request for the Royal Accolade. This was passed on to various bodies for their opinions. One of these was the Royal College of Physicians where it came before Comitia in the writer's presence. It caused some amusement and Comitia passed on to the next business. The other was the matter of the 'obligation': the altered By-Laws required every Fellow to sign a form of obligation promising that he would, to the utmost of his power, promote the honour and interest of the Society and observe the By-Laws both as they were then and as they might from time to time be altered. The vast majority of signed forms came back quickly. Some never signed but this did not seem to matter.

Everything was now ready for October 1950. The re-formed Society, called the 'Manchester Medical Society' entered the new phase of its existence with Sections of Medicine, Surgery, Pathology, Anaesthetics and Odontology. By means of an illuminated address dated 4 October 1950 signed by its President, Joint Honorary Secretaries and Secretary, the Royal Society of Medicine (then comprising 9000 Fellows) expressed to the re-formed Society its good wishes for 'the greatest possible success in its future life and development'. This framed document hangs proudly in the Society's offices to this day.

WB

**The President and Council**

of the

**Royal Society of Medicine,**

on behalf of its nine thousand Fellows, extend

**Greetings**

to the

**Manchester Medical Society**

on the occasion of the reconstitution of the Medical Societies
of Manchester as the MANCHESTER MEDICAL SOCIETY.

The Greetings of the Council of the Royal Society of Medicine are the more cordial since the Manchester Medical Society, in uniting an important group of Medical Bodies with similar Objects, has followed the principles which guided the Royal Medical and Chirurgical Society, when in 1907 it happily brought about the fusion of most of the leading Medical Societies of London to reconstitute itself as the Royal Society of Medicine.

The history of the Royal Society of Medicine since that date gives its Council great confidence in wishing the MANCHESTER MEDICAL SOCIETY the greatest possible success in its future life and development. The Royal Society of Medicine is proud to think that it has contributed by example to the formation of a Body whose bright future cannot stand in doubt and whose constitution has been moulded on that of the Royal Society of Medicine.

It is hoped that, in the abundant activity which will undoubtedly characterise the life of the Manchester Medical Society, place may be found for frequent and friendly liaison with the Royal Society of Medicine.

*Walt. Johnson* · President ·

*J. M. Wilson*

*J. C. Ainsworth Davis* Honorary Secretaries.

*Geoffrey R. Edwards.* Secretary.

The fourth day of October, 1950.

5. The illuminated address dated 4 October 1950 by which the Royal
Society of Medicine expressed to the re-formed Manchester Medical
Society its good wishes for 'the greatest possible success in its
future life and development'. See chapter 3.

CHAPTER 4

THE FORMATION OF NEW SECTIONS SINCE 1950

The by-laws of the Society included the following provision:

> The Council of the Society may from time to time create new Sections upon such terms and conditions as it may determine, provided that the Council shall in some suitable and sufficient manner announce to the Fellows its intention so to do, and if, within three months after such announcement, no written objection be received, such new Section or Sections shall thereupon be *ipso facto* established ...

On four occasions since 1950 this provision has been invoked. The Section of General Practice was formed in 1951; that of Paediatrics in 1964; Psychiatry in 1970; and Community Medicine in 1976. In none of these instances was any objection raised to the formation of the proposed new Section. In this chapter the events leading to the formation of each of these new Sections are related, and in those cases where there were antecedents these are described.

## General Practice

General practitioners in Manchester seem to have shown a relatively low motivation towards association. It is therefore interesting to note one early *ad hoc* grouping, notwithstanding that it appears to have been shortlived. On 20 May 1834 - five months before the Manchester Medical Society came into existence - a meeting was called in the name of the 'Associated General Practitioners in Medicine of Manchester and its Neighbourhood' at the Mosley Arms Hotel, Piccadilly in order to make representations to the Parliamentary Committee on the subject of the recognition of medical qualifications.[1]

We recommend the abrogation of the existing Medical Incorporations, and the formation of a general National Faculty privileged to confer Diplomas, entitling to practise in all branches of the Profession, leaving it to the choice of each individual to select a branch for himself ...

Pressure of this kind led eventually to the reform, by means of the Medical Act of 1858 and the setting up of the General Medical Council, of the chaotic situation in regard to recognition of medical qualifications which is described in the essay on Thomas Turner (1793 -1873) in chapter 7.

Sir James MacKenzie (1853-1925) of Burnley and Sir William Coates (1860-1962) of Manchester may be taken as examples of outstanding local general practitioners of a bygone age. Dr H W Ashworth recalls how the idea of forming a Section of General Practice within the Manchester Medical Society came into his mind through conversation with Dr William Brockbank, who, as related in the last chapter, had contributed so much to the re-formation of the Society, and who served as its honorary secretary between 1950 and 1954. He says that Dr Brockbank came to see him at his practice house on Stockport Road, Ardwick, and invited him to take on the task of organising a Section of General Practice within the Manchester Medical Society. The first meeting of the council of the new Section was held in the Committee Room at the Private Patients' Home, Manchester Royal Infirmary on Monday 8 October 1951 at 9 p.m. Dr Ashworth wryly comments, 'Note the time of the meeting - 9 p.m. - for in those days every surgery started between 6 and 6.30 p.m. and finished between 8 and 8.30 p.m.' Dr John Kerr of Hyde was the first president of the Section and Dr Ashworth its first honorary secretary. The council of the Section comprised 17 Fellows. A sub-committee was appointed to draft the regulations of the Section, and these when finally adopted stated that the Section existed to 'cultivate and promote General Practice by reading papers, discussions and demonstrations'.

## Paediatrics

The Section of Paediatrics of the Manchester Medical Society was inaugurated at a meeting on 9 July 1964 in the large Anatomy Theatre of the old Medical School. For some months there had been discussion amongst paediatricians concerning the formation of a specialist section of paediatrics. Although the amalgamation of other specialist societies in Manchester had taken place some fourteen years before this, the paediatric society (the Manchester Paediatric Club) had not joined.

The Manchester Paediatric Club had been founded in 1948 in the mould of the British Paediatric Association with the object of 'the promotion of friendship among paediatricians and the advancement of the study of paediatrics'. At the time of its formation the number of practising paediatricians was still small; the membership was therefore limited but from the start included colleagues in other disciplines who 'held a substantial clinical responsibility for children'. It was a significant and in those days an advanced attitude which led to the election in 1951 of Dr Winifred Kane, Senior Assistant Medical Officer for Maternity and Child Welfare for the City of Manchester as the fourth president. The first president had been Dr Catherine Chisholm, of whom a biography is included in chapter 7. The Club has always been a vigorous organisation loyally supported by all paediatricians. Academic meetings form the basis of its activities and these are usually followed by a social occasion. The promotion of friendship has certainly been achieved and the academic standard is of the highest.

It was therefore understandable that clinicians in paediatrics, having access to the meetings of the Manchester Medical Society, should not feel that the formation of a paediatric section of the Society was a pressing matter. The practice of paediatrics was however becoming much more than a hospital clinical exercise, and the years between 1948 and 1964 had seen the establishment of paediatrics as one of the four main academic medical disciplines; it therefore appeared anomalous that the Medical Society did not have a section to cater specifically for paediatrics.

The initiative to form a Section came from within the Paediatric Club. Members were aware that the Club was not open to all who might have a paediatric interest. Was a second organisation needed? Would the functions of the two societies overlap or compete? Was there sufficient interest to support a second paediatric activity? Would there be too many meetings? Should the scientific programmes differ in content or standards? All these questions and others were openly debated within the Paediatric Club for some months. They were not debated elsewhere because there was no other forum and because the

Club was respected with no-one wishing to appear to be undermining its influence. Eventually a consensus was reached and on 20 February 1964 the Secretary reported to the Council of the Society receipt of a letter from Professor Wilfrid Gaisford, Honorary Secretary of the Paediatric Club, carrying the proposal to form a Section of Paediatrics. At the inaugural meeting in July the late Professor Aron Holzel was elected the first president and Dr G V Feldman secretary.

After the event, the Paediatric Club has continued to prosper. The membership has grown with the growth of paediatrics, colleagues in disciplines allied to medicine have been admitted to membership, and a vigorous academic and social programme has been continued. The Section of Paediatrics of the Society has maintained regular programmes presenting distinguished local and visiting speakers to attentive and appreciative audiences of undergraduates and postgraduates. The Section meetings are open to a wider audience of members and fellows of the Society than is likely to be able to attend meetings of the Paediatric Club. Facilities for discussion of paediatric topics have been extended and the doubts of 1963 have been laid to rest.

RIM

## Psychiatry

The essay in chapter 7 on Samuel Gaskell (1807-86) shows how one enlightened doctor attempted to ameliorate the lot of the mentally ill in the lunatic asylums of his time. The planned systematic development of psychiatry in the general hospitals in Manchester and Salford began only after the second world war. Before this, mental illness and mental subnormality were treated in the County mental hospitals and County subnormality hospitals with a small number of patients admitted into Local Authority observation wards. Outpatient clinics were held in neighbouring towns and staffed by the doctors from the nearest mental hospitals; for example staff from Prestwich Hospital held clinics at Oldham.

Just before the War, the Manchester Royal Infirmary appointed the late Dr E H Kitching as a psychiatrist attached to the neurological department under Dr F R Ferguson. It was the second world war that stimulated the development of psychiatry in the three Services – with the result that hospitals became more psychiatrically minded at the cessation of the war. In 1947 two appointments were made by the Health Committee of the Manchester Corporation, Dr Kitching to Withington Hospital and Dr N J de V Mather to Crumpsall Hospital and the adjoining Park House, the mental observation ward of Manchester. It was the success of the department at Crumpsall Hospital that led the Manchester Regional Hospital Board (created with the National Health Service in 1948) to develop its pioneering scheme of peripheral psychiatric units in the major general hospitals in this Region: this pattern was then followed by other regions in the country.

There was little contact with the Manchester Medical Society. The University was developing a department of psychiatry at the Manchester Royal Infirmary under the guidance of the late Professor E W Anderson and Dr (now Sir William) W H Trethowan. At the re-formation of the Medical Society in 1950 it was felt that if too many sections were created initially attendances at meetings would be inadequate, and on Professor Anderson's advice a section of psychiatry was not recommended. This lack was compensated for to a considerable extent by the existence of the Manchester Psychiatric Association which was formed by the psychiatric consultants in the Manchester Region to provide a forum for professional psychiatric matters and academic lectures. Meetings took place in the psychiatric departments of the general hospitals in the Manchester Region.

The rapid increase in the number of medical staff in the University Department of Psychiatry however, together with the new postgraduate training course in the newly opened Withington Hospital and the increase in consultant appointments to district and general hospitals in the late 1960s, all demanded a new and more central forum for psychiatric meetings in the Region. The Manchester Medical Society was therefore approached about the setting up of a Section of Psychiatry. Dr John Johnson, a consultant at Withington Hospital, played a prominent part in the initiation of the Section. The Society's Council on 5 June 1969 supported the proposal, and formal notices were sent to all fellows with the October diary card. No objections were received, and the inaugural meeting of the new Section took place on Tuesday 24 February 1970 with Dr A Morgan Jones in the Chair.

NJdeVM

## Community Medicine

The Section of Community Medicine of the Society formally came into being on 5 August 1976 (the day after the last day for receipt of objections to the proposal that it be constituted). Its origins lay in the public health practice of the nineteenth century. Dr Thomas Percival (1740-1804) of Manchester (who is referred to in chapter 1 as one of the founder members of the Manchester Literary and Philosophical Society) had been a true apostle of preventive medicine;[2] with his support along with that of John Ferriar and others of the informal 'Manchester Board of Health' and his advocacy of the 'House of Recovery' for the isolation and treatment of cases of infectious disease he anticipated later accepted practice by a century. In spite of this early lead however Manchester Corporation was slow to be convinced of the desirability of appointing a medical officer of health such as Liverpool, the first in the country – and indeed in the world – to do so, had done in 1847. Eventually in 1868 Manchester did appoint Dr John Leigh (1813-88) as its first medical officer of health – only four years before it became a statutory duty of all local authorities to have a medical officer of health.

In 1875 a voluntary society, the Manchester and Salford Sanitary Association, was instrumental in bringing into being the North Western Association of Medical Officers of Health; and in 1888 this local group amalgamated with several other similar groups to become the North Western Branch of the Society of Medical Officers of Health.[3] Throughout the 101 years of its existence this North Western group held regular meetings, often in the fine town halls which local authorities were building from the 1870s onwards,[4] which were the bases from which medical officers of health operated. The Branch covered a wide area extending to Yorkshire, Liverpool and North Wales. The membership of the Society initially comprised almost exclusively medical officers of health or their deputies and assistants, and in chapter 7 the lives of James Niven (1851-1925) and John Lancelot Burn (1902-73) are presented as examples of doctors who held such appointments with distinction. From the early years of the present century they were joined on an increasing scale by doctors working in the fields of infectious diseases, tuberculosis and the maternity and child welfare services. The minutes show that in 1905 the application of the first woman doctor to be proposed for membership of the North Western Branch was accepted only after reference to the committee and a delay of some months. In October 1948 the Society opened its membership to professors and lecturers in social medicine, child health and allied subjects (who had hitherto been eligible only if they held the Diploma in Public Health or other public health qualification or some actual appointment under a local authority). In 1951 Colin Frazer Brockington was appointed to the newly created Chair of Social and Preventive Medicine at Manchester University. Later national developments, notably the foundation of the Faculty of Community Medicine in 1972 and the reorganisation of the National Health Service in 1974 initiated closer relationships between traditional public health doctors, health service administrative medical staff, and academics. In 1973 - somewhat belatedly one might think with hindsight - the Society of Medical Officers of Health changed its name to the Society of Community Medicine.[5]

Following the 1974 reorganisation of the National Health Service the North Western Branch of the Society of Community Medicine separated organisationally into two branches to cater for the new National Health Service regions of Merseyside and North Western. Several joint meetings were held between the two branches, notably an outstandingly successful centenary dinner at the Bull and Royal Hotel, Preston on 10 April 1975 which was attended by 120 members and guests with Sir John Brotherston, FRS (then Chief Medical Officer, Scottish Home and Health Department) as principal guest.

It was against this background that at an informal meeting on 17 July 1975 between Dr Philip Wood, Director of the Arthritis and Rheumatism Council's Epidemiology Research Unit in Manchester, Professor Alwyn Smith, Professor of Community Medicine at Manchester University and Dr Willis Elwood (then the centenary president of the North Western Branch of the Society) the idea of forming within the Manchester Medical Society a Section of Community Medicine was examined. The idea was ventilated, put to members of the Branch by a circular issued in March 1976, and formally accepted at the last annual general meeting of the Branch, which was held at the Heinz Factory at Kitt Green near Wigan on 1 July 1976.

Notice of the proposed formation of the new Section was given at the annual general meeting of the Manchester Medical Society on 4 May

1976; a provisional steering committee was elected for the new Section at a meeting held at the Medical School on 15 July which was attended by 37 members; and the first meeting of the Section with Dr James Haworth Hilditch (1917-83) as the first president was held on 28 October 1976, when the speakers Professor Alwyn Smith and Dr Alastair Ross, Area Medical Officer for Bolton, expounded the theme 'Putting community medicine on the map'. Some years later, Dr Wilfrid Harding, second president of the Faculty of Community Medicine, remarked to the writer, 'What you have done in Manchester' (i.e., in forming a Section of Community Medicine within the Manchester Medical Society) 'is analogous to what we have done nationally in forming the Faculty of Community Medicine within the three Royal Colleges'.

WJE

CHAPTER 5

ACTIVITIES SINCE 1950

Chapter 3 brought the reader up to 4 October 1950, the date of the
re-formation of the Society with its five foundation Sections of
Medicine, Surgery, Pathology, Anaesthetics and Odontology.

The inaugural meeting of fellows, held in the Physiology Theatre of
the old Medical School at 4.30 p.m. on that date, was an impressive
gathering. The President, Mr Wilson Hey, was in the Chair, and it is
recorded that about 300 fellows and guests were present including: the
Lord Mayor and Lady Mayoress of Manchester, Alderman and Mrs Percy
Dawson; the Vice-Chancellor of the University, Sir John (later Lord)
Stopford; the President of the Royal Society of Medicine, Lord
Webb-Johnson; the President of the Royal College of Surgeons, Sir
Cecil Wakeley; the President of the Royal College of Obstetricians and
Gynaecologists, Professor Hilda Lloyd; Professor Crighton Bramwell,
representing the Royal College of Physicians; and the President of the
Liverpool Medical Institution, Dr David Johnston.

It has been the usual pattern that meetings have been held from
October to May, some arranged by the Council of the Society and some
by the councils of its several sections. With five sections there were
37 meetings in the 1950-1 session; with nine sections this had grown
to 66 meetings in the 1982-3 session. Credit for the quality of the
programmes is due to those who down the years have served the Society
and its sections as officers or members of council. Meetings arranged
by the Society and those arranged by some of the sections were called
in the earlier years for 4.30 p.m., but in later years for 5 p.m. or
5.30 p.m., have been preceded by tea, and frequently followed by a
dinner or buffet supper. Meetings arranged by other sections, notably

Surgery, Anaesthetics and General Practice, have been called for
8 p.m. or 8.30 p.m. (or even 9 p.m. in the earlier years) so as to
allow time for an arranged dinner preceding the meeting. During the
fifties and sixties the majority of the meetings of the Society and
its various sections were held in the old anatomy lecture theatre
which was near the Society's reading room and the University Medical
Library in Coupland 3 Building which then accommodated much of the
medical school. The Society's single-roomed office was also in this
building. Dr Leslie Doyle recalls:

> Prior to the meetings, tea was graciously served just below the
> steps in the lesser reading room. The inclusion of chocolate cake
> was a special feature. At the appropriate time a signal was given
> to indicate that the meeting was about to start. Those present then
> moved up the steps and through the reception and enquiry area
> towards the theatre. At this point a tradition was enacted: the
> retired and senior members entered the theatre at the ground or
> rostrum level and then took their places on the lower series of
> benches. At the same time the majority of members and guests
> entered the theatre by means of stairs which led up to the top of
> the theatre. With its steeply racked rows, its hard wooden benches,
> straight backs to the seats and its many deeply incised initials,
> names and dates, this theatre was itself a memorial to many past
> generations of medical students. When the audience was large, those
> already present were asked to move towards the centre of the
> benches; some members stood or sat on the gangway steps; while
> others stood, perhaps two or three deep, on the passageway at the
> top of the theatre. In a curious way, this close packing often
> engendered a heightened expectation and friendliness in the
> audience.

Since 1973 the majority of the meetings have been held in the Medical
School (the Stopford Building) where tea (without chocolate cake!) has
been available at the teabar adjacent to the main lecture theatres.
Meetings of the Section of Odontology have however been held in the
Cordingley theatre in the Architecture Building which is close to the
Turner School of Dentistry. These modern lecture theatres with their
functional design, comfortable seating and electronic equipment are a
far cry from the old anatomy and physiology theatres. Nowadays however
they are seldom crowded as those used to be - due in part no doubt to
the greater availability of medical meetings at the local postgraduate
centres which were progressively developed in the Region from 1965
onwards.

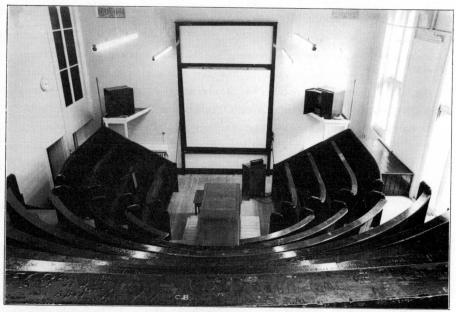

6 and 7. Two views of the old Anatomy Theatre in Coupland Building, where meetings of the Society were regularly held until 1973. See chapter 5.

Meetings of fellows

There have been three fixed events in the calendar for each session:
(1) the presidential address of the in-coming president, usually at
the first meeting in October or early in the session; (2) a joint
meeting with the Liverpool Medical Institution during the first week
of March; and (3) the annual general meeting during the first week of
May, for which it has been customary to invite a speaker of
distinction. In addition each session included in the earlier years
one or two ordinary meetings of fellows; since 1964-5 the Telford
Memorial lecture; and since 1975-6 a Christmas lecture for young
people. The presidential address has generally been in the field of
clinical interest of the speaker, though some have drawn from a wider
field, e.g., Dr William Brockbank on 'Old anatomical theatres - and
what happened therein' (1955-6 session) or Professor George Mitchell
on 'Evolution and man' (1964-5 session). The joint meeting with
Liverpool Medical Institution carries on a tradition which goes back
to 1920: the meeting is held alternately in Liverpool and Manchester,
the visiting society providing the speakers and the hosts the
hospitality. Speakers at the annual general meetings of the Society
have included presidents of each of the Royal Colleges. Details of the
Telford bequest are given in the next chapter: in some respects the
Telford memorial lecture has been the highlight of the Society's year,
and it is possibly worth setting out for the record the names of the
guest lecturers and the titles of their addresses as an indication of
their scope, interest and variety:

| | |
|---|---|
| 1964-65 Sir JAMES LEARMOUTH | Surgery in a Developing Society |
| 1965-66 Dr F J CRICK | The Genetic Code |
| 1966-67 Dr RICHARD DOLL | The Geographical Distribution of Cancer |
| 1967-68 Professor E B CHAIN | Biochemical Research and Progress in Medicine |
| 1968-69 Professor J Z YOUNG | Logic and Language in relation to Brain Structure |
| 1970-71 Sir SOLLY ZUCKERMAN | Two Manchester Anatomists |
| 1971-72 Sir DERRICK DUNLOP | The Problem of Modern Medicines and their Control |
| 1972-73 Hon.Sir JOSEPH CANTLEY | Treatment of the Offender |
| 1973-74 Professor DOROTHY HODGKIN | Insulin |
| 1974-75 Dr H YELLOWLEES | To promote the Establishment of a Comprehensive Health Service |

| | |
|---|---|
| 1975–76 Professor R Y CALNE | The Current State of Organ Transplantation |
| 1976–77 Professor W S PEART | The Kidney as an Endocrine Organ |
| 1977–78 Sir RODNEY SMITH | The Patient with Cancer and his Doctor |
| 1978–79 Sir DOUGLAS BLACK | Medicine and Society |
| 1979–80 Sir ALEC MERRISON | Patient and Provider: the idea of a Health Service |
| 1980–81 Professor ALAN EMERY | Medical Genetics – The Preventive Medicine of the Future? |
| 1981–82 Professor JOHN A DAVIS | The past, present and future neonatology |
| 1982–83 Prof. Sir WILLIAM TRETHOWAN | Growing old gracefully |

For the Christmas lecture for young people the Society has drawn generally on the expertise of members of the academic staff of the University; aimed at 16–18 year olds, primarily the sons and daughters of fellows, this annual event has usually drawn audiences of 100 to 300.

Reminiscences of each of the sections are now presented in turn.


## Section of Medicine

During the third of a century since the Society was re-formed (1950), significant changes have taken place in the practice of medicine; in part, these have been due to the great increase in biological and medical knowledge that has accumulated over this period. Writing in The Canadian Medical Association Journal of 1952, Sir Francis Walshe observed

> Medicine has a changing and unchanging face, and it is as necessary to learn the meaning of the first as it is to recognize and to cherish the second.

Over the years, the Section of Medicine has kept this fine balance. During the fifties, the average size of the audience at the section meetings was about 140. At the larger meetings, up to 250 were present – coming from near and far in the North West. Some of the more memorable meetings were:

Professor Sir Geoffrey Jefferson, FRS            (1952)
Varying behaviour of pituitary adenomas
(This was based on 316 cases of which he had operated on 250)

Professor G W Pickering            (1954)
Benign and malignant hypertension

Dr Charles Dent                                (1955)
Cystinuria

Dr Sheila Sherlock                             (1956)
Acute hepatic failure

Professor M L Rosenheim                         (1962)
Phaeochromocytoma

For a number of years, clinical meetings were held annually at one of the main Manchester hospitals. These included the presentation of patients with a well documented history and commentary for each, as well as relevant X-rays and histology slides for viewing. By this means some rare conditions were demonstrated.

Medicine today lies at the focal point of many diverse disciplines. The Section of Medicine provides a forum in which these same disciplines and their clinical implications can be explained and discussed by both physicians and medical scientists.

LD

## Section of Surgery

Surgeons who have attended the Section of Surgery with some degree of regularity over the years have had the major advances in surgery brought to their notice, often with considerable operative and clinical detail. They have been able to discuss and perhaps criticise changes. There have also been regular reviews of treatment of most of the common surgical problems and diseases. All this has been done comfortably and pleasantly during two to three hours a month, producing a stimulus for surgical advance.

Men such as R L Holt, Ian Orr and H T Cox commenting on peptic ulceration or Wilson Hey, D S Poole-Wilson and Thomas Moore on urological problems come to mind. Not less memorable was Professor A M Boyd who was never averse from lightening discussion with a waft of humour. Presidential addresses, usually at the opening meeting of the session, have generally covered the particular surgical interest of the president. Peter McEvedy was a modest but enthusiastic early president, a distinguished teacher and a meticulous operator: he was especially notable for his regular use of local anaesthesia in both major and minor surgery. One recalls some surgeons working in the periphery who have given most interesting presidential addresses:

I W Ball's paper on 'Observations of emergency surgery' being a notable case in point. Not all presidential addresses have been on surgical subjects: Oliver Jelly for example explained the field of 'Art and medicine' in his address in 1965. One remembers the clear exposition of the surgery of parathyroid adenomata by Frank Nicholson and the meticulous operative approach to parotid tumours described by Alan Nicholson in their presidential addresses.

At ordinary meetings thoracic diseases such as tuberculosis, diaphragmatic hernia and closed chest injuries, the surgery of childhood and the management of head injuries have been some of the various subjects discussed. Plastic surgery has been well represented by contributions from Randall Champion on cleft palate and Frank Robinson on burns and scalds. The doyen of the Section, Sir Harry Platt, has given wide ranging comments on surgery in general and John Charnley has outlined progress in hip surgery in particular.

The programmes of the Section has always included a lecture and an after-dinner speech by a distinguished guest invited by the president. The Section has thus had the benefit of listening to some of the foremost and most knowledgeable surgeons in the United Kingdom describing their special interests. Professor Milnes Walker (1952) on the surgical treatment of portal hypertension, Professor Rob (1953) on arterial grafting, Harold Edwards on Crohn's disease (1960), Professor L N Pyrah (1961) on renal calculi, Professor J C Goligher on peptic ulcer and York Mason (1977) on Quain's peculiar tumour are recalled not only for the indications for operative treatment in each subject, but also for the vividness and enthusiasm with which the lectures were delivered.

NFK

## Section of Pathology

The first council meeting of the Section of Pathology was held, antepartum, on 6 March 1950 in the Library of the University Department of Bacteriology, then in York Place. Dr G J Crawford of Salford was elected the first president. On Wednesday 4 October 1950 the Pathological Society of Manchester merged with the new Manchester Medical Society. (It took six years to amend the entries in the 'Handbook of Scientific and Learned Societies'.) From this fusion and subsequent fission pathologists emerged as the Section of Pathology, complete with president, council and regulations - the latter surviving, with only minor modifications, to the present day.

Monthly meetings were held - lectures usually in the large Anatomy Theatre of the old Medical School and laboratory meetings in York Place. The minute books of the Section give the reviewer a sense of déja vu. On 4 January 1951 the Section joined with Medicine to discuss 'The role of asphyxia in foetal and neonatal mortality'. Thirty-two years later, in 1983, the presidential address to the Section was, 'Asphyxia - the truth - the whole truth?'. In 1952-3 the Section heard: Dr J L Burn's condemnation of the archaic sanitary fittings in the old Medical School - long before the collapse of Manchester sewers excited the attention of the media; a trio of distinguished haematologists recommending that blood refrigerators should be kept locked; another trio discussing laboratory facilities for general practitioners; and W C Cockburn of the Public Health Laboratory Service speaking on 'Field investigations of whooping cough vaccines'. One wonders if it can really have been 30 years ago? In 1963 M F A Woodruff had a large audience in the Physiology Theatre to hear his 'Experiences with the transplantation of the kidney in man'; he quoted with evident relish Marion Walker's verse from Punch,

> My true love hath my heart and I have his donated kidney -
> That's what marriage means to simple folk like me and Sidney.
> We twain 'one flesh until us death do part': for who, we wonder,
> Whom surgery hath joined, would care to start to put asunder?

Eleven years later in December 1974 A R Mainwaring's subject was 'The pathology of renal transplantation'.

In 1963 R W Fairbrother and H B Maitland were elected honorary members of the Section; the Section held its first annual dinner; a presidential medallion was donated anonymously to the Section; and Dr T H Blench made a bequest to the Section for social and convivial purposes: the latter was used to purchase two decanters which are in use at the Section's festive occasions to this day. In 1965 J Chapman spoke on 'Electron microscopy': with dramatic licence he told his audience that although only a few cubic millimetres of tissue had by then been sectioned the resulting photographic plates placed end to end would span the Atlantic! In 1980 the Section made a presentation to Mrs E Johnson, Secretary of the Society for 23 years, and had the pleasure of her company at dinner. After the laboratory meeting in

1981 Dr J F Wilkinson, who for years had been responsible for the minutes of the Section's meetings, regaled members by showing his unique collection of 'Painted pots' ranging from a Babylonian prescription tablet of 4000 BC to drug jars down the ages.

On 12 May 1982 the Section joined with the University Department of Pathology in its centenary celebrations. The monthly meetings of the Section continue and are well attended. If the quantity of exhibits at the laboratory meetings seems to have dwindled from the level of the 1950's it may well be that the quality is higher. The Section of Pathology has always been a society of friends. Long may it continue!

JEH

## Section of Anaesthetics

The Section of Anaesthetics continued to meet in very much the same circumstances as those of the meetings of the Manchester and District Society of Anaesthetists - initially in the Staff House of the University, and from 1973 onwards in the new Medical School. In recent years a tradition of the predecessor Society has been revived - that of holding one or two meetings each session in peripheral centres such as Preston, Lancaster, Bolton or Blackburn and, by special invitation of Dr Ward, in Huddersfield.

The Section has made it possible for visitors from abroad to be heard by the members; the individual speakers are too numerous to mention in detail. Among speakers from within the United Kingdom have been such distinguished guests as Professor Mushin from Cardiff, Professor (now Sir William) Paton from Oxford, Professor Nunn from Leeds and his colleague Dr Gordon McDowall who is a world authority on cerebral blood flow, not to mention Professor Payne whose early career in the specialty was in the Department of Anaesthesia at the Royal Infirmary in Manchester. Appropriately for an organisation in the home town of James Braid (1795-1860) his subject of hypnosis has been discussed on more than one occasion.

In 1971 ICI (Pharmaceutical Division) agreed to fund a prize of £50 for the best account of an original investigation presented to the Section by a registrar in training in the Northwest Region on a subject related to anaesthesia. Shortly thereafter Abbott Laboratories made a similar sum available for an account of a clinical study or a review of a clinical subject. Almost without exception these prizes have attracted high quality entrants. In the year 1982-3 no fewer than six papers were offered, and it is a testimonial to the quality of these entries that the winner subsequently offered his paper to the Section of Anaesthetics of the Royal Society of Medicine for a similar competition and again it won first prize.

The work of the Section has expanded in another direction. It was felt that the longsuffering spouses of the members deserved some special consideration and for the last three years a summer meeting of the Section has been held, to which they have been invited and at which the subject discussed has been of a general nature. The first such meeting, held at Hope Hospital, was addressed by Dr David Anderson; it was a most successful occasion and it is hoped that such an event will take place annually.

ARH

## Section of Odontology

Since the nucleus of the Section within the re-formed Society was composed of staff of the Dental School and the Dental Hospital, there was some anxiety that general dental practitioners might perceive it as essentially created for academics. Efforts were therefore made both to formulate programmes which would encourage the attendance of all dental surgeons irrespective of their professional interests; and to ensure that not only would they attend meetings as members or fellows but would also take an active part in the government of the Section and possibly of the Society as a whole. These objectives have to a great extent been realised; the council of the Section has a balanced membership of University, consultant and general dental practitioners; and the Section has provided an honorary treasurer and two presidents of the Society.

In compiling its programme of speakers, the council of the Section has naturally had the interests of its own members foremost in mind: it is however gratifying to note that many of the speakers have attracted members of other sections. Some of these speakers have been of national and international reputation, and on two occasions the Section has been honoured by the presence of deans of the Faculty of Dental Surgery of the Royal College of Surgeons of  England.  A recent innovation has been the inclusion of a members' evening, when younger members of the Section are encouraged to present a preliminary or final report on any research or clinical project leading to a postgraduate degree. This has proved useful to them in that it has added to their training experience and has helped their supervisors to assess the quality of the presentation.

If one bases one's opinion of the success of otherwise of the Section on membership alone there is no doubt that the original concept was sound, for a membership of 35 in 1957 has grown to 131 in 1982, and many dental surgeons have been attracted to the Section as a means of providing themselves with postgraduate education. As a founder member of the Section, it gives the author of this brief report great satisfaction to see the earlier hopes materialised, and there is no evidence to suggest that there is any decline in interest.

JKH

## Section of General Practice

The presidential address of the inaugural session was given in May 1952 by Dr John Kerr of Hyde on the topic 'Influence and status of the general practitioner'. This theme has been discussed repeatedly since then; it was however found necessary in the early years to restrain a tendency for discussion to move into the medico-political field since the Society exists to promote medical and scientific discussion and is not a political forum.

It was a great encouragement to the Section when Dr Hugh Patrick Fay of Stockport was elected President of the Society for the 1954-5 session - the first general practitioner since 1936 to hold this office.

One of the liveliest meetings the writer can recall was in 1957 when J H Cyriax came from London to talk on 'Manipulative medicine'. The talk was followed by a demonstration on the writer, who, pinned to the post-mortem trolley by two callous colleagues, submitted himself to repeated pulling and twisting by the operator, clad only in rolled up shirt sleeves and trousers. The event was hilarious.

During the writer's presidential year, 1959-60, ladies were invited to the council dinner for the first time, and in the following year Dr Jean Broughton took office as President of the Section - the first woman to do so.

Dr M Balint of the Tavistock Clinic came to speak in 1960, and few who heard him would have believed he was going to have such an effect on general practice. His philosophies became almost a cult, and Balint groups were set up throughout the length and breadth of the land so that general practitioners could analyse together their own disappointments, frustrations and inner feelings vis-à-vis their patients.

In 1961 Lord Taylor spoke about his 'Harlow experiment', describing how a new town was to be supplied with co-ordinated medical services delivered from purpose-built health centres. Little did his audience imagine that it would be a further ten years before such health centres (which had been envisaged as an essential component of the National Health Service under the Act of 15 years earlier) became popularised and programmed by the Robinson Administration.

27 January 1969 provides a final example of an outstanding meeting, when Dr (later Dame) Cicely Saunders came to speak on 'Caring for the dying'. Famous as the founder of the hospice movement, she spoke to a full house which included the Bishop of Manchester. It was decided after that meeting to go ahead with the provision of a hospice in Manchester. The results of that decision are seen today at Heald Green, where St Ann's Hospice was opened in 1971; and at Little Hulton, where a new purpose-built hospice was completed in 1979. If the Section of General Practice were to fold up tomorrow, the establishment of our hospices would stand as a permanent testimony today in the Greater Manchester area.

HWA

## Section of Paediatrics

Dr (later Professor) Aron Holzel gave the inaugural presidential address on 'Sugars, enzymes and malabsorption' on 11 February 1965. This was an outstanding contribution which introduced a whole new concept in the diagnosis and management of diarrhoeal disease in infancy. For the second presidental address Professor Wilfrid Gaisford reported on some aspects of his work on BCG and measles vaccination. Later the same year (1966) Professor Donald Court gave a survey of the needs of children in a hypothetical group practice and discussed the ways in which these needs might be met by changes in general practice. Obviously the Section was then privileged to hear the beginnings of the thinking which went into the setting up of the Committee under his chairmanship, whose report he returned to discuss in March 1977. In 1968-9 Dr Duncan Macaulay had been leader of the British Paediatric Team working in the Children's Hospital in Saigon and visiting Professor at the University there. He returned to Manchester in 1970 and gave a most interesting lecture on the way of life of the children of South Vietnam during the war, and showed that as long as a child had the support of his family group his tolerance of adversity - even serious illness and grave injury - was quite remarkable.

Over the years not only have distinguished paediatricians in Manchester and the United Kingdom given papers at the meetings, but also have distinguished specialists in allied branches addressed the Section. Thus in 1969 Dr Oliver W M Wrong of the Department of Medicine spoke on 'Renal tubular acidosis' and Professor C I Phillips gave an address on 'Paediatric ophthalmology' - a completely new subject for many people. Again to show wider interests, Dr Brenda Hoggett, Senior Lecturer in Law at the University of Manchester, spoke on 'Battered babies and the law' in 1981; and 'Adoption practice' was discussed by Dr Christine Cooper in 1975 and by Dr Basil Wolman when he was President in 1978.

In November 1974 Dr Elsie Widdowson of Cambridge, a well-known international figure, gave an outstanding talk on infant foods and their effects. Professor H A Visser of Rotterdam addressed the Section in 1972 on 'Abnormalities in sexual differentiation in the new-born'; and Professor D L Miller, Professor of Community Medicine at the Middlesex Hospital spoke about measles vaccination.

Our own professorial staff have made distinguished contributions over the years: Professor Dobbing on 'Foetal growth restriction and brain development'; Professor Houston on 'Renal function before and after birth'; Professor Taylor on 'The sick child's predicament'; and Professor Boyd asked 'Is the placenta a barrier?'

We were very pleased in 1978 to welcome Dr Helen Holzel, daughter of our first President and a consultant bacteriologist at King's College Hospital, who addressed the Section on the role of 'E coli in gastro-enteritis'.

BW

## Section of Psychiatry

The inaugural meeting took place on 24 February 1970 with Dr A Morgan Jones in the chair. The inaugural address, 'Behavioural science teaching in the medical curriculum', was given by Professor G M Carstairs in the large Anatomy Theatre of the old Medical School: an audience of over 100 was present of whom 49 were foundation members of the Section. Since then six meetings each year have been arranged with invited guest speakers. In addition, a clinical meeting each year was organised in a district general hospital in the region, but attendance was poor and this was abandoned after two years. The Section of Psychiatry has been in existence for 14 years; since its inception it has continued to grow and there are now well over 100 members.

NJdeVM

## Section of Community Medicine

During the seven years from its inception to the time of writing (Summer, 1983) 57 papers were presented to meetings of this, the newest Section of the Society. Besides nationally known speakers like Dr A M Adelstein who spoke on 'Medical aspects of the work of the Office of Population Censuses and Surveys', Sir Richard Doll who gave an assessment of the risks of cancer and Sir George Godber who outlined the scope and means of prevention, opportunity was given to newly qualified doctors and graduate trainees in community medicine to present papers. The papers presented may be classified as follows:

| | |
|---|---|
| Environmental health | 2 |
| Infectious disease and foodpoisoning | 3 |
| General aspects of community medicine | 5 |
| Prevention (including vaccination and immunisation) and screening | 10 |
| Epidemiology and research | 11 |
| Social, economic and political topics | 11 |
| Services for particular care groups | 15 |
| Total – papers presented, 1976–1983 | 57 |

It is interesting to note that 12 out of the 15 papers in the last mentioned classification were presented by colleagues in the training grades or recent graduates. The Section at the end of the 1982–3 session had 119 members and was in good heart.

WJE

CHAPTER 6

DEVELOPMENTS SINCE 1950

Membership

It will be recalled from chapter 3 that the Society started the
re-formed phase of its existence with five sections. The total
membership reported at the first annual general meeting in 1951 was
1178. By 1961 membership was 1490, by 1971 1603 and since 1981 it has
been over 2000. With nine sections the membership at April 1983 was as
follows:

| | |
|---|---:|
| Honorary fellows | 10 |
| Honorary members of sections | 6 |
| Life fellows (not being honorary fellows) | 184 |
| Fellows | 1761 |
| Temporary members | 10 |
| Associates | 98 |
| Members of sections (not being fellows) | 15 |
| | 2084 |

Revisions of by-laws

The original by-laws based on those of the Royal Society of Medicine
were finally formally adopted at a special meeting of fellows in the
1953-4 session: they proved eminently satisfactory for a good number
of years. They were modified in 1964 mainly in order to create a
category of 'temporary member' which it was thought would prove
attractive to junior doctors. They were again revised in 1980, when
the need to define more clearly the mechanism for the admission of
non-medically qualified 'associates' (which had occasioned some
difficulties) provided opportunity for a complete revision and
re-writing in more modern English with the advice of the Society's

honorary legal adviser Professor Harry Street. One casualty of this
revision was the 'Obligation' which all fellows had formerly been
required to sign,

> I, whose name is hereunto subscribed, being a Fellow of the
> Manchester Medical Society, hereby promise that I will, so long as
> I continue to be a Fellow, to the utmost of my power promote the
> honour and interest of the said Society, and will observe the
> By-laws, both as they are and as they may from time to time be
> altered.

This was considered by many members to be archaic and was dropped;
instead a general requirement to be bound by the by-laws of the
Society was laid upon all classes of member.

## Presidental medallions

Towards the end of chapter 1 an account is given of the beautiful
presidential badge which was presented to the Society by Dr and Mrs E
Bosdin Leech and first worn at the annual general meeting on 5 May
1937. At the time of writing the presidents of seven of the nine
sections of the Society have the privilege of wearing medallions.
These became available in various ways - through personal gift, by
money from a legacy, or by means of the use of the medallion of a
predecessor society.

## Royal title

Since its constitution had been modelled on that of the Royal Society
of Medicine, two attempts were made, in 1951 and in 1975, to obtain
for the Society the accolade of the title 'Royal'. On the latter
occasion the approach to the Home Office which deals with such matters
was made informally by Mr Thomas Moore, the then President of the
Society. The reply stated,

> The application has been very carefully considered, but I am sorry
> to have to inform you that the Home Secretary, consistently with
> the long established practice in these matters, would be unable to
> submit a formal application from the Society for the title Royal to
> the Queen with a favourable recommendation.
> I realise that you will be disappointed, but the title Royal is
> now granted very sparingly, and I can assure you that the decision
> in no way reflects upon the standing of the Society.

## Finance and the Telford bequest

The standard rate of subscription for fellows, which for very many years had stood at two guineas (£2-10) per annum, was raised to five pounds from the beginning of 1977, ten pounds from 1980 and fifteen pounds from 1984. That it has not reached a much higher level has been due to a most generous bequest to the Society following the death in 1961 of Professor E D Telford. It was during the session 1963-4 that the Society learned that it was to inherit about £55,000 with interest and without any conditions. A sub-committee was appointed to decide how best to deal with the bequest. It was decided to keep the capital intact in the hands of three trustees, to leave the Treasurer to deal with the annual interest, and to found with a fee of £100 an annual Telford Memorial Lecture. (This fee has subsequently been increased – first to £150, then to £250). The Telford lecture has been one of the highlights of the Society's annual programme, and the lecturers invited and the subjects presented have been noted in chapter 5.

Besides a fixed amount of £500 per annum which the Society has paid to the University since 1950, a discretionary grant is made each year by the Society for University Library purposes. This discretionary grant has been increased from time to time and in 1983 it was £6000. In that year in agreement with the University Librarian, Dr M A Pegg, arrangements were made to provide part of the grant as service in lieu of cash by making part-time secretarial support available to University library staff. With cuts in University grants and the freezing of many vacant posts this has been a means of practical assistance which has strengthened in the world of today the historic links between the Society and the University Library.

## The Library

Designed by Sir Hubert Worthington, the handsome traditional building at the foot of Lime Grove on the University campus was brought into use in 1936 as the then Arts Library. In 1956 an extension in the same style was added. The planning of a further major extension was begun in 1968; this, proposed for 1974, had to be postponed for financial reasons until 1977; designed by Dane, Scherrer and Hicks, this modern extension eventually came into operation on 1 September 1981, and was officially opened by HM The Queen on 5 May 1982.

From the time of the 'arrangement' between the Society and Owens College in 1875 until the summer of 1981 the main medical library collection was in Coupland 3 Building. One of the troubles in this building was that the large room which served as a fellows' reading room and in which many journals were kept on the central table was directly beneath the pharmacology laboratory. On several occasions carelessness in leaving taps running meant that water dripped through the ceiling doing irreparable damage. It also happened that the Library suffered from flooding due to blocked drains, and on one occasion water from fire hoses caused further havoc. It was with all this in mind that the present medical faculty library was planned to be sited on the top floor of the Stopford Building.

Various moves of parts of the library collections took place over the years to accommodate the growing demand for space, e.g., in the 1968-9 session some medical books together with an enormous quantity of early journals were transferred to the main library; in the 1972-3 session when the Stopford Building became available a proportion of the medical books and journals were transferred to the new faculty library; and in 1976-7 use was made of space at the famous John Rylands Library in Deansgate (which had merged with the University Library in 1972) for the storage of early medical books and manuscripts. Much manpower was needed for these moves. They were facilitated by carrying the books in boxes measuring just under one metre in length, 38 centimetres in width and 30 centimetres in depth. They had ropes for carrying at each end, fitted in the Library's van, and were officially known as 'coffins'. One elderly member of the Society who helped in these moves said that he had filled more coffins with books than he had filled with bodies during the whole of his professional career.

Eventually the need for ad hoc interim moves came to an end, and by the summer of 1981 all the medical books (apart from those which remained as the faculty library in the Stopford Building) were in place in Worthington's 1936 building or its newly commissioned extension. At last medicine, science and the humanities were housed in the same building. There was an abundance of space – both on the shelves for books, in the racks for journals, and at tables throughout the building for study. Not everyone however was pleased with the

8. The Medical School of the University of Manchester (the Stopford Building), where most of the meetings of the Society have been held since 1973.

9. The John Rylands University Library of Manchester main building. Worthington's 1936 building (in which the Society's office has been accommodated since April 1982) is in the foreground; and the frontage of the huge extension which was opened by HM The Queen on 5 May 1982 can just be seen in the background. See chapter 6.

changes: what had been a medical library had become a section of the main University Library, and its physical separation from the Medical School (with the need to maintain in the School a separate small faculty library) made older members look back with nostalgia to the days before 1973 when the medical library, the medical school and the Society were all under the same roof in Coupland Building and the library staff there were dedicated exclusively to medicine.

Reference has been made in chapter 1 to the 1930 agreement for the medical library to be managed by a Committee consisting of 'five representatives nominated by the University and three representatives nominated by the Society'. This Committee, now regarded as a Sub-Committee of the University Library Committee, has met regularly down the years. Its representation has been widened by the simple expedient of co-opting colleagues in medical specialties and University Departments in the Faculty of Medicine other than those to which the formally appointed representatives belong - so that the total membership of the Committee may be of the order of 25 to 30. It is serviced by the Registrar's Department of the University, and it currently fulfils a useful role in continually keeping the interests and points of view of members of the medical and dental professions in the Region before the mind of the University Librarian and his staff.

Personnel

The Society has been faithfully served over the years by its officers, both honorary and paid. A list of its presidents is given in Appendix 1. Of its paid officers special mention must be made of Mrs Elsie Johnson, who retired in 1980 after having completed 23 years as secretary: the Society owes her a great debt of gratitude for the smooth and efficient manner in which its business was handled throughout her term of office.

1967 saw the retirement of George Wilson, the University's Medical Sub-Librarian, after 54 years of service part of which had been on the Society's pay-roll. He was internationally recognised as a medical librarian and was president of the medical section of the Library Association. He was awarded an honorary degree by the University and honorary fellowship by the Society. Sadly he did not live long to enjoy his retirement. His successor Mr David Frederick Cook  served as

Medical Sub-Librarian from 1967 until his retirement in 1983. The honorary fellowship of the Society was conferred upon him at the annual general meeting on 4 May 1983.

## The Society's offices

For many years the Society's office was one small room on the ground floor of Coupland 3 Building. Though small, this had until 1973 the advantage that it was in the building which accommodated both the medical library and the greater part of the Medical School. In that year the Medical School moved to occupy the newly commissioned Stopford Building, and over the course of the next few years other University departments gradually moved into Coupland 3. Eventually on 14 April 1982 it was possible for the Medical Society to take over as its offices a handsome suite of rooms within the John Rylands University Library of Manchester main building - rooms on the second floor of Worthington's 1936 building which had been allocated to the Society on the recommendation some four years previously of Dr F W Ratcliffe the then University Librarian. The availability of these rooms and of capital released by the Society's trustees has made possible their furnishing in an appropriate style and the acquisition of the kind of office machinery and equipment which has moved the office and its procedures in a series of rapid leaps from the 1950s to the 1980s.

WB/WJE

CHAPTER 7

SELECTED BIOGRAPHIES

The reader of the preceding six chapters will have appreciated that
the life of the Manchester Medical Society has for the 150 years of
its existence been closely bound up with the life of the medical
profession in Manchester and the region of which it is the centre.
This was particularly true in the period before post-graduate centres,
which were provided in districts from 1965 onwards, began to develop
as local foci of medical activity. The Society has had strong links
with the Manchester Royal Infirmary throughout its history, with Owens
College particularly since 1875 and with the Victoria University of
Manchester from 1904.

The biographies which follow are intended to give a cross-section
of doctors who achieved eminence in their several fields. They are to
be regarded as representative of their disciplines and of their
periods rather than as having been included simply because of their
connection with the Manchester Medical Society. Ten of them became
presidents of the Society and 13 were professors of the University.
But general practitioners, medical officers of health and
representatives of the radicals and reformers of the nineteenth
century have also been included. They are here presented in
chronological order of year of birth. The closing contribution, by Sir
Harry Platt, is the address which he gave in Manchester Cathedral in
1982 to commemorate the life of Sir John Charnley, 1911-82. About half
of the lives have been written up by colleagues who like Sir Harry
have personal recollections of their subject. But all have been
included primarily on the grounds of their inherent interest and
variety. We hope that our readers will agree.

7.1 JOSEPH JORDAN, 1787-1873

    FRCS

Joseph Jordan deserves a modest niche in the medical history of England because he was a pioneer in creating the foundations of our provincial medical schools and in breaching the monopolistic attitudes of the London Colleges and the Society of Apothecaries. As this is his main claim to fame a disproportionate part of the ensuing review of his life and work will deal with this achievement.

His forbears arrived in Hull from Holland in the fourteenth century and some went to Monmouth and others to Carlisle. The latter group ultimately became calico printers and William Jordan, grandfather of Joseph Jordan, moved to Manchester in 1745;  by 1772 he was well established as a linen and cotton printer in the area known as St Mary's Churchyard. One of his sons, also named William, married a Mary Moors and they had four sons and two daughters; the youngest son, born on 3 March 1787, was the Joseph of this story.[1]

Joseph's preliminary education was at a school owned by the Rev. J Birchall. Although diligent he confessed in later life that he 'had many a good thrashing or had been kept locked up in school without dinner' for getting involved in various scrapes. However when he tried to satisfy his curiosity about the anatomy of the school clock the result was disastrous for both the clock and Joseph, as the irate Mr Birchall ordered him to leave the school forthwith. His age at the time of his expulsion is not recorded, but when 15 he was apprenticed to Mr J Bill, a Manchester Infirmary surgeon. His initial experiences as a medical apprentice were unhappy. He had to spend most of his time washing bottles in a gloomy cellar and making pills and plasters, so his indenture with Mr Bill was cancelled and he was placed in the tutelage of Mr W Simmons,[2] another Infirmary surgeon. Although Simmons was a disputatious character, he was a good and kind master to Jordan who eagerly seized the ample opportunities provided to study the activities in all departments of the Infirmary. He remained with Mr Simmons until he was 19 and then went to Edinburgh where he studied anatomy under Alexander Monro (Tertius) and (Sir) Charles Bell. He also studied other subjects and received the diplomas of the two Royal Edinburgh Colleges.[3]

This was the time of the Napoleonic Wars and, as usual at such times, there was a crying need for Army surgeons.    Jordan responded and joined the 1st Battalion of the Royal Lancashire Regiment as an Ensign on 12 December 1806, becoming Assistant Surgeon the following year on 8 April 1807.

Letters to his mother and to Mr Simmons indicate that Jordan found his military service only mildly attractive as he had no opportunity to go on active service. He met some distinguished officers, however, such as General England, Admiral Young and (Sir) James McGrigor who became Director General of the Army Medical Service under Wellington and one of his most trusted advisers. Between 1806 and 1811 Jordan moved with his Regiment to various places - Exeter, Milford Haven, Kidderminster, Bristol, Worcester, Nottingham, Hull, York, Berwick, Haddington and Dalkeith where he was in medical charge of some French prisoners. He did some private work 'on the side' and received fees of 2-5 guineas 'which is very pleasing to a young man'. At Kidderminster he operated for cataract on a gentleman who had been blind for 20 years and 'the patient was so pleased with the result that he rewarded the Surgeon with a handsome present and gave a dinner to the whole Regiment'. He also did some inoculations and vaccinations. Even during his army service he continued his studies, especially in anatomy. In Kidderminster he somehow obtained the body of a child for dissection, but the parents discovered what was going on, and Jordan had to beat a precipitate retreat from the town.

In a letter to his mother in 1807 he surmised that an army career 'is not that to be wished by a young man who intends to get well forward in life', although he added that if he became a full army surgeon on pay of 12/6 per day it would allow him to be of some assistance to her. Several years later, apparently disillusioned by being shunted around home bases and seeing no real action (except riots in Nottingham), he resigned his commission.    In 1811  he went to

London for a year to continue his studies and widen his experience, and he returned to Manchester in 1812 to become junior partner in a well-established practice belonging to Messrs Stewart and Bancks. Perhaps he found practice less satisfying and rewarding than anticipated, or maybe he had an unfulfilled desire to teach, for within two years he had retired from the partnership and on 14 September 1814, the following advertisement appeared in Wheeler's Chronicle:

> To Students of Anatomy
> Mr. Jordan will open rooms for the study of
> Anatomy on the 1st of October.
> Bridge Street.

The same advertisement was repeated in 1815, except that the word 'open' was replaced by 'reopen' and the number '69' was inserted before Bridge Street. Initially the lectures and demonstrations were devoted mainly to anatomy, but subsequently instruction was provided by Jordan or an assistant in a few other subjects such as surgery and pathology. Thomas Turner opened a second medical school in Pine Street, Manchester, in 1824. From its inception it had a wider curriculum than Jordan's, and Turner deserves the credit for creating the first more or less complete provincial medical school in England. Jordan attempted to counter the threat produced by Turner's school by erecting a new purpose-built school in Mount Street, which he opened in 1826 'for the express purpose of teaching Anatomy, Surgery, Medicine, Chemistry and other branches of Medical Science'. It was larger and much better equipped than the Pine Street school, and even included private dissecting rooms for doctors - the first medical provision in Manchester for postgraduates. Turner employed more and better lecturers, however, and his school flourished as Jordan's declined. Eventually it engulfed Jordan's school and in 1836 it became the Royal Manchester School of Medicine and Surgery, which was finally absorbed into Owens College,[4] the precursor of the Victoria University of Manchester, as the basis of its Faculty of Medicine. (For more details see essay No. 7.2 on Thomas Turner.

Jordan conceived the idea of providing his courses of lectures with three objectives in mind: to spare students the considerable expense of their obligatory attendance at such courses in London if they wished to obtain a diploma from the College of Surgeons or a licence from the Society of Apothecaries, to guard the youths from exposure to the moral and social dangers in the metropolis at an impressionable age, and to increase the number of qualified medical men to the advantage of country towns. His course was therefore designed to conform with the requirements of the London College and the Apothecaries' Society, comprising 140 lectures, with demonstrations and dissections, extending from 1 October in one year until the end of April in the next. Readers will appreciate his innovation better if they recall that, prior to the eighteenth century, most medical practitioners had no university, college or society qualifications. A minority had Oxbridge, Scottish or Continental university degrees, others had diplomas from London, Edinburgh or Dublin Colleges, and those dispensing medicines required a licence from the Society of Apothecaries. The majority of intending doctors, however, became indentured to established physicians, surgeons or apothecaries for 5-7 years from the age of 15-20. The apprentice received instruction in medicine, surgery, midwifery and dispensing from his master and gained practical and clinical experience by assisting him in his practice. Any theoretical instruction on principles was rudimentary, suitable books were scarce, and lecture courses in medical subjects were available only in the few British Universities in existence before 1800 or in private schools (like that of the Hunter Brothers) in the capital cities of London, Edinburgh and Dublin. This is why Jordan's innovation was so significant, and within 10-20 years it was followed by the founding of similar or more complete schools (like Turner's in Manchester) in many other provincial towns such as Sheffield, Birmingham, Bristol, Leeds, Nottingham, Liverpool, York, etc.

Jordan's success brought him both profit and prestige. This aroused jealousy and hostility in some quarters which became manifest, for example, when he tried unsuccessfully to be elected as an Infirmary surgeon in 1828 and 1833. It was then suggested to him that, if he closed his school, any subsequent application he made for election as an Infirmary surgeon would not be seriously opposed: he did close his school in 1834, though probably the increasing success of Turner's school was already turning his mind in that direction. In 1835, owing to the unexpected death of Mr Whatton who had been the successful candidate in 1833, the Infirmary post again became vacant. Jordan applied anew, along with three other candidates, and this time he was appointed – despite attempts to sabotage his chances by allegations that he was making false and unjustified claims. Evidence of this persists in a letter published in the *Manchester Guardian*,[5] as the following extracts reveal:

> Sir – It having been repeatedly alleged during the present canvass for the vacant surgeoncy at the Royal Infirmary by the friends of one of the candidates, that he has greater claims upon the trustees than the other candidates, on the ground of his having been the originator or founder of the Anatomical, Surgical, and Medical Schools, in this town, and believing that such assertions have originated in inadvertence, and not from any wish to misrepresent, or to assume for such candidate merit to which he is not fairly entitled. ... In Manchester, Schools of Anatomy, Physiology, Medicine and Surgery have long been established. The celebrated Charles White, Mr. Gibson, Dr. Roget, and Messrs. Ransome and Ainsworth, gave annual public courses of lectures upon Anatomy, Physiology and Surgery, and they are the true founders of Anatomical, Surgical and Medical Schools in this town.

The writer(s) must have known that these were half-truths. All the above-mentioned doctors, and others such as Drs G Bell and T Percival, gave sporadic or short courses of lectures on medical topics before Jordan opened his School in 1814. Thus Dr Bell gave the inaugural lecture to the Manchester Literary and Philosophical Society in 1781 against a hypothesis that the animal body can generate cold.[6] In 1783 Dr Charles White and his son Thomas gave a course of lectures on anatomy and physiology to the same Society, and four years later they gave a course on midwifery in Charles White's house. Doctors B Gibson, P Roget (of Thesaurus fame), J A Ransome and J Ainsworth gave lectures on anatomy, surgery, physiology and other subjects on various dates prior to 1814, but none approximated in scope or duration to Jordan's courses; none was supported by dissection facilities or by a museum comparable to the one Jordan assembled in his School; and none of the courses given by these presumed 'true founders of ... Medical Schools in this town' was approved by the College of Surgeons or Society of Apothecaries – whereas Jordan's were reputedly approved by the Society in 1817 and by the London College of Surgeons in 1821: London College recognition was probably delayed because Jordan then possessed only the Edinburgh diploma.[3] Approval meant that Jordan's certificates for the non-clinical parts of the medical course were accepted as the equivalent of those obtained from London Schools and his students were allowed to take the appropriate examinations. The London examiners (many were also London teachers) noted that the Manchester entrants 'were particularly well equipped in anatomical knowledge' and 'during the time Dr Jordan lectured in anatomy (upwards of 20 years) he never had a student rejected in this subject'. Dr John Hull, First President of the Manchester Medical Society, wrote several letters to the Apothecaries and Surgeons in support of Jordan's applications and played an influential rôle in their successful outcome. Incidentally Drs Hull, Jordan, Simmons, Brigham and Stewart were co-founders in 1819 of the Manchester Lock Hospital for unfortunate women (later called St Luke's) and Jordan acted as its surgeon until 1835, when he gave up this post on becoming an Infirmary surgeon.

In 1854 Mr Wilson, then senior Infirmary surgeon recalled Jordan's earliest teaching efforts in a small place in Back Queen Street and described himself 'as an early participator in the benefits conferred by Mr Jordan on the whole profession'. Mr Brigham attended Jordan's opening lecture 'when we only mustered a dozen, Anatomy and Surgery being at that time the *principal* pursuits and the *principal* sources of study'. They do not mention dates, but an article in the Manchester Guardian[7] says 'Jordan's work as a teacher in Manchester began in 1812 in a small place in Back Queen Street (now Lloyd Street) off Deansgate'. As stated earlier, his advertised courses of study in 1814 and 1815 were given at 69 Bridge Street, but by 1816 he had to rent more spacious premises at 4 Bridge Street (later renumbered as No. 70). The dissecting room at No. 4 was on the first floor and the only access for living and dead was by a ladder from the back yard. Increasing numbers of students necessitated further expansion, so Jordan rented the entire house next door (No. 68) and the upper part of No. 66. The upper floors of all three houses were then converted into two large rooms, one serving as a dissecting room and the other as a museum for his ever-increasing number of specimens. These rooms were isolated from the others (which were occupied by Jordan and his domestic staff) by an internal enclosed staircase. They were regarded as haunted by the servants and this 'was the cause of a good deal of domestic trouble for the servants were continually leaving'.

One special advantage was claimed by Jordan for his school: bodies or subjects for dissection could be obtained very easily. Before the Anatomy Act was passed in 1832 regular supplies of human bodies could not be obtained legally for dissection. Some of the older universities had the right to claim the bodies of a limited number of executed criminals every year for dissection, but students at Jordan's and other similar schools had no such rights and had to rob graves and gallows.[8] A few ruffians, like Burke and Hare in Edinburgh, committed murders to provide bodies for sale, but there is no evidence of such crimes in connection with the Manchester medical schools. A footnote in Jordan's biography[1] reveals, however, that he sent surplus bodies to Dr Knox, who ran a similar but much larger school in Edinburgh.

Jordan admitted his own involvement in a speech at a prize-giving ceremony in the Chatham Street School of Medicine in 1854 when he said:

> You have heard of body-snatching, but you have not been behind the scenes. The students in my time were obliged to steal bodies themselves, and I am not ashamed to say that I was one of the very parties. You were required to understand your profession, but you were utterly forbidden to dissect. You had no means of obtaining subjects, you were prosecuted if you robbed the churchyards. Here you were; the public and the Legislature demanding of you a knowledge of your profession, and yet the law utterly prevented you obtaining that knowledge.

In the earlier days of his school Jordan and his students stole the bodies themselves, but later most or all of these macabre activities were performed by professional 'resurrectionists' who charged about £10 per body. Jordan was once fined £20 for instigating body-snatching and a 'resurrectionist' he employed was sentenced to a year's imprisonment. The magistrate was 'reluctant' to fine Jordan as he recognised that medical students must dissect as part of their training, while lacking legal provision to obtain bodies for such purposes. This judicial restraint was not shared by the public. On one occasion when Jordan sent a barrel containing 10-12 bodies to a carrier it was not forwarded promptly and the resulting stench aroused suspicions. Inquiries revealed the nature of the contents and the identity of the consignor and angry crowds smashed the windows of Jordan's Bridge Street houses, while he did not venture outside for several days. The *Manchester Guardian*[9] records the 'great ferment' caused in the town by the detection of two resurrection men; and in the *Lancaster Gazette*[10] there is a report of an inquest on an unknown woman and child whose bodies had been discovered in a box consigned from Manchester to Edinburgh by a New Times coach. A pamphlet printed by J Pratt[11] gives an account of the trial in 1827 of John Eaton, Sexton of St George's Chapel, who was accused of assisting in body-snatching. Other events could be cited showing that body-snatching was common in and around Manchester, and that some attempts were made to prevent this foul trade, although a contemporary Liverpool paper stated correctly: 'The difficulty of obtaining bodies in Scotland, for the anatomical lectures, is chiefly owing to the vigilance with which the churchyards are watched. The surgeons are therefore obliged to send their agents to England, where less precaution is generally taken, and the recompense, which is now £10-£15 per body, never fails to procure a sufficient supply'.

After the closure of his School in 1834 a dinner was given in Jordan's honour[12] when about 130 attended. After several laudatory speeches he was presented with a massive inscribed silver vase and salver, and in an emotional response he declared it was the proudest moment of his life. There were thirty toasts! He rejected various invitations to teach in the Pine Street School until the session 1838-39 when he acted as co-lecturer in surgery with Mr Ransome Jun., and following renewed requests he lectured on surgery again in 1850 and 1851. Thereafter he confined his teaching entirely to clinical lectures at the Infirmary.

When Jordan was appointed as an Infirmary surgeon in 1835 he remarked 'I now have reached the height of my ambition, I will retire from practice, enjoy mine ease, and keep my carriage'. However, apart from retiring from his post as surgeon to the Lock Hospital, little is known about his later years. His biographer states that 'his professional work filled his life and it was only later in life that he indulged in recreational pursuits'. He and his yellow carriage were well known in the town and his hospital visits took precedence over his private practice. He was always kind and considerate to patients, especially to women and children, with a reputation as a good diagnostician and a cool operator. A great favourite with students, 'his class at the Infirmary was always the most largely attended'. His achievements were recognised by the award of the FRCS (Hon.) in 1843,[13] and of an illuminated address in 1862 from the Royal Society of Medicine. On retiring from the Royal Infirmary in 1866 he received 'a testimonial expressed in unusually cordial terms and signed by the whole staff' and made an Honorary Consultant, and in 1869 he was appointed as Consulting Surgeon Extraordinary to the Salford Royal Hospital. Mr Wilson, the Senior Infirmary Surgeon and some of Jordan's

MP admirers proposed in 1859 that some mark of Royal favour should be solicited for him, but he modestly asked them to desist from this proposal.

He was not noted as a research worker or writer. He was fluent in French, and so competent in the Classics that he could converse in Latin. He began translating Galen *On the Hand*, but it had to be finished by T Bellot;[14] and a planned treatise on human physiognomy (he had 'some pronounced views on the nose' - not surprising when one studies his portrait!) was never started. He visited Paris annually over an unspecified number of years and was very friendly with Professor Nélaton and Dr Béraud. With their help a treatise entitled 'Traitement des pseudarthroses par l'autoplastie périostique' was produced in 1860, and a case report on 'Oblitération de l'aorte' in a man aged about 40 was communicated in Jordan's name to the Société de Biologie and appeared in the *Gazette des Hôpitaux* No. 108, 14 September 1858. At an earlier date he had published another report on 'A case of obliteration of the aorta';[15] this condition had been detected in a  man aged 21 whose body had been 'raised for the purpose of dissection'. He intended to produce a work on 'Diseases of the Testis' and showed his specimens to his friend Sir Astley Cooper (who once suggested he should move to London), but no evidence of this work has been traced.

Apart from his portraits, a picture of his physical and personal characteristics can be composed from descriptions and remarks made by his biographer, colleagues and former students. He was tall and thin and had a dignified and commanding presence. He was very active, a stickler for good discipline and time-keeping, but he had a buoyant and happy disposition, a sense of humour, the gift of quick repartee, an infectious laugh, and he was very popular with his patients, students and most of his colleagues. Despite these mainly attractive qualities he never married; perhaps any lady friends, like his servants, were repelled by the prospect of sharing a home with a dissecting room and museum!

Like many bachelors his home was rather untidy and his furniture and furnishings old-fashioned and uncomfortable. He slept on a camp bed with bones underneath, in a bedroom lined with bookshelves, and an overflow of books on every chair and covering most of the floor. His habits were methodical and abstemious. He did not smoke but was an

inveterate snuff-taker, and it was only in later life that he allowed
alcoholic drinks at his dinner parties. Maybe these austere habits
explained why he enjoyed such good health for most of his life.
However, after living for sixty years in Bridge Street, his health
began to fail. Assuming the Manchester air was to blame he transferred
for short periods to Salford and then to Stroud. Finally he removed to
Hampstead to be near an old friend, Mr Gay, who attended him in his
last illness. He died, aged 86, on 31 March 1873. The following
remarks are part of the tribute to him in the *Manchester Guardian*:[16]

> Mr Jordan's nature was most simple and gentle, and yet he was
> possessed of perfect coolness and determination. Without ever being
> a brilliant surgeon, he was to the last a thoroughly large-minded
> and large-hearted medical man. Never prejudiced against a project
> because it was new, nor bigoted in its favour because it was old.
> Indeed, of him it might truly be said, 'Both gladlie would he
> learne and gladlie teache'.
>
> > GAGM

7.2 THOMAS TURNER, 1793-1873

   FRCS, FLS


Thomas Turner was born on 13 August 1793 in Truro, youngest of the
five children of Edmund and Joanna Turner. Edmund Turner was a banker.
His forbears came to Cornwall from Hempstead, Hertfordshire, when the
Reverend John Turner, MA,(Cantab) became Vicar of Treneglos and
Warbstow in 1635. Turner was educated at Miss Warren's day-school and
Truro Grammar School and in 1811 he was apprenticed to Mr Nehemiah
Duck, one of the surgeons of St Peter's Hospital, Bristol. There he
completed a course in anatomy and physiology and his diligence
attracted the attention of the Governor and Medical Officers of the
Hospital, who 'promoted him to several appointments in the Hospital'
including four years as post-mortem examiner.[1] In October 1815, Turner
became a student at the (then) united Hospitals of Guy's and St
Thomas', under Mr Astley Cooper, (later Sir Astley Cooper, PRCS). He
became MRCS, and LSA, in 1816, and in August of that year, with an
introduction from Astley Cooper, he went to Paris, where he spent a
year as the pupil of Professor Roue. He attended the clinics of
Champier, Richerand, Dupuytren and Boyer. Early in 1817, he prepared a
paper on medical education for presentation to one of the medical
societies in Paris, to several of which he belonged. This paper marked
the beginning of a lifelong interest in the teaching and examining of
students. He was reading for a medical degree having settled the
preliminaries with the College, when his youngest sister and her
husband, resident in Manchester, urged him to apply for the vacant
post of house surgeon to the Lunatic Hospital and Infirmary (from
1830, Manchester Royal Infirmary). He was appointed in 1817 and soon
afterwards he wrote to his former teacher, Mr Nehemiah Duck,
describing the busy practice of the Infirmary and the  development  of

his clinical experience. A severe illness in 1820 kept him from his work for three months so that he resigned in September and toured the Isle of Man, Scotland and London. In Glasgow he visited the teaching hospitals, and in Edinburgh the Royal Infirmary, the Royal College of Surgeons, and the museums of Doctors Barclay and Munro. In London he visited Hunter's Museum and attended lectures by Astley Cooper. He returned to Manchester on 5 October 1820 and settled into independent practice at his house in Piccadilly. In 1821, he was elected a member of the Manchester Literary and Philosophical Society and Secretary of the Natural History Society. At these meetings he was introduced to many eminent doctors and scientists, including John Dalton, and on the 1 November 1822, he delivered the first of a series of lectures on anatomy, physiology and pathology to an audience of members of the Literary and Philosophical Society and medical students. The last lecture of that series was delivered on 17 March 1823, and at a dinner at the Albion Hotel on 16 July, he was presented with a richly chased antique gold vase, by the members and students who had attended his lectures. His diary records the completion, on 20 September 1822, of 'An Epitome of Anatomy and Physiology in the application to Medicine and Surgery', and it was published later that year. He continued to lecture at the Literary and Philosophical Society and in 1824, he delivered an address there proposing the establishment of a preparatory School of Medicine and Surgery in Manchester. The background to this proposal relates to the conditions then prevailing for the examining and licensing of medical students. Five classes of practitioner cared for patients in the United Kingdom at that time (1824), physicians, surgeons, surgeon-apothecaries, apothecaries, and unlicensed 'practitioners'. Apothecaries greatly outnumbered physicians and surgeons and unqualified practitioners outnumbered them all.[2] The urgent need for naval and military surgeons during the Napoleonic wars added to the confusion because their examinations were much less rigorous than were those of candidates for the ordinary diploma. Having been approved for naval or military service, the returning surgeon could enter civilian practice without further examinations.[3]

On the 1 August 1815, a month after the Battle of Waterloo, the Apothecaries Act became law. This Act, 'for better regulating the Practice of Apothecaries throughout England and Wales',[4] was the

10 and 11. Two silver medals awarded to Mr John Wood in 1832 and 1833. Some of the rival medical schools which flourished in Manchester about the time of the formation of the Manchester Medical Society are referred to in the essays on Joseph Jordan (7.1) and Thomas Turner (7.2).

catalyst for future reforms and it greatly influenced and encouraged the development of provincial medical schools.[5] Unfortunately for Turner and other provincial teachers, the regulations made by the Court of Examiners of the Society of Apothecaries and the care with which they discharged their new responsibilities stimulated the London and Edinburgh Colleges of Surgeons to alter their regulations. In 1820, the Edinburgh College of Surgeons required that candidates studied under *resident* Fellows or Licenciates of the Colleges in London, Dublin, Edinburgh or Glasgow[6] and the London College of Surgeons made similar regulations in 1824.[3]

Turner and his colleagues opened a *preparatory* School of Medicine and Surgery in Pine Street, Manchester, in October 1824. The first lecture of the winter course was given on the 8 November, the lecturers being Turner (Anatomy), J L Bardsley (Principles and Practice of Materia Medica), Ransome (Surgery), John Dalton, FRS, (Chemistry), Kinder Wood (Midwifery), and Thomson (Botany). Turner addressed the staff and students in January, 1825;[1]

> If you neglect to lay the foundation you will find, when the time comes to lay the superstructure, that your basis is so sandy as to discourage you in your proceedings ... on the other hand, young men who have had the advantages of elementary instruction have entered on their studies at the superior schools with avidity and success.

The 'superior schools' were the Colleges noted in the regulations of the London and Edinburgh Colleges of Surgeons. Turner's claim that 'The Company of Apothecaries receive our Certificates of Lectures and our Certificates of Attendance at our Infirmary and public institutions' was true. They had never sought to establish a monopoly but had endeavoured, as the Apothecaries Act required, to ensure that only properly apprenticed and properly educated people practised as apothecaries; the annual reports of their Court of Examiners make it quite clear that candidates for the diploma of apothecary had to be *examined*, but not necessarily taught, in London.[7] Indeed, in evidence to a Select Committee of the House of Commons, in 1828, John Watson, the Secretary of the Society of Apothecaries said,[8]

> no young men came before the Court of the Society of Apothecaries better qualified in every respect than those who had been entirely educated at Manchester ...

But Turner's claim that 'the opposition which might on some accounts have been expected from the Colleges of London and Edinburgh has not been made' was ambiguous. He wrote to, and visited, the Presidents of both Colleges. On 1 March 1825, the President of the Edinburgh College 'moved that Mr Turner's lectures be received as a course of anatomy and that attendance on the Manchester hospital be admitted ...'.[9] He was less successful in London. On the 6 October 1826, the Secretary of the Court of Examiners of the Royal College of Surgeons of London was instructed 'to inform Mr Turner that this Court regret that they cannot allow his Certificates to be so admitted, because if they allow it to him they must allow the same to every person who shall lecture in any provincial Town, which, in the opinion of this Court, would be detrimental to scientific professional education'.[10] Turner persisted with applications to both Colleges and the Edinburgh College recognised the teaching at Pine Street School of Medicine and Surgery *for one year's course of study* in anatomy, midwifery and 'attendance upon the hospital', in November 1829.[9] The London College recognised only anatomy and physiology, on 5 March 1830.[10]

Apart from his teaching and his surgical practice, Turner was active in other directions. In 1828, Henry Warburton's Committee at the House of Commons was charged 'to Inquire into the manner of obtaining subjects for dissection in the Schools of Anatomy ...' and Turner was invited to submit evidence. He noted that the original draft made no provision for supplying subjects to the Anatomy Schools and his recommendations, based on his experience in Paris, were included in an amended Bill. The Anatomy Act became law on the 1 August 1832, and it had an early and considerable effect on provincial schools. Turner's School was not the first to teach anatomy in Manchester. Joseph Jordan opened a School of Anatomy in Bridge Street, Manchester in 1814 and in 1826, he took larger premises and included pathology and clinical subjects in the curriculum (see essay No. 7.1 on Joseph Jordan). According to Jordan's biographer, his nephew F W Jordan, the School 'broke up on account of petty jealousies of the lecturers ... they intrigued and opposed his efforts to get into the Infirmary'.[11] These were Jordan's colleagues in his own School, not the lecturers at Pine Street. Turner was elected to the surgical staff of the Manchester Infirmary on 4 August 1830 and Jordan applied unsuccessfully in 1828 and 1833. Jordan's biographer claimed that a proposal was made that if Jordan gave up his School and joined Pine Street, all opposition to a further application would disappear.[11]

This claim is difficult to understand because candidates were then elected by vote of the Trustees and at Jordan's (1833) unsuccessful application, 732 votes were cast, of which Whatton, the successful candidate gained 419 and Jordan 277, 36 going to a third candidate. Jordan applied successfully on 31 December 1835, when 900 votes were cast, 466 to Jordan.[12] Because pre-election canvassing was accepted and widely practised, it is possible that the votes could be influenced as Jordan's biographer suggested but it seems unlikely. After his election to the Infirmary staff, Jordan agreed to join Turner and his colleagues at Pine Street. So did Thomas Fawdington who had been one of Jordan's lecturers at Mount Street in 1826, and had left, with others, to found another School of Anatomy, in 1828, in Marsden Street nearby. Fawdington was one of three unsuccessful candidates when Jordan was elected to the Infirmary Staff in 1835, but he was successful in 1837. Neither Fawdington nor anyone on his behalf suggested that he must join his School with Pine Street in order to get on the Infirmary Staff. Almost certainly, the reason why Jordan and Fawdington joined Turner's School was the report of Doctor Somerville, the first Inspector of Anatomy appointed by the Home Department following the Anatomy Act of 1832. Doctor Somerville reported to the Secretary of State on 12 September 1832, only six weeks after the Act became law,

My Lord,
Having completed the inspection of the Schools of Anatomy in the Provincial Towns in England, I have the honour to submit the following report to your Lordship's Consideration ... The existence of two or more Schools of Anatomy in some of the smaller Towns is an Evil the more to be regretted when there is a small supply of dead bodies. I have therefore, endeavoured to impress upon the minds of the Teachers the necessity of a coalition and in some instances, I hope with good effect.

Doctor Somerville inspected three Schools in Manchester. Turner's, 'the most complete School in all its departments'; Thomas Fawdington and John Boutflower's School, 'these gentlemen originally lectured in conjunction with Mr Jordan'. Of 'the third' School, Somerville said 'Mr Jordan being in London, I had only an opportunity of seeing his premises which are very extensive'. On the 16 November 1832, the President of the Royal College of Surgeons of London laid before the Court of Examiners a letter written by Doctor Somerville enclosing a list of the Teachers of Anatomy in the Provincial Towns of England licensed by the Secretary of State:[10]

Manchester: Thomas Turner
John Boutflower
Thomas Fawdington
Joseph Jordan
Edward Stephens
Edward Blackmore

Here was the lever that moved Jordan's School into Pine Street, no doubt primed by Messrs Fawdington and Boutflower. Somerville's approval now conferred a legal right to obtain subjects for dissection but should he withhold a licence, a School could not lawfully teach practical anatomy. Fawdington and Boutflower clearly went willingly to Pine Street with their School, leaving Jordan with the possibility that his School would not gain a licence. His School closed in April 1834 and he joined the staff of Pine Street. Having obtained royal patronage in March 1836, the Pine Street School became the Manchester Royal School of Medicine. Surgery lectures were then given by Arthur Dumville, MRCS, and George Southam, MRCS, both of whom were prominent in establishing a rival School of Medicine and Surgery in Chatham Street in 1850. This and the Royal School amalgamated in 1858, the newer premises in Chatham Street being used until 1861 when the combined School returned to Pine Street. The Dumville Surgical Scholarship was founded by Dumville's second wife in his memory. George Southam followed Turner on the Council of the Royal College of Surgeons of England. He was Honorary Surgeon to the Royal Infirmary as were his son, Frederick, and his grandson, Arthur.

In 1843, approval was given for changes in the Charter of the Royal College of Surgeons of London, two results of which were a change of title to 'The Royal College of Surgeons of England' and the creation from existing Members, of 'Fellows'. The first 300, with Turner and Jordan among them, were elected on 11 December 1843. In July 1865, Turner was elected to the Council of the College, with Mr James Paget (later Sir James Paget, PRCS). Turner evidently contributed little to the business of the College and Sir James Paget did not mention him in his Memoirs. In 1852, he founded, with Canon Richson, the Manchester and Salford Sanitary Association and in 1859 he raised enough money to establish an infant school for the deaf. He resigned from the staff of the Royal Infirmary in 1855 but maintained his interest in the Royal School of Medicine and in environmental and industrial causes of disease. The Royal School was incorporated into Owens College* in August 1872, and Turner gave the Inaugural Address. An agreement was made between him and Mr Southam the surgeon for the purchase of their interest in the property of the School, the income being applied as the 'Turner Medical Prize'.

He married Anna, only daughter of James Clarke of Medham, Isle of Wight, in March 1826. There were two sons and three daughters. The eldest daughter married the Rev. W H Hamilton, Curate (later Rector) of the Parish of Marton, near Skipton in Craven, Yorkshire in 1850. She died in 1858 and was buried in the churchyard there. Her mother died in 1861 and was buried beside her daughter. Turner busied himself with patients and lectures after his wife's death until 1873 when a few months gradual deterioration ended with his death in December, in his eighty-first year. He was buried with his wife at Marton.

Jordan was undoubtedly the pioneer of organised medical teaching in Manchester and perhaps in the provinces. Turner was the acknowledged leader of those whose long exertions led to the establishment of a University Medical School, some of whose students would achieve great distinction. One would be known as the Prince of Vice-Chancellors, some would be Fellows of the Royal Society of London, and one would be President of the Royal College of Surgeons into whose Council Turner had been admitted nearly a century before. The Medical School, the springboard of these achievements, was not the creation of one man; he did not pretend it to be, but it owed much to the drive and vision that were expressed in a paper on Medical Education written in Paris in 1817.

LT

*Opened on 12 March 1851, it later became the Victoria University of Manchester.

## 7.3 JOHN ROBERTON, 1797-1876
### MRCS, LSA


Of the original members of the Manchester Medical Society, none attained distinction over a wider sphere than the Scottish surgeon, John Roberton. A devout Nonconformist, he combined a distinguished career in obstetrics and gynaecology, with campaigning for over half a century on many aspects of social reform. He wrote on philosophy, paediatrics, midwifery and hospital design, and produced a steady stream of political pamphlets.[1]

He was born on 20 March 1797 at Earnoch, Hamilton, in Lanarkshire, the second son in a family with a long yeoman ancestry.[2] After training as a surgeon at Glasgow and Edinburgh, he qualified MRCS at Edinburgh in 1817 and came to England the following year. As a student he had been influenced by the physician and philanthropist William Pulteney Alison, whose dedicated care of the sick poor became a model for Roberton's later work.

His first practice was at Warrington where he achieved a high reputation and married Mary Bellhouse, the daughter of a successful entrepreneur. The Bellhouses had extensive business interests in Manchester, and it was at their suggestion that Roberton and his wife moved to the 'shock city' in 1825, shortly after the early death of their first child.

Within two years of his arrival Roberton had been elected to the honorary medical staff of the Lying-in Hospital (now St Mary's), one of the largest domiciliary midwifery charities in Europe, delivering 4000-5000 infants a year in some of the worst housing conditions in Manchester. His appointment as a man-midwife, as the obstetricians were called, marked the turning point in his professional life, for until his election he had no particular leanings towards midwifery and little experience. He was required to train himself on complicated cases requiring the use of instruments; straightforward deliveries were left to the female midwives.

After seeing his colleagues apply a variety of instruments, sometimes with disastrous results, Roberton decided to develop his own. With the advice of Thomas Radford (1793-1881) he constructed a pair of craniotomy forceps and later designed a perforator, a blunt hook, a pair of long forceps and a foetal respiratory tube. This was an ingenious contrivance, devised in an emergency to save the life of a child. It was inserted into the mouth of the foetus to induce respiration and was used when feet or breech presentations occurred in a first labour.

Some of his inventions were probably unique though most of the instruments for which he became well known were refinements of those commonly available. His forceps were made by a Manchester firm which sold about two hundred pairs between 1830 and 1850, and were so popular that the makers asked him to prepare a book of instructions to accompany his instruments. In it he included six golden aphorisms. The sixth was: 'Better flee midwifery than injure, by the use of instruments, the organs of a wife and mother'.

For several years Roberton taught midwifery and medical jurisprudence at the Marsden Street School of Medicine after Radford had transferred to the rival Pine Street School. He enlivened his teaching with descriptions of the midwifery practices and puberty rites of foreign cultures, a subject on which he was an authority. His research showed that, contrary to travellers' tales, parturition among primitive peoples was not always natural and easy, but often highly dangerous because of the customs practised. His investigations into midwifery around the world were linked to his interest in the effects of climate, and the heat of cotton mills, on female puberty. He was the first doctor to challenge the orthodox medical belief that warmer climates produced earlier puberty. To establish that the age range of menarche in Britain was much wider than believed, he questioned a sample of patients from St Mary's, a novel method of research in 1830. Then he extended his enquiries by contacting doctors and missionaries as far away as Greenland and Polynesia, amassing a wealth of fascinating detail. By his studies Roberton overturned the current belief that factory girls were precocious.

For over twenty years Roberton wrote on midwifery and puberty in leading medical journals. In 1851 he collected his papers into *Essays and Notes on the Physiology and Diseases of Women, and on Practical Midwifery*, a work which was highly praised in this country and America. One of his papers, an account of an epidemic of puerperal fever in Manchester, was of such importance as to be later cited by authorities like Sir James Young Simpson and Oliver Wendell Holmes as evidence that childbed fever was contagious.[3] The outbreak had originated in the patients of one of the midwives of the Lying-in Charity in December 1830. She was removed from the district when it was discovered that of the thirty women she had delivered in one month, sixteen had died. But the fever spread through the town in a wave of destruction for a further six months. Roberton estimated that hundreds of mothers died in the epidemic and many more made a lingering recovery. This harrowing experience convinced him that puerperal fever could be transmitted from one patient to the next by a doctor or midwife, a conclusion few doctors were then prepared to accept.

The destitution and foul conditions he encountered in his daily round for the Lying-in Hospital disturbed him profoundly and he began to agitate for public health reforms. Few writers were so familiar with the insanitary cellar-dwellings of Manchester and Salford, or were more committed to speak out on behalf of the poor. Roberton's work had an authenticity which commended it to contemporary social commentators such as Leon Faucher, Kay-Shuttleworth and Frederick Engels, who quoted from his writings.

When, in 1831, it was claimed by some political economists, that people were living longer and must therefore be healthier, he countered publicly that life for many textile workers was one long disease. He recognised that many of the poor seeking relief from medical charities needed not medicine, but food and rest; he advocated convalescent homes by the sea, where the sick poor could receive a nutritious diet and breathe fresh air, if only for a few weeks.

His first book, published in the year he was elected to St Mary's, had drawn attention to the high infant mortality of the new industrial towns. With data extracted from burial registers he demonstrated that the infant death rate in Manchester was much higher than in rural areas. His figures pinpointed the enormous loss of life immediately after birth, especially among boys, and the great mortality under the age of two. Since the introduction of smallpox vaccination more children were surviving beyond two years, but Roberton calculated that this left more children to die between the ages of two and ten from measles, scarlet fever, whooping cough and croup. This book was also a child-care manual, based on the belief that many infant deaths could be prevented by more careful management. It gave advice on breast-feeding, weaning, teething and dress. The regimen he recommended of a plain diet, daily cool baths and no swaddling or coddling was followed by his own large family, two of whom died in infancy. His first son, born after six girls, died of croup at the age of five months, despite his own efforts and those of his colleagues to save him. He was so concerned by his inability to cure the boy that he had the body dissected and reported the findings in a medical journal.

In all his writings Roberton attempted to bring about improvements to the quality of life, by raising the standards of medical practice and by stirring the public conscience. He was a deeply religious man, who believed it was his duty to help the weak and to fight social injustice. Whether he was combatting child neglect, or calling for better housing, safer working conditions or changes in the hospital services, it was his religion and humanity which spurred him.

The majority of his patients were women, and repeatedly in his pamphlets he questioned their subordinate position, their lack of rights and education. It was recognised at that time that there were more women in the population than men, but Roberton was the first to examine the question in detail, by comparing statistics from Britain, Europe and America. He calculated that the excess of females over males was much greater in some English towns than the generally accepted figure of two per cent, and that a large proportion of these women were unmarried or widowed. The plight of widows with dependent children particularly attracted his sympathy. He attacked the harsh treatment meted out to widows with young children by the Poor Laws, and even criticised his own church for not being sufficiently charitable to widows, orphans and the aged. In contrast, he gave his medical services to the poor of his church and to the patients of the Town Mission and he supplied mothers with free milk and other necessities.[4]

His duties at the Lying-in Hospital undermined his health and, after eleven years service, he resigned. This gained him more time for his large private practice and for his writing. He joined the Manchester Statistical Society and was President from 1844 to 1847. In his twenty-seven years membership he presented more papers than anyone in the history of the Society.[5] During the 1840s his demands for public health reforms were ably supported by the impressive mortality tables he prepared for the Health of Towns Commission.

His involvement in the movement for reform earned him the respect and admiration of some of the leading figures of his day – men like Richard Cobden, MP who corresponded with him for many years, and Edwin Chadwick the sanitary reformer. In 1846 Roberton enlisted Chadwick's help and the backing of the Manchester Statistical Society to expose the conditions of the railway navvies working on the Summit Tunnel. Almost a thousand men were engaged on the line. Their squalid, makeshift camp, devoid of all amenities, covered three or four miles of desolate moorland. There were no safety regulations to protect railway labourers and the number of fatal accidents on the excavations was high. When Roberton made the issue public the *Manchester Guardian* rallied to his cause and the surgeon who attended the navvies agreed to give evidence against the railway company. With Chadwick lobbying intensely at Westminster they procured a Parliamentary Enquiry which confirmed the accuracy of Roberton's allegations. But they could achieve nothing more because of the power of the railway companies.

Against such vested interests less determined men retreated but Roberton continued to inspect mines, workhouses, prisons and hospitals, prodding those responsible into introducing changes. He called for improved accident services and for more and better hospitals. In his opinion conditions in hospitals were so unhygienic that accident victims were more likely to die from the effects of the polluted wards than from their injuries. The Manchester Royal Infirmary did not escape his criticism, indeed the medical committee was forced into a public rebuttal of his charges.[6] They nonetheless improved conditions very much as Roberton suggested. This did not entirely satisfy him; he thought that the Infirmary should be rebuilt out of town, away from the noise and dirt of Piccadilly.

Roberton's greatest contribution to hospital reform was in the introduction to Britain of the pavilion system of hospital construction.[7] He had seen hospitals built on the pavilion pattern in

France and was so impressed that in 1856 he published plans of the hospital at Bordeaux. To Roberton, the new French hospitals, erected in single storeys around peaceful gardens, appeared as havens of tranquility. They were carefully designed to ensure maximum natural cross ventilation so as to prevent the build-up of a foul 'hospital atmosphere', and it was this feature which Roberton set about promoting in this country. His ideas were taken up with so much enthusiasm that he went on to design warehouses, schools and public buildings, based on the system of natural ventilation; but it was on hospital construction that he made the most impact. The type of ward he advocated is now known as the 'Nightingale ward', although it owes as much to Roberton as to Miss Nightingale, who referred to him as 'our greatest hospital authority'. His advice was sought in the building of many local hospitals, including the voluntary hospitals at Blackburn, Ashton under Lyne and Macclesfield, and the Chorlton Union Workhouse Infirmary, now Withington Hospital, which he regarded as, 'one of the best planned in the kingdom'.

In the mid 1860s he retired to New Mills, in Derbyshire, but returned to Manchester frequently to read the prayers at the Female Penitentiary and to continue his works of charity. He died at New Mills on 24 August 1876 and was buried at Rusholme Road Cemetery, Manchester. In his will he left six hundred pounds to the poor of his chapel.

JM

7.4 SAMUEL GASKELL, 1807-86
   FRCS


Samuel Gaskell (SG) was born in Warrington in 1807. In the latter part of the eighteenth century, this town had become a centre of learning, scientific education and printing; its Academy was founded in 1757 by unitarians, and there was a library and dispensary. It also became a manufacturing centre which for a time rivalled Birmingham and Manchester. SG's father, William Gaskell senior, was a manufacturer of sail canvas, and was one of a complicated network of inter-related families (all Dissenters), including the Darwins, Wedgwoods, and Hollands, who were active in all humanitarian concerns. The father died at the age of 42, leaving three sons and two daughters.

It was said to have been due to the self-denial and good sense of Mrs Gaskell that the family received the best education possible locally; she later married the unitarian minister, Rev. Dimock. From an early age, SG had wanted to become a doctor, but the family doctor discouraged this because an attack of measles had caused a weakness of SG's eyes. Therefore - perhaps paradoxically - he was bound for an apprenticeship to William Eyres, a publisher and bookseller in Liverpool, where he continued to study in his spare time. When any important news arrived from America, he was employed to take it to London by post-chaise, and is said to have used these long journeys for studious reading.

However, his drive to enter medicine did not diminish and, being recognised by his master, resulted in several years of his apprenticeship being remitted, so that he became free to follow his original bent. At the age of 18, he moved to Manchester, which by then had become an outstanding centre of both science and industry; he became apprentice to Mr Robert Thorpe at the Manchester Royal

Infirmary. In 1831, he moved to Edinburgh and returned the following year, having obtained the LRCS (Edin.) and MRCS (Eng.). In that year, cholera - which had been travelling westwards across Europe - arrived on the East Coast of England. SG was appointed Resident Medical Officer at the Cholera Hospital, Stockport, one of two special hospitals for it in the Manchester area.

Two years later, SG was appointed Resident House Apothecary at the Manchester Royal Infirmary, in succession to Mr Lloyd, and he became increasingly involved in the Lunatic Division of the hospital. The many references to him in the minutes of the Board meetings include his initiative in starting a library in 1839; he was said to have never lost his temper with the apprentices (which was presumably unusual). When he left the Manchester Royal Infirmary, its physician wrote that 'it is impossible for any public medical officer to have excelled him in the exercise of (his duties)'. Meanwhile, his brother William had been appointed minister of the Cross Street Chapel and had married Elizabeth, who became the famous novelist; SG remained a bachelor, but always had a happy association with his sister-in-law and her children.

In 1840, SG became Resident Surgeon at the Lancaster County Lunatic Asylum, which had been founded in 1816; it had fallen into stagnation since the first superintendent had left. On arrival there, he found 29 patients wearing instruments of restraint, and 30-40 more chained down to special seats during the day; all epileptic and violent patients were secured to their beds during the night. SG expressed the hope 'to follow in the steps of Pinel and Esquirol', though he was not prepared to abolish restraint completely. He placed great importance on the selection and instruction of the attendants. During his stay, there was a visit of inspection by Lord Shaftesbury, one of the Commissioners in Lunacy, a body which had been established in 1828; SG had given 40 female patients the exclusive care of an equal number of orphan children, 'to develop in the women the great principle of maternal love'. Shaftesbury was so impressed by this arrangement that he determined that SG should become a Commissioner when a vacancy occurred, which was achieved in 1849. The Commission reported in 1843 that 'the tranquility and orderly conduct are remarkable' at the Lancaster Asylum; in that year, the FRCS was conferred on SG.

In 1841, SG had been one of six superintendents who responded to a circular letter from Dr Samuel Hitch, and met at the Gloucester Asylum to discuss setting up a professional association. As a result, the first meeting of the Association of Medical Officers of Asylums and Hospitals for the Insane was held at Nottingham later the same year. This later became the Royal Medico-Psychological Association, and eventually the Royal College of Psychiatrists. Though SG found difficulty in managing on his salary of £400 per annum and the matter of expenses 'most hateful', he arranged for the second meeting of the Association to be held at his hospital in 1842. He was anxious to prevent the number of patients in the hospital from rising uncontrollably, but there was a constant pressure of new cases and of mentally ill paupers transferred from workhouses; in spite of these efforts, the population of the asylum increased from 559 to 758 during his period of office. SG was also most concerned to separate quiet from violent patients, and to improve living conditions, since 200 patients were still sleeping on loose straw at this time. A programme of extensions was carried out, a library and other forms of occupation introduced, and such crude physical treatments as purging and bleeding abolished. SG also became interested in mental retardation, since many patients of this kind found their way to the asylum; he started an enquiry on the problem nationally, and went to Paris to visit the Bicetre.

Having become a Commissioner, SG visited nearly every workhouse in England and Wales, as well as the asylums, since Poor Law Authorities tended to ignore their legal responsibilities for the mentally ill. In 1852, he was appointed to the Royal Commission on Lunacy in Scotland, and in 1859, gave evidence to the Select Committee on Lunatics. He continued to urge the need for the separation of different types of patients, and this was helped by the opening of Broadmoor Hospital in 1863. His practical experience as a psychiatrist added much weight to his efforts to improve standards of care, in which he strongly supported Lord Shaftesbury.

The obituary in the *Journal of Mental Science* records of SG's work as Commissioner that

he was highly esteemed, both by his colleagues in office and by the superintendents of the institutions of the insane, although the latter were at times disposed to resent his very thorough and minute examination of the institutions he inspected from floor to ceiling. His influence, however, was excellent, (and he gave) sound advice ... to assistant medical officers to associate familiarly with patients, and accompany them in their walks ... In no particular matter did he effect so great a change in asylums as in the matter of dirty bed-linen, which he maintained from his own experience could be reduced to a very small item if the superintendents insisted upon proper precautions being taken with dirty patients before they retired to rest, and their being systematically roused in the night to attend to the calls of nature.

In 1865, while crossing a street, Gaskell was knocked down by a vehicle (presumably horse-drawn). It was stated that from that time, he 'experienced so much discomfort in the head that it was not only impossible for him to pursue his work, but painful to enter into social life. Consequently, he became, to a great extent, a recluse, although he maintained his mental faculties to the close of his life'. He died on 17 March 1886 at his home in Walton, Surrey, at the age of 79. His relatives established an annual prize in his name, which is still awarded by the Royal College of Psychiatrists.

Apart from the annual reports of the Lancaster Asylum, and contributions to the reports of the Lunacy Commissioners, and on mental defectives in *Chambers' Journal*, his only published work was an article 'On the want of better provision for the labouring and middle classes when attacked or threatened with insanity', which appeared in the *Journal of Mental Science* in 1860. However, this was a remarkably progressive piece, proposing for the first time that voluntary admission should be possible and that there should be public hospitals for milder cases of psychiatric disorder, which would be acceptable to those who were not paupers but could not afford private care. In fact, it was not until 1930 that voluntary admission to public hospital became possible, and not until the 1950s that any substantial number of psychiatric beds were provided outside mental hospitals.

SG was not an innovator of the first rank, such as William Tuke or John Connolly; however, he was certainly an outstanding figure in the early development of British psychiatry. He can best be regarded as one of that group of supremely energetic mid-Victorians whose administrative and lobbying skills, together with an insatiable drive to discover the facts, laid the foundation for a modern and humane system of health care in this country. As such, his name deserves to stand beside those of Edwin Chadwick, Florence Nightingale and Lord Shaftesbury.

HLF

## 7.5 ARTHUR RANSOME, 1834-1922
### MD, MA, FRCP, FRS

Arthur Ransome, who practised as a G.P. and physician in the Manchester area between 1858 and 1894, gained a national reputation for his pioneering public health work and for his writings and research on respiratory diseases, particularly tuberculosis.[1] He was an active member of the Manchester Medical Society for a large part of his medical career, contributing nearly twenty papers to society meetings and serving as vice-president in 1874 and 1878 and as president in 1876-7.[2]

Ransome was the third generation of his family to practise in Manchester. His grandfather, John Atkinson Ransome MRCS (1779-1837) and his father, Joseph Atkinson Ransome FRCS (1805-67), were consulting surgeons during the first half of the nineteenth century, each in turn a member of the honorary surgical staff of the Manchester Royal Infirmary, and both taking prominent positions at the foundation of the Manchester Medical Society in 1834, John as one of the first vice-presidents and Joseph as one of the first members of council. The Ransome family was one of a number of medical families at a time when continuity, contacts and patronage could be powerful determinants of success. The medical careers of the three Ransomes together spanned nearly the whole of the nineteenth century, and the career of Arthur presents some interesting contrasts with those of the earlier two.[3]

Arthur Ransome received a long and thorough education, beginning as a boy in Manchester where he studied chemistry and natural history under local experts. Like his father, he attended a Manchester medical school, but for him this was only the start of a more varied training. He was sent to Dublin to study at Trinity College, and while there he attended midwifery practice at the famous Rotunda Hospital and acted as clinical clerk for a short time at Meath Hospital. From Dublin he went to Cambridge, then becoming more popular with provincial dissenting families because of its new regulations and improved medical teaching. He was a distinguished student at Caius College, winning scholarships in anatomy and chemistry. As a Cambridge undergraduate he took the standard qualification of a mid-nineteenth century general practitioner - viz. the MRCS (in 1855) and the LSA (in 1856) - and spent a year in clinical studies at St George's Hospital London and at the Children's Hospital, Great Ormond Street. In 1857 he spent three months in Paris studying surgery, and finally graduated MB Cambridge in 1858.[4]

Ransome's father had trained as a surgeon by apprenticeship and in a proprietory medical school. Arthur Ransome, who qualified just before the 1858 Medical Act was passed, received the broader education already characteristic of the profession by mid-century. In addition he had a more advanced academic training which equipped him to be a consultant physician if he so wished. However, after surveying the consultant market in Manchester, Ransome decided that there were no possible openings for him in that quarter, so in 1858 he settled as general practitioner in nearby Bowdon in Cheshire, while at the same time taking a small share in his father's practice in central Manchester. Bowdon was a rural area with a large proportion of wealthy residents and he quickly prospered. In his first year of practice he earned only £70, but by his fourth year he was already making £500. In 1866, he took on a partner, W O Jones, who probably dealt with a large amount of the routine work, and who continued the practice after Ransome's retirement. Ransome kept on his father's rooms in central Manchester after the latter's death, and was there consulted by a high-status clientèle. Ransome earned an extensive reputation through his work on public health and because of this he became rather more than an ordinary general practitioner.[5]

Though never a physician at Manchester Royal Infirmary, he did have some minor hospital attachments, one of which provided a basis for his important work on tuberculosis. Early in his career he was offered a post as medical officer to a small voluntary hospital at Altrincham, the Lloyd's Hospital and Dispensary. He accepted on condition that in his first year of office he might put forward the advantages of the provident system of administration, for he was already interested in such medico-social questions. Ransome's persuasion was successful and by the end of the year the charity became a provident dispensary. In 1883, he was appointed physician to the Manchester Hospital for Consumption and Diseases of the Throat. At that time tuberculosis was attracting more medical attention: Koch's work on the tubercle bacillus was becoming known and sanatoria were being introduced into Britain. The Manchester Hospital was the only one of its kind in the district, having been founded in 1875, but it was situated in an insalubrious part of central Manchester and in a very poor condition at the time of Ransome's appointment. Ransome persuaded the hospital authorities to move the institution out to new and larger premises in the fresh air of Bowdon, retaining a dispensary in town but ensuring that cases with hopes of recovery were sent to the country.[6]

Ransome's interest in respiratory disease predated his appointment to the Manchester Consumption Hospital. Early in his career, he invented a stethometer which he used in the scientific measurement of respiration. In 1876 he published an account of his work, *On Stethometry*, and for this he was made a Fellow of the Royal Society. In his work on tuberculosis, Ransome stressed and investigated the role of external and environmental factors, though he remained convinced that the 'seed' as well as the 'soil' played a part in the spread of disease. He was one of the first to take up Koch's work on the tubercle bacillus, and he sent one of his three medical sons to Berlin to study Koch's methods of research, Ransome's many papers on tuberculosis were later collected together in *A Campaign Against Consumption* published in 1915. His other works on tuberculosis included *On the Relation of Chest Movements to Prognosis in Lung Disease* (1882), *On the Causes of Consumption* (1885), *The Treatment of Phthisis* (1896), and *The Principles of Open Air Treatment of Phthisis and of Sanatorium Construction* (1903). He was appointed the first Milroy Lecturer on tuberculosis at the Royal College of Physicians in 1890, despite his non-membership of the College and his provincial location. He later became a member of the College, after examination, in 1895, and became a Fellow in 1899. Ransome retired to Bournemouth in 1894, but remained active, taking on another honorary hospital appointment as Consultant Physician to the Royal Boscombe and West Hampshire Hospital. He received the first Weber-Parkes prize in 1897 for his essay *Researches on Tuberculosis*.[7]

Arthur Ransome's work on tuberculosis was only one facet of his predominant interest in public health reform. He joined the Manchester and Salford Sanitary Association in 1859, and quickly became one of its leading spirits. He served on its committee for thirty-eight years and was its chairman for fourteen. The Association was a voluntary movement of medical and lay people formed in 1852 to improve the sanitary conditions of Manchester and Salford by education and persuasion. At the time when Ransome joined, its chairman was in favour of its disbandment, considering its work done. However, the vigorous efforts of Ransome and others ensured its survival. Under the new chairmanship of Thomas Turner (1793-1873), Ransome as honorary secretary was able to give a new direction to the Association's work. The cumbersome machinery of local sub-committees reporting on the health of their districts to a central committee was abandoned, and Ransome instituted a system of weekly statistical returns of diseases from the local medical institutions, which were then published. This system, a basis for statistical analysis by Ransome and others, was imitated elsewhere, and foreshadowed the later campaign for a national system of notification and registration of diseases. Ransome had a lifelong interest in medical statistics and believed that their scientific analysis might answer many questions about the causes and propagation of disease.[8]

Ransome encouraged the Manchester and Salford Sanitary Association to promote nurse training in Manchester. They managed to establish Nightingale nurses in some of the medical institutions in Manchester, thus originating the Manchester District Nursing Service. Ransome also took a prominent role as lecturer in the courses of 'Health Lectures for the People' regularly delivered by Association members to the working classes. Previously he had lectured in physiology at the short-lived Working Men's College run by the Mechanics Institute. In 1876, soon after the amalgamation of Owens College with the Manchester Medical School, Ransome was appointed lecturer in hygiene and medical jurisprudence; after the creation of the Victoria University, he occupied the Chair of Public Health. He became examiner in hygiene to both Cambridge and Victoria Universities, and claimed to have initiated the scheme for the Cambridge Diploma in Public Health, the first to be offered by a British university.[9]

Despite spending the whole of his career in the provinces, Ransome had a cosmopolitan reputation. In Germany, in particular, he was recognised as a pioneer in the study of tuberculosis, and he was an associate editor of *Zeitschrift für Tuberculose*. His obituary in the *British Medical Journal* commented that he had filled in important gaps in the masonry of human knowledge and enjoyed the doubtful privilege of being ahead of his time.

In Arthur Ransome's career we see a double transformation of public health. Through the Sanitary Association he developed notification and disease statistics which built on the earlier work of pioneers like Percival and Kay-Shuttleworth, preparing the ground for the full-time, specially trained medical officer of health. In Ransome's later work we see how bacteriology brought the laboratory into public health, linking medical officers of health to university medical scientists such as Sheridan Delépine. Ransome saw both these transitions, and the associated specialisation, but he remained a general practitioner. That was not an anachronism, for general practitioners still have much to contribute to the study of disease in the community and to the protection of the public health.

KW

7.6 JAMES NIVEN, 1851-1925

MA, MB, BCh, LLD

Despite its unenviable reputation as the 'shock city of the age' in the mid-nineteenth century, Manchester was late in appointing a medical officer of health. Liverpool had led the way in 1847 with the appointment of Dr William Henry Duncan, and was closely followed by the City of London which appointed the famous Dr (Later Sir) John Simon. It required intense political pressure from the Manchester and Salford Sanitary Association before the Corporation of the City of Manchester acknowledged the need for a medical man to spearhead its public health effort, and Dr John Leigh did not take up office until 1868, and then initially only in a part-time capacity. However, it is remarkable that from 1868 until the abolition of the office in 1974 with the Reorganisation of the National Health Service, only six doctors held it, Leigh, John Tatham, James Niven, Robert Veitch Clark, Charles Metcalfe Brown and Kennedy Campbell, spanning 106 years. Only Leigh, who was born in Middleton, received his medical training in Manchester. Tatham, though of English birth, trained at Trinity College, Dublin, and the last four have been members of that happy band of brothers who have contributed so much to English and world medicine not least in the public health field, the expatriate Scots.

The longest serving, albeit by a 'short head', and therefore taken as representative of a devoted line of public health doctors who have served the City with distinction, was Dr James Niven, who served in the office of medical officer of health for the City of Manchester for 28 years, from 1894 to 1922. Niven was born in Peterhead, Scotland on 12 August 1851. He graduated in Arts at Aberdeen University in 1870, and then entered Queen's College, Cambridge to study mathematics. He was eighth wrangler in the mathematical tripos in 1874 – a family tradition, for his three brothers were also Cambridge mathematical wranglers. He then took up a Fellowship in his College, with the intention of studying engineering, but after proceeding to the Master of Arts degree in 1877, he decided to study medicine and entered St Thomas's Hospital, graduating MB in 1880. His first appointment was with the Metropolitan Asylums Board where he specialised in infectious diseases, but he soon moved to Manchester to private practice.

After four years practice, in 1886, Niven was appointed medical officer of health for the Borough of Oldham, and medical superintendent of the Westhulme Fever Hospital. On taking up his appointment, he immediately set about the task of identifying the public health priorities in Oldham, and in the 8 years of his appointment was instrumental in improving the standard of housing, of sewage and refuse disposal, of the milk and water supply, in reducing smoke pollution, and containing the spread of infectious disease. He graduated BCh in 1889, having been the author of several papers on infectious disease.

In 1894, whilst he was serving as president of the North-Western Association of Medical Officers of Health, the fore-runner of the Section of Community Medicine of the Manchester Medical Society, Niven was appointed from amongst 33 applicants to succeed Dr Tatham as medical officer of health for the City of Manchester at a salary of £850 per annum. During his 28 year term of office, despite a falling birth rate, the population of the City increased from 517,000 to 770,000. On appointment, as in Oldham, he concentrated on identifying priorities, and continued the sanitary reform of the City initiated by his predecessors. He is considered to be mainly responsible for the fall in death rate from 24.26 per 1,000 population in the year before his appointment, to 13.82 per 1,000 in 1921, through his intense zeal, perseverance and courage of conviction. He accelerated the City's slum clearance programme, and over 23,000 houses were demolished or modified, and 85,000 converted from pail-closet to water-closet systems. In collaboration with Professor Delépine of the University of Manchester, he achieved immense improvement in the City's milk supply, and made considerable progress against the ravages of tuberculosis.

In 1896, since the City had no isolation hospital of its own, he arranged the purchase of Monsall Hospital by the Corporation from the Trustees of the Manchester Royal Infirmary. Monsall, Manchester's

major infectious diseases hospital which had been opened in 1871, was
the direct successor to the Manchester House of Recovery, the first
general fever hospital in the country founded in the City centre in
1796 by the voluntary Manchester Board of Health. In 1897, he drew
attention to shellfish as one source of infection in enteric fever,
and with Delépine advocated the routine use of the Widal reaction to
ensure better diagnosis of the disease. He later participated in
epidemiological investigations into poliomyelitis and meningitis, and
into immunity following the influenza pandemic of 1918-19.

He worked strenuously to reduce smoke pollution in the City, and to
improve maternal and child health. In 1907, the health visitors
employed by the Ladies Public Health Society, as successors to the
Ladies Sanitary Reform Association which pioneered health visiting in
Manchester and Salford in 1862, were transferred (not without
difficulty) to the employ of the Corporation, and 1914 Niven arranged
for an increase in their numbers, and an expansion of welfare centres
and clinics. His mathematical training was utilised in his
presentation of statistics in his plans and reports. He was a prolific
writer, much sought after in national councils; he was president of
the Epidemiological Section of the Royal Society of Medicine,
president of the Manchester Statistical Society, examiner in sanitary
science at Cambridge, and lecturer in public health in Manchester. He
was also president of the Section of Public Health at the Annual
Meeting of the British Medical Association in Manchester in 1902; and
his 'alma mater', Aberdeen University, conferred upon him the honorary
degree of Doctor of Letters. He was awarded medals for his service to
preventive medicine by the Royal Institute of Public Health and other
bodies.

On his retirement in 1922, the City of Manchester presented him
with a formal resolution of thanks for his long and devoted service to
the City. In his *Observations on the History of Public Health Effort
in Manchester* published in 1923, he gave an account of his work in
Manchester from his appointment until his retirement, with suggestions
for the future management of the public health effort in the City.
Sadly, he died by his own hand on 30 September 1925 whilst on a visit
to the Isle of Man.

WPP

7.7 SIR JAMES MACKENZIE, 1853-1925
    MD, FRCP, FRS


Born in the small Scottish parish of Scone on 12 April 1853, the third child and second son of a farmer, James MacKenzie ultimately proved to be one of the most remarkable men in British medicine during the late nineteenth and early twentieth centuries.

## The Young MacKenzie

MacKenzie's school record was unremarkable and at the age of 15 he left to become an apprentice to a pharmacist in Perth. This brought him into contact with medicine and by the age of 20 MacKenzie had resolved to enter medical school. This he did a year later at Edinburgh, a now highly motivated mature student. His student career was good but not outstanding. He was probably in the upper 20 per cent of his year but there is no record of any honours or prizes coming his way. During his Edinburgh student days his friend and mentor was a Dr John Brown who, by the time MacKenzie had qualified, had settled in general practice in Burnley. MacKenzie joined him in that practice in August 1879.

## Dr MacKenzie in Burnley (1889-1910)

General medical practice in the slums of nineteenth-century Burnley, at a time when the crude death rate was 30 to 35 per thousand, and over 15,000 people were in receipt of poor law relief, appears an unlikely setting for original research. Apart, however, from the quality of MacKenzie himself he was fortunate in joining a practice with two outstandingly able partners, Dr Brown and a Dr Briggs, the latter being the surgeon of the trio. The conjunction of three good and enquiring minds was a powerful stimulus to young MacKenzie and perhaps, too, the very lack of investigative facilities sharpened his clinical acumen. Within three years of settling in general practice, MacKenzie had his first paper accepted by the *Lancet* - the first of a string of publications and writings, many of the highest possible quality.

## MacKenzie the Cardiologist

MacKenzie's first publication on a cardiological topic was in the *Caledonian Medical Journal* in 1891 on the significance of venous pulsation in the neck; and his second paper (a case report) was published in the *Manchester Medical Chronicle* a few months later. The real output began when he devised a means of simultaneously recording venous and arterial pulsation. The development of 'Dr MacKenzie's ink polygraph' based on the Dudgeon sphygmograph and its manufacture by Mr B Shaw, watch maker of Padiham (price £10.10s.0d. net complete in plush lined box with two sets of pens, one dozen rolls of paper and a bottle of writing fluid and a brush) enabled him to begin the serious analysis of cardiac arrhythmias.

And analyse them he did. All forms of cardiac irregularity were investigated in meticulous detail. Auricular fibrillation in particular was recognised as a condition in which there was no auricular systole: MacKenzie called it auricular paralysis, a perfectly correct description in terms of pathophysiology. (The term auricular fibrillation was introduced by Thomas Lewis following the development of the electrocardiogram.) MacKenzie studied the action of, and indications for, digitalis, and showed that it was of primary clinical value in cases of heart failure associated with a rapid irregular pulse, i.e. atrial fibrillation - a view anticipating modern thinking on the indications for digitalis by some 80 years. He co-operated with Sir Arthur Keith on studies on the conducting tissues of the heart. He formed a close friendship with the German cardiologist, Wenkebach, which led to several joint papers on extrasystoles and their nature. During his 20 years in practice in Burnley MacKenzie published some 36 papers on cardiological topics and published three books, *The Study of the Pulse*, 1902, his superb

# "DR. MACKENZIE'S INK POLYGRAPH."

Maker - - Mr. S. Shaw, Instrument Maker, Padiham, Lancashire.

## Description and Management.

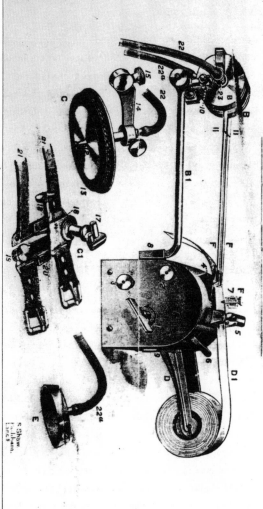

12. Part of the first page of the instructions for using Dr MacKenzie's ink polygraph. This ingenious mechanical device, manufactured to MacKenzie's specification by a local watchmaker about the turn of the century, anticipated the modern electrocardiograph. See the essay on Sir James MacKenzie (7.7).

*Diseases of the Heart*, 1908, and *Symptoms and their Interpretation*, 1909. From his general practice in Burnley Dr MacKenzie had founded the specialty of cardiology.

## Dr MacKenzie in London 1910-19

Obviously Burnley was becoming too small and MacKenzie began to consider moving to one of the major cities. Manchester was the obvious choice but was rejected, I think, because it did not really fulfil his ambitions. He looked closely at Edinburgh but in the end the call for London won and in 1910 he joined the staff of a London hospital as Lecturer in Cardiac Research. The London hospital, however, was by no means keen to appoint a provincial general practitioner, no matter how famous, to its consultant staff and for three years MacKenzie was denied consultant status. However, in 1913 he achieved this being appointed as physician in charge to the department for cardiac research with an allocation of 15 beds and a seat on the Medical Board.

The relationship between Dr MacKenzie and the London hospital was, however, not a happy one and probably had been soured by his initial disappointment in being denied full consultant status. He was a simple man, much less sophisticated than his colleagues, but with a world wide reputation which far exceeded theirs and of which they were jealous. Undoubtedly MacKenzie did not possess a great deal of tact and, consequently, relations remained rather prickly. During the 1914-1918 War MacKenzie described irregularities of the heart, a syndrome of irregular cardiac action under the name 'Soldier's Heart', subsequently also called 'Da Costa's syndrome'. This was a functional stress related disturbance of rhythm thought not to be due to organic heart disease. Rumours began to circulate in London that MacKenzie was providing certificates exempting young men from military service because of this rather ill-defined condition. Almost certainly these accusations were unjustified. I am sure that he did make the diagnosis of soldier's heart more frequently than was justifiable but there is no evidence that he ever used this to his financial advantage. It seems very unlikely that a man of his enormous reputation and with a very large and successful private practice in the West End of London would descend to rather petty crime.

About this time MacKenzie was also becoming a vascular invalid. He had had his first myocardial infarct at the age of 47 but made a complete recovery from it. Between 1910 and 1920 he was becoming progressively incapacitated by angina and claudication and in part because of his ill-health and in part because perhaps of his relative unhappiness in London he decided to leave. In 1919 he resigned his London appointment to move to St Andrews as Director of the Sir James MacKenzie Institute for Medical Research. This was an astonishing undertaking for a 67 year old man with severe generalised arterial disease and was almost certainly an unwise decision.

## MacKenzie at St Andrews 1919-1925

Although a noble vision, the St Andrews' Institute was not a success. The intention was to go back to what one might call the grass roots of medical practice, looking at symptoms and signs as they occurred in general practice and using this data as a basis for epidemiological studies. MacKenzie, however, no longer had the necessary drive and he also lacked the training. He was essentially an individual descriptive physician with a highly enquiring turn of mind best equipped to handle adhoc clinical research. He was ill-equipped to handle quantitative data and unused to handling and directing a large research team. The topics selected for investigation were generalised, the question asked unlikely to permit satisfactory investigation or solution and no major original research emanated from the institute during his six years as Director. Some outstanding books were published, in particular *Heart Disease in Pregnancy* and *Angina Pectoris*. They were, however, based on work done by Dr MacKenzie during his Burnley and London days. His health steadily deteriorated and he died of a further myocardial infarction in 1925. The influence of the Institute steadily faded after his death and it had ceased to be a force in British Medicine before the onset of the Second World War.

## MacKenzie and the Manchester Medical School

MacKenzie's first paper was published in the *Lancet* in 1883, a case report of paradoxical contraction following spinal injury. Between 1889 and 1891, four papers were published in the *Manchester Medical*

*Chronicle*, a publication closely linked with the Manchester Medical Society. One of these was his second paper on a cardiological topic, a case of aneurysm of the heart with symptoms of angina pectoris during life. After 1891 all his publications were in National journals. It is said that he demonstrated his polygraph to the Manchester medical students but so far as I am aware he never communicated formally to the Manchester Medical Society and was never an office bearer of this Society.

The genetic mix which goes to make a man like MacKenzie is rare. Perhaps too a man of his make-up requires a certain cultural background to flourish. I wonder how MacKenzie would fit into the modern medical scene with its emphasis on team work and the multi-disciplinary approach to problems so that even a simple case report requires half a dozen authors. I do not feel that it would be to the independent MacKenzie's liking.

EGW

## 7.8 AUGUSTE SHERIDAN DELEPINE, 1855-1921
   MB, ChM, MSc

Auguste Sheridan Delépine came to Manchester in 1891 as Procter
Professor of Pathology and remained here until his death in 1921.
While not contributing to any fundamental new discovery in medicine,
his great achievement was to establish one of the first laboratories
in this country devoted to the application of bacteriology to public
health. He was an outstanding teacher and, under his influence,
Manchester became a major centre for the training of medical officers
of health, state veterinary officers, and sanitary chemists, so that
during those 30 years nearly one thousand postgraduate students were
taught in his department. His scientific publications were
considerable, covering a wide range of topics including morbid
anatomy, laboratory methods, tuberculosis, water supplies, the
diagnosis of typhoid and cholera, arsenic poisoning, disinfection and
sterilisation, and medical education.

Sheridan Delépine was born in 1855 at Perroy which is a noted
beauty spot by Lake Geneva and close to the birthplace of his Swiss
mother. His father, Antoine Delépine, was a Parisian who owned
property in Faubourg St Antoine where two courtyards are still named
after him. Why their firstborn was given an Irish name is obscure.

His early education was at the Collège Charlemagne in Paris where
he lived until 1870. He then obtained a BSc from the University of
Lausanne, gaining distinction for studies in physical and natural
sciences, and was subsequently awarded a prize for research. This led
to his appointment as Curator of the scientific collection of M.
Schlumberger in Alsace. During 1876 he studied at the University of
Geneva, and in the following year, at the age of 22, he went to
Edinburgh University to study medicine. He distinguished himself by

passing all the professional examinations with first-class honours. He was Senior Mackenzie Bursar for proficiency in dissection, first Senior Medallist in Pathology, and he graduated MB, CM in 1882. During the next two years while working with Professor Hamilton in pathological research at Edinburgh he made the drawings of the reflections of the peritoneum which appeared in the first edition of Cunningham's *Guide for Dissectors*.

In 1884 he moved to St George's Hospital in London where he had been invited to the post of demonstrator in normal and pathological histology and pathologist to the hospital. Two years later he was made lecturer in physiology and organised that department in the medical school. As pathologist to the hospital he was for a time curator of the museum but gave this up when he was placed in sole charge of the Pathology Department. For several years he also assisted the eminent physician, Sir Andrew Clarke, in his scientific work. This was a very active period in his career, for in addition to his official appointments he also had to establish himself and earn his living by private practice. He also had increasing family commitments, for in 1884 he had married Florence Rose whose family were well-to-do pianoforte manufacturers whose products were marketed under the 'Underwood' trademark. Their first child, Eliza Helen, was born in 1884 and their second, Helenus George, in 1888. He was devoted to his children and it was a great tragedy to him when Helenus died of wounds in 1915 at the battle of Ypres.

Towards the end of his time at St George's, Delépine was elected to the London Pathological Society to which he contributed numerous case reports many of which were beautifully illustrated by himself, for he had considerable artistic talent. He established a private laboratory in his own house where he undertook microscopical, chemical, and bacteriological investigations because he was dissatisfied by the incompleteness of clinical diagnosis. This became generally known and his consulting practice became quite large. Unfortunately, patients did not understand the value of these investigations and few were willing to pay for them. He thus became convinced that no private individual could take the risks involved and that pathological investigations would need to remain the province of hospitals or alternatively special laboratories would have to be endowed for the purpose. He recalled later that during his time in London he had personally examined over six thousand specimens in his practice.

In the nineteenth century there were very few full-time medical professors and these were usually dependent upon charitable endowments from private philanthropists. This was true not only of the clinical chairs of medicine and surgery, which were usually filled part-time by the honorary staff of the teaching hospital, but it also applied to pathology which was usually taught by physicians and surgeons. The Manchester Medical School was no exception to this when Julius Dreschfeld was appointed as its first Professor of Pathology in 1882.

However, in 1890, a legacy of £6,000 from the estate of Daniel Procter, a wealthy local merchant, endowed a whole-time chair in the subject to which Delépine was appointed. Amongst his other duties, he was informed that one would be to provide a course in bacteriology applied to public health, and opportunities for research were also offered in the new bacteriological laboratories provided in the 1894 extension to the Medical School buildings. At the time, these were the only laboratories of their kind in the north-west of England and Delépine was quickly beset by requests for assistance in investigations from doctors and public authorities. Although they were quite willing to defray any expenses incurred, there were a number of difficulties in meeting these demands.

In the first place, there was a heavy teaching load for both undergraduate students in pathology and postgraduate teaching in public health. In this, his only assistant was a part-time demonstrator, Dr T N Kelynack, who was also pathological registrar to the Infirmary. Within a few months of his arrival in Manchester, Delépine found that if he were to undertake any commitment for consulting work he would require further assistance, or else shut his laboratory to enquirers. The terms of his appointment to the College, however, precluded him from undertaking practice of any kind, so that he could not in the circumstances obtain any fee for the payment of an assistant. At the same time, the College was hardly likely to provide him with this help for the sole object of allowing one of their professors to give scientific advice to people other than students. He brought these considerations to the attention of his colleagues and their importance was quickly recognised by the Principal, Professor Adolphus Ward, and by Professor Daniel Leech, but there were many difficulties to be surmounted before a practical solution could be found. For nearly two years he was obliged to provide what help he could without assistance. In 1892 he joined Dr Arthur Ransome of the Consumption Hospital at Baguley and Dr Tatham, then Medical Officer of Health for Manchester, in an investigation into the prevention of tuberculosis by voluntary notification and the disinfection of the homes of consumptives with chloride of lime. He found, however, that any ongoing commitment to provide diagnostic services was impossible within the time at his disposal.

Crisis came in 1893 when suspected cases of cholera appeared in this country. During the previous summer the disease had spread across Europe reaching the North Sea ports of Germany and Holland, and there was intense public concern about its possible arrival in this country. Because of the prevalence of diarrhoeal diseases at the time it was almost impossible to differentiate cholera nostras from the dreaded cholera asiatica on clinical grounds alone. When suspected cases of Asiatic cholera appeared in Manchester in the middle of September, Delépine, who was on holiday at the time, was summoned by a telegram from Dr Tatham to provide bacteriological confirmation. This he was able to do, but only because the call came during the vacation when unencumbered by his teaching commitments.

The occurence, however, dramatised the need for readily available diagnostic services. Lengthy discussions took place about this and it was eventually agreed in March 1895 that fees could be accepted from public authorities, subject to the approval of a committee appointed by the Council of the College. This did not entirely solve the problem, for unless he was assured of a steady income it was difficult for Delépine to take on regular paid assistants without serious financial risk to himself. He was fortunate, however, in having amongst his pupils Dr E J Sidebotham, a man of independent means, who offered to give his services free during the initial stages of the scheme. In the event, he continued unpaid for over 25 years and it is doubtful whether the Public Health Laboratory could have been established without his help.

Provided with this base, the success of the laboratory was assured and applications came in rapidly from local authorities wishing to take advantage of the scheme. Within five years there were 61 sanitary authorities making use of the laboratories and the annual number of investigations had risen to 4,652 in 1900 which provided an income of

£1,374. This rapid growth in the work of the department highlighted the need for better accommodation than the two small rooms which were available in the Medical School, and it was clear that alternative arrangements would have to be made. Delépine's solution to this problem was to rent a house on the Stanley Grove estate, where the medical corridor of the Manchester Royal Infirmary now stands, which he occupied himself and built a laboratory extension which was funded by a loan of £2,300 from the College. These new premises were opened in May 1902. By this time the staff engaged in public health work consisted of three permanent assistants, Dr Sidebotham, Dr Carver and Dr Sellers, supplemented when help was needed by occasional assistants. There was also a full-time departmental secretary, Miss E C Iliff, who continued on the staff until she retired in 1946.

Until October 1903 the financial responsibility for the department rested solely upon Delépine, but from then it was officially recognised by the University who appointed him Director responsible to an Advisory Committee, and changed his title to Professor of Comparative Pathology and Bacteriology. This left vacant the chair in pathology which was filled in the following year by Lorrain Smith.

Soon after the move to Stanley Grove it became known that the Infirmary had now decided to rebuild on what has since become known as the 'Island Site' so that the search began once again for new premises. At the same time, discussions were held with the Royal Infirmary which led to an agreement that bacteriological work for the hospital would be carried out under Delépine's direction. The new laboratories, therefore, had to be close to the Infirmary, and for this reason a rather expensive site in York Place was chosen for the new building within which a room was set aside for hospital use. In the event, this arrangement was never taken up because Dr George Loveday, who was Director of the Clinical Laboratories, preferred to be independent and to continue his work on vaccines and opsonins within the confines of the hospital where, in 1908, it was minuted that the new pathological block 'could be made to do for clinical pathology'. It has been doing so ever since.

The new laboratory in York Place was a masterpiece, designed by Delépine, into which many of the fixtures were transferred from Stanley Grove. Work on it had started in March 1904 and the first classes in the building were held in January 1905. The construction costs were £21,000 of which £13,000 was raised by compensation from the Infirmary, and from various donations and grants, the University contributing a mere £1,200. Within this new building, the work of the department flourished so that by the time of Delépine's death the original loans had been paid off, and all other expenses including equipment, materials, and salaries, excluding the professor's, had been met out of income. In later years it made a considerable profit for the University who had acquired a valuable asset at little risk to itself.

The work fell into two categories; routine and special investigations. The routine work consisted mainly of Widal reactions for typhoid, throat swabs for diphtheria, sputum for the diagnosis of pulmonary tuberculosis, also milk for tuberculosis, and Wassermann tests for syphilis. Special investigations for local sanitary authorities were numerous and covered a wide range of subjects. Among these were a study of the role of houseflies in the spread of disease; the dangers of breathing air in sewers for which a special laboratory was built; the outbreak of arsenic poisoning in Salford during 1900 from the chemical contamination of brewing sugars; and the disposal of carcasses of animals infected by anthrax in the County of Chester.

There were, of course, many more, and one of Delépine's main crusades was in the cause of clean, safe, milk. He was convinced that dirty milk was an important factor in the spread of tuberculosis and intestinal disease. This was in the face of opposition from various sources, including Robert Koch himself who had declared in 1901 that bovine tubercle bacilli were not pathogenic to man. Nevertheless, Delépine's enthusiasm was passed on to Dr James Niven, Medical Officer of Health for Manchester, who initiated measures aimed at the segregation of infected cows and cleanliness in milking and the distribution of milk.

In the investigation of disease and in the teaching of students, Delépine always had round him a remarkably loyal and devoted staff; indeed, he seems to have inspired great affection amongst all his colleagues and the students who came for instruction within his department. The memorial bust by John Millard, to which so many of them contributed, and which now stands in the Stopford Building, bears witness to this.

RMS

7.9 SIR WILLIAM COATES, 1860-1962
     KCB, CB, CBE, VD, TD, O St J, FRCS, DL


William Coates was born in Derbyshire on the 14 June 1860. He trained
in medicine at the London Hospital where he was greatly influenced by
Hughlings Jackson. Moving to Manchester in 1884 he practised in Moss
Side, then a fashionable suburb on the outskirts of the City. However
he moved to Whalley Range in 1891 where he lived at 'Ingleside' until
his death in 1962. A modern block of flats named 'William Coates
Court' occupies this site today. His contribution to medicine and
other allied interests in Greater Manchester is quite remarkable.
Engaged in general practice until his 90th birthday, he also had a
consulting practice in Market Street from 1905 and at 17 St John
Street from 1935. Throughout his life a firm believer in the Christian
faith, this slightly built but enormously energetic man was able to
perceive a need, conceive a solution and provide the means to achieve
success. This is amply illustrated by his protean interests.
   Joining the Manchester Medical Society soon after his arrival he
was its Secretary from 1894 to 1898 and President in 1909.
Disagreement over Lloyd George's Medical Insurance Proposals led to
his becoming Secretary of the National Medical Union formed to counter
this legislation. In 1885 he joined the 20th Lancashire Rifle
Volunteer Corps. Earlier he had seen the attempts by Sir James Cantlie
and Surgeon Major Evatt in London to found the Volunteer Medical Staff
Corps. Following a visit to Manchester when Cantlie and Evatt
addressed a meeting at Owens College, Coates was instrumental in
founding the Manchester Volunteer Medical Staff Corps in 1886. He
commanded this unit from 1897 and raised £6,000 by voluntary
subscription to help build the Drill Hall in Kings Road, Stretford,
which was opened in 1904. This building and the adjacent land is still

occupied by the RAMC (V) today and houses the oldest RAMC Officers Mess in the Corps. Coates held a bazaar in Hulme Town Hall in 1887 (Jubilee Year) and Miss Florence Nightingale sent a letter and a tea cosy she had made for sale at that event. The original letter is with the British Red Cross Society (BRCS) in London but a photograph of it is held in the Mess at Kings Road. The Volunteers became the Royal Army Medical Corps in 1898 and 450 all ranks served in the South African War.

Haldane undertook to re-organise the Reserves in 1907 and addressed a meeting in Manchester in that year; Coates was then President of the Volunteer Officers Association. Sir Alfred Keogh, then Director General RAMC, formed a committee including Coates which drew up the Regulations for the Territorial Force – little changed to this day. This early scheme had deficiencies in that it lacked nursing help. To fill this need Voluntary Aid Detachments were recruited under the control of the BRCS. So Coates founded the BRCS in East Lancashire in 1908. Retiring from the Territorial Force in 1908 he was recalled in 1914 to help organise hospital facilities in the North West, for the duration of the First World War. The BRCS ran all the ambulance trains and they were met at Mayfield Station and Winwick Warrington; 1032 trains came to Mayfield and 300 to Winwick. On one occasion 6 ambulance trains came from Southampton in one day! On visiting the Star and Garter Home with Sir Frederic Treves, Sir William was so impressed he founded the Totally Disabled Soldiers Home at Broughton House in Salford and another at Southport. Later, in 1924, seeing the need for a sanatorium for ex-servicemen, he founded the Barrowmore Tuberculosis Colony near Chester.

Sir William continued in active practice until his 90th year, but Lady Coates died in 1949. Though he later became totally blind he retained a lively interest in affairs through the radio and readings by his chauffeur from the daily papers. His honours and decorations are probably unique. He had the KCB (Civil) and the CB (Military). (There have been only five holders of these twin decorations of the Order of the Bath.) The BRCS awarded him their badge; there are only ever 25 holders of this much prized honour at any one time. He also had four Coronation Medals – for King Edward VII, King George V, King George VI and finally Her Majesty Queen Elizabeth. He held both the Volunteer Decoration and the Territorial Decoration. The Royal College of Surgeons elected him to a fellowship in 1905.

Truly his was a remarkable career and a massive contribution to the medical affairs of Manchester. In a fascinating scrap book compiled by his son Col. J B Coates, CBE MC DL there is a letter (amongst many congratulating him on his centenary) from his Insurance Company informing him that the Directors were happy to say his premiums had now been waived!! He replied personally to the many letters and telegrams on 14 June, 1960; the range and scope of his friends and colleagues were enormous. He died peacefully nearly two years later; truly one could say of his long career that he had 'filled the unforgiving minute with sixty seconds' worth of distance run'.[1]

WME

7.10 & 11 ARCHIBALD DONALD, 1860-1937

        MA, MD, FRCP, Hon FRCOG, Hon LLD, and

        WILLIAM EDWARD FOTHERGILL, 1865-1926

        MA, BSc, MD

AND THE MANCHESTER OPERATION

Manchester has been endowed with many competent and skilful obstetricians and gynaecologists but only a few have risen to eminence outside the city or been remembered long after their time; but among such we must count Archibald Donald and William Edward Fothergill who together developed the Manchester operation for pelvic floor repair. Donald who devised the operation originally and demonstrated it frequently wrote little about it; but Fothergill wrote extensively about the technique of pelvic floor repair with the result that for many years (and even occasionally today) the operation was known by his name. Despite this there was no personal antipathy and on a number of occasions they collaborated in other aspects of gynaecology. Perhaps this was because they were both aliens in a foreign land, Edinburgh graduates in sassenach Manchester, but more probably because their personalities were complementary.

Donald

Although Archibald Donald was born and educated in Scotland he was really an Irishman who possessed the best qualities of both races. It is thought that he owed his boyish spirits and youthful outlook to Ireland. Certainly his love of golf he owed to his Scottish inheritance. A love which took him back to Scotland at frequent intervals to play with Robert Muir, author of a classical *Textbook of*

*Pathology*. It has been suggested that the stern and uncompromising look which came into his face when subjects about which he held strong views were being discussed was also a product of his Scottish ancestry. He graduated to MB, CM in Edinburgh in 1883 and MD in 1886. After a resident post at the Royal Maternity Hospital, Edinburgh, he had a voyage to India as a ship's surgeon. In 1885 he was appointed resident obstetrical assistant surgeon at St Mary's Hospital in Quay Street, Manchester, and house surgeon to forty gynaecological beds. He held this dual post for three years but shortly after vacating it, in 1888, he was appointed to the staff of St Mary's when Cullingworth left Manchester for St Thomas' Hospital. In 1912, on the death of Sir William Sinclair, he was appointed professor of obstetrics and gynaecology. Systematic lecturing, however, did not appeal to him, so he persuaded the University to bring obstetrics and gynaecology into line with medicine and surgery by making a second chair in clinical obstetrics and gynaecology, which he held until his retirement in 1925. Donald joined the honorary staff of the Royal Infirmary in 1895 on the retirement of Lloyd Roberts as consulting gynaecological surgeon, having become a member of the Royal College of Physicians which at that time was a prior requirement.

In his private life Donald was kindly and genial and generous to minor failings, but he was forceful in stating and supporting his convictions. In 1901, taking part in a debate on 'Medical Etiquette', he stressed that the prime duty of a medical man is to his patient. A doctor also has a duty to his profession but 'if public convenience is ignored we may be sure something is wrong'. Fletcher Shaw records him refusing a large country fee because it would prevent him giving his clinical lecture the next morning. 'Woe to the man', Donald wrote, 'who suffered his professional opinion to be biased by hope of pecuniary gain'. Donald was a man of great modesty. At the outbreak of the Great War, at the age of 54, he joined the à la suite staff at the Second General Western Hospital with the rank of captain, becoming junior to most of those considerably junior to himself in civil practice. For some months, in addition to his other military duties, he took time to 'live-in' and do what was, in reality, merely the work of a house surgeon - an admirable instance of his loyalty and devotion to what he thought was his duty. In 1922 Donald delivered the first Lloyd Roberts lecture in St Mary's Hospital: it was entitled

'Transition'; and Judson Bury re-reading it after his death commented, 'Although there is ample acknowledgement of the investigations of his colleagues I can see no reference to his own'.

Early in his career in Manchester, Donald was anxious to undertake gynaecological surgery and although as a full member of St Mary's staff he was entitled to do so his senior colleagues found ways of restricting the activities of this young and venturesome surgeon. There was only one theatre at this time in Quay Street and the senior surgeons were granted priority. At times when Donald had planned an operation for a particular day, he found that one of his seniors had already operated on a septic case and by the rules of the hospital no further operating was permitted that day. It seems that because of these restrictions he turned his attention to the problems of prolapse of the uterus which was then a common and challenging condition. Probably because operating on this condition was considered minor surgery, not requiring the aseptic precautions of abdominal surgery he was allowed to proceed, and on 28 July 1888 he performed his first pelvic floor repair. At the turn of the century the theatre in Quay Street was on the top floor, unheated and poorly lit except by natural light. The table was flat and it was impossible to use the Trendelenberg position for pelvic surgery. Fletcher Shaw, who was his assistant from 1904 to 1906, had a vivid memory of Donald tackling difficult pelvic operations. Except that he had discarded his frockcoat and vest he was dressed in his usual walking garments with his neck encircled by a very tall stiff collar which prevented him bending his neck forward in comfort. He was

> an operator of the first flight. His long thin hands could work through an incision which was the envy of his more sturdily built contemporaries, while his long thin fingers ... were enabled to dissect from the pelvis with the minimum of damage adherent tumour which was inseparable by those less skilled.

When Donald was appointed to St Mary's Hospital change was in the air and this suited Donald who was a great innovator. The teaching of Lister was gradually permeating each centre. Antisepsis was the keynote; the carbolic acid spray was in full blast; and instruments, surgeon's hands and patient's skin were prepared with carbolic acid solution. There were no sterilised gowns and no reliable sutures. In his first two colporraphies he used silver wire as a suture, but this has obvious drawbacks. Fortunately in the same year he heard that some German surgeons were using catgut and he obtained a supply of this for his third case. Never again did he use any other material in his pelvic floor repairs except for silkworm sutures for the perineum. Catgut was obtained from Germany in small bottles of carbolic acid. He was so impressed with the material that he experimented with other methods of sterilisation; and even at the end of his surgical career catgut was prepared for him in iodine and spirit by his theatre sisters. In the whole of this time, including the early days when catgut was improperly prepared, he had only one case of tetanus. His interest in asepsis extended to obstetric practice as evidenced by his clinical lecture to medical students recorded in the Manchester Royal Infirmary *Students Gazette* for 1899. In it he gave detailed instructions to the obstetric attendant for the preparation of the patient and his own hands. He held the view that there would be little puerperal sepsis if attendants used a plentiful supply of an efficient antiseptic for their hands and he favoured perchloride of mercury. This interest led him to be appointed to the Departmental Committee of the Ministry of Health on the Causes and Prevention of Puerperal Sepsis.

Donald had a large clinical practice both in hospital and in private and it is said that this did not leave him much time for writing. Nevertheless until the outbreak of the first World War he would present two or three case reports each year to the North of England Obstetrical & Gynaecological Society. In the discussions at the Society's meetings, no matter how abstruse or rare a case was, he could generally call to mind one with similar features, often seen many years earlier. In 1896 he read a paper to the Society on three cases of symphysiotomy, pointing out that although there had been a recent revival of interest in this procedure on the continent, the operation had found little favour to date in this country. About the same time Fothergill was experimenting with Walchen's position in parturition which changes the size of the pelvic outlet by rotating the pelvis on the sacrum. In 1895 he described to the Society a new flushing curette. He was a strong advocate of curettage but he did not use it indiscriminately - only with well defined indications. Whether or not at this stage histological examination of curettings was a regular practice, it certainly became so early in the next century.

The appearances must have presented many problems since it was not until 1908 that Hitschmann and Adler recognised the cyclical changes in the endometrium and in 1915 that Schröder related these to changes in the Graafian follicles. In 1904 he published a description of 'Chronic endometritis and chronic metritis in virgins'. The curettings were examined by Fothergill and the paper was illustrated by good photomicrographs although of rather low-power. He returned to the topic in 1910, when he published a paper with Fletcher Shaw. He concluded by saying, 'From this confusion we cannot hope to emerge completely till uterine pathology has made great advances'. Perhaps we might still say the same today.

He was active in writing and analysing his results up to the time of his retirement. Soon after Sampson's description of external endometriosis in 1922 he wrote a series of three papers describing his experience of the condition. But, perhaps, his major literary achievement was his textbook *An Introduction to the Study of Midwifery for Medical Students and Midwives*. The first edition appeared soon after his appointment to St Mary's Hospital. It was written with clarity and amply illustrated and ran through eight editions until he retired.

## Fothergill

William Edward Fothergill was born in Southampton in 1865 but was brought up in Darlington where his ancestor John Fothergill had settled as a surgeon. This Fothergill was brother to Dr John Fothergill FRS (1712-80) who practised in London and had one of the finest botanical gardens in Europe. In 1748 he wrote 'An account of Sore Throat' which was the first recognition of diphtheria in England. The Fothergill family produced many influential members of the Society of Friends.

William was educated in Edinburgh where he graduated to MB, CM in 1893 and MD in 1897. While at the University he took part in founding Edinburgh University Union. He also became secretary of the Athletic Union when it was in severe financial difficulties and handed over the office three years later in a sound condition. After a period of study at Jena and Paris he returned to Edinburgh and became house physician and clinical assistant to Professor Simpson, first in the gynaecology wards of the Royal Infirmary and then in the Royal Maternity Hospital. However, despite his brilliant academic record, there was little chance of advancement and so he moved to Manchester in 1895. Fothergill's first hospital appointment was to the Northern Hospital for Women and Children in 1896. In 1899 he was appointed as the first director of the clinical laboratory of the Manchester Royal Infirmary, then on the Piccadilly site, and this he held until 1904 when he was appointed to the staff of the Southern Hospital and, after the amalgamation of the two hospitals, to the staff of St Mary's Hospitals. In 1907 he became assistant gynaecological surgeon to the Royal Infirmary and full surgeon in 1919. Successively he held the posts of lecturer in obstetrics and gynaecology (1901), professor of systematic (1920) and clinical (1925) obstetrics and gynaecology.

In his private life he was a delightful host with a fund of anecdotes. He tramped the countryside with his wife, sketching in the Lakes and the Yorkshire Dales. He used his artistic ability to illustrate his case reports.

Fothergill was a friend to students in all faculties and threw himself whole-heartedly into the undergraduate life of the University, serving for several years as president of the Athletic Union, the football and other clubs. Familiarly known as 'Bill Fothergill', he was at the service of any student who sought his help. One of his greatest assets was his command of the English language and his ability to express himself both in speech and writing by the apt phrase or a memorable story. He gave many lectures to students and was always sure of a packed theatre. His material was excellent and garnished with anecdotes, many quite outrageous. The women students would protest, but to no avail. There was the story of how he once diagnosed hydramnios when he entered the house and saw the amniotic fluid flowing down the stairs. At Board meetings he would work with pencil and paper to express exactly the consensus opinion about a complex issue. At scientific meetings he could use the succinct phrase to express a comparison or clinch an argument with a devastating comment. On one occasion he described death from a gestational choriocarcinoma as matricide, but from a testicular choriocarcinoma as fractricide. At the British Congress of Obstetrics and Gynaecology in 1921 he poured vials of scorn on those who still practised abdominal fixation for uterine prolapse. One speaker said that there were more ways of killing a dog than by hanging it. He replied that it was not a case of other ways of killing a dog than by hanging, but first killing the dog and then trying to inflict further punishment by hanging. Fothergill was a prolific writer. In the Manchester Collection there is a group of fifty papers and communications he published between 1895 and 1908. In the same period he also published *A Manual of Midwifery*, *Golden Rules in Obstetric Practice* and *Lectures to Midwives and Maternity Nurses*. Later he also published a text book of gynaecology.

Among his more interesting papers are two on the use of Senecio in disorders of menstruation. The second of these formed part of a dissertation for which he had been awarded the Milner Fothergill Gold Medal in Therapeutics at Edinburgh. In these articles he discussed the botany of the Senecio group of plants (which include groundsel and ragwort) and the chemistry of the various extracts made from them. He concluded his 1898 paper writing,

> Lastly if no drug may be used until its action is definitely known, and its indications clearly defined, there is an end to the introduction of new therapeutic agents. All that the most exacting can demand is that the introducer of the drug shall give a working hypothesis according to which the drug may reasonably be supposed to act.

There was no committee concerned with the safety of medicine then! He discussed whether extracts of Senecio acted directly on the uterus as ecbolic agents or whether they are true emmenagogues. He concluded that they act on a nervous mechanism which initiates menstruation through a centre in the lumbar spinal cord. It is interesting that in the first edition of his *Manual of Diseases of Women* (1916) he argued strongly against the idea that menstruation is related to ovulation. This position he continued to hold even in the 1922 edition, but then the physiology of menstruation was only clearly elicited later by the work of Allen and Doisy (1923), Zondek and Aschheim (1927), and Corner and Allen (1929).

Fothergill's interest in pathology led him to develop a classification of gynaecological disorders. In 1912 he wrote,

> Classification marks the transition of any subject of enquiry from being a mere collection of observations and theories into being a science ... gynaecology as a science is very young. As an art it has, of course, reached a high level.

Having discussed a number of classifications then in use, he continued,

> For some years the writer has been using six main divisions in
> clinical teaching and in his systematic work. They were suggested
> by the arrangement of specimens introduced by Professor Lorrain
> Smith in the Pathology Museum of Manchester.

These were: (1) developmental errors, (2) vascular changes, (3)
mechanical conditions, (4) results of infection, (5) progressive
conditions and (6) retrogressive conditions. He used this
pathological, rather than an anatomical, arrangement in his *Manual of
Diseases of Women*. His interest in pathology is also shown in his
careful records of interesting specimens. One of the most interesting
of these records concerns two solid ovarian tumours (1902). A
photomicrograph of one clearly shows it to have been a Brenner tumour.
This was one of three such tumours recorded in some detail before
Brenner's description in 1907. The nature of such a tumour was not
then understood so he sent material from one of the specimens to
Orthmann in Berlin and Schröder in Bonn for a second opinion. Almost
the last paper published by Fothergill was in the *British Medical
Journal* of 13 February 1926, entitled 'History and development of
vaginal operations for genital prolapse'. In it he outlined the
various procedures used in the nineteenth century and gave full credit
to Donald for his work.


The Manchester Operation


Neither Donald nor Fothergill invented the procedure of colporraphy.
Earlier work on the anterior repair for prolapse has been attributed
to Heming (1831) and Marion Sims (1866), on repair of the posterior
wall to Emmett (1864) and Hegan (1836) and of the perineum to Baker
Brown (1852), while Huguier (1848) amputated the cervix and Schröder
(1888) attempted a combination of these procedures. Donald, in 1888,
was among the first operators to attempt pelvic floor repair by a
combination of anterior and posterior colporraphy with amputation of
the cervix and, in 1894, he discussed the procedure at a meeting of
the North of England Obstetrical and Gynaecological Society. Thus
Donald was actively developing the operation before Fothergill came to
Manchester. In 1908 he published a short paper entitled 'Operation in
cases of complete prolapse', which was illustrated by sketches made by
Fothergill during the course of an operation. Although the basic

features of the Manchester operation remained the same, both surgeons developed it in line with their own experience and the clinical indications. In later years this gave rise to minor disputes between their successors about details of Fothergill's procedure or Donald's procedure, which were of considerable amusement to the less well informed members of St Mary's staff.

The operation outlined by Donald is empirically based but over a number of years Fothergill endeavoured to establish a theoretical basis. In 1907 he read a paper to the Royal Society of Medicine entitled 'The support of the pelvic viscera: a review of some recent contributions to pelvic anatomy with a clinical introduction'. It was well illustrated by a number of his own sketches as well as by diagrams culled from the literature. 'If asked to say how the pelvic viscera are supported in their usual position', he said, 'a modern student of medicine describes all the structures of the pelvic floor ... He concludes that the pelvic organs are partly propped up from below and partly suspended from above'. Fothergill argued that while this is true in a general sense, it lacks accuracy if a clinician is to have a real grip of his work. Extreme laxity of the pelvic floor when the perineum is badly torn can exist without descent of the viscera. 'Even in virgins careful examination shows the cervix does not lie on the pelvic diaphragm any more than the bottom of a hansom cab rests on the ground'. He argued that the main support of the viscera was the parametrium, defined by Virchow as the loose connective tissue, with abundant blood vessels and lymphatics which surround the lower part of the uterus and upper part of the vagina.

Fothergill's views however were strongly attacked by R H Paramore in a paper in 1908 who argued that the pelvic viscera were maintained in position by two sets of forces - the intra-abdominal pressure from above and the pelvic muscles especially the levatores ani reflexly responding below. Paramore quoted Tandler and Halban who pointed out that when the fourth sacral nerve is included in the meningocele in patients with spina bifida there is paralysis of the pelvic floor musculature and descent of the pelvic contents. The controversy rumbled on over the years but it seems that the electromyographic studies of Porter and Parks (1962) lend support to the importance of the rôle played by the muscles of the pelvic floor.

Justification of the Manchester operation for prolapse rests not on theoretical considerations but on its results. In 1921, Lacey read a paper to the British Congress of Obstetrics and Gynaecology, reviewing the results of the treatment of 750 women during the years 1914, 1915 and 1916. A letter was sent to all the patients asking five questions, and 521 replies were received. Of these 87 per cent said that their womb kept up well. Of those who replied that the operation was not a success, Lacey saw and examined 29 and of these 17 had some prolapse. There was a more critical examination of the operation in 1961 at a meeting of the North of England Obstetrical and Gynaecological Society by gynaecologists from outside Manchester. It emerged that provided the type of case for which it is suitable was identified the operation remains the one of choice, and it still retains this position in the present day textbooks of operative gynaecology both here and in America. For an empirically based operation devised nearly a century ago, this is no mean achievement.

Here then are two men whose names live after them because of a surgical operation they mutually developed; an operation which may not have saved many lives but has given relief to many women suffering the consequence of childbirth. Both were insistent on the unity of obstetrics and gynaecology. But their memorial lies not only in this achievement but also in their contributions to discussions on puerperal sepsis, endometritis and other problems and concepts of their time which helped to clarify and advance an understanding of these conditions − an understanding which they conveyed to their students in the lecture theatre and at the bed side.

FAL

7.12 ALFRED ERNEST BARCLAY, 1876-1949
    OBE, MA, MD, FRCP, DMRE, DSc(Hon)


When the Manchester Medical Society was founded, radiology did not exist. Nowadays it is difficult to imagine a diagnostic service in the Western world without X-ray facilities, ultrasound, and radio-nuclide imaging, not to mention computed tomography and nuclear magnetic resonance.

    Two people in the United Kingdom are known to have received copies of Roentgen's original paper published on 28 December 1895: Lord Kelvin in Glasgow and Arthur Schuster, Professor of Physics in the University of Manchester. The first photographs of the effects of X-rays were sent by Roentgen only to Schuster. On 7 January 1896, C H Lees, an assistant to Schuster, spoke to the Manchester Literary and Philosophical Society and showed some of these photographs. The photographs have survived and probably represent the earliest evidence to be presented publicly in support of Roentgen's discovery. In a special meeting held on Wednesday, 18 March 1896 in the Chemical theatre at Owens College, Schuster delivered an address to the Manchester Medical Society making special reference to the medical and surgical applications. He described the problems of examining patients in physics laboratories and suggested that until a suitable place in a hospital could be provided, some rooms nearby should be fitted up. An offer from Mr W J Chadwick, of 2 St Mary's Street, who photographed patients in his rooms by the Roentgen ray process was accepted by the House Committee of the Manchester Royal Infirmary on 21 December 1896, on the following terms:

| | |
|---|---|
| Hands, feet, ankles and elbows | 5s. each |
| Shoulders, hips or the body | 10s. each |

terminable by 3 months notice on either side. The arrangements were indeed terminated on 23 December 1898. X-ray equipment was installed in the old Piccadilly Infirmary in 1900 and its medical control rested in the hands of Dr C H Melland of the staff of the clinical laboratory, followed by Dr E Bosdin Leech. The partitioned-off gallery of the chapel was considered a suitable place for radiography in 1904. There was no window, no ventilation and all was painted black. Messrs Mottershead & Co., Chemists, of 7 Exchange Street sold and hired equipment for both radiodiagnosis and treatment. Arrangements between Mottersheads and Manchester Royal Infirmary were formalised on 29 May 1905 when the Board of Management resolved that radiographic work should be carried out by them both in the Infirmary and in their shop 'upon payment of £35 per annum'. The 'new' Royal Infirmary in Oxford Road was opened in 1908, and although it was at that time the last word in hospital design no provision whatever had been made for an X-ray Department. On 26 January 1909 Mr A E Barclay was appointed medical officer in charge of radiography and electricity at a salary of £100 per annum. The accommodation allotted to Barclay was a basement designed for Russian and mud baths.

Alfred Ernest Barclay was born in Manchester on 30 September 1876, second son of Robert Barclay, founder of one of the great mercantile companies, Robert Barclay and Sons, with branches in Montevideo and Buenos Aires. The eldest son became Lord Mayor of Manchester and the youngest spent most of his life directing the South American branches of the firm. Alfred entered medicine seeking his education first at Cambridge. His clinical studies began in Manchester in 1897 and were completed in the London Hospital. During his student days in Manchester he was instrumental in the establishment of the Medical Students Representative Council and indeed became its first president in 1901. He qualified in 1904. In 1906, after various house appointments, he returned to Manchester to set up in private radiological practice. Radiology was not then a speciality and to attempt, as he described later, 'to challenge the stranglehold of a chemist without any hospital appointment was indeed a venture of faith'. The first real X-ray department in Manchester was established in Ancoats Hospital and Barclay was invited to join the honorary staff. This dignity was dictated primarily by the precarious financial position of the hospital. It was here, however, that he made his first experiments with bismuth meals and realised the great dividends to be obtained from correct and painstaking radiological examination of the gastrointestinal tract. When in 1909 he was appointed to the Infirmary he established in the basement under the receiving room two X-ray rooms, one specifically for the investigation of disorders of the alimentary tract. To have two rooms, one dedicated to screening, was a new feature in X-ray department design. He was criticised for taking up a 'vast' space and horrified the hospital authorities by ordering nine new X-ray tubes at £2 each. Some of the early fragile and erratic tubes responded to kind treatment but there were others he recalled 'that sulked or were even spiteful'. Nevertheless it was in Manchester Royal Infirmary in these primitive conditions that the early history of the opaque meal was written and the methodology firmly established. It was Barclay who first appreciated that 'living anatomy' was different from that of the dissecting room and that the physiology being witnessed by radiology was not in accord with the text books of the day. Throughout his life he pursued a campaign for the better understanding of normal bodily structures and function. In 1912, in association with Bythell, who succeeded him at Ancoats, he published a monograph on *X-ray Diagnosis and Treatment*. This book attracted worldwide attention and became the 'Bible' of those in training for many years.

During World War I, Barclay was commissioned as a Captain in the RAMC and with one colleague to assist him was responsible for the X-ray services of the hospital unit which eventually grew to 35,000 beds in and around Manchester. Most of the work was concerned with fractures and with the localisation of foreign bodies for which he invented an ingenious extraction instrument which rang a bell on contact with a metallic foreign body. His wartime work brought a realisation not only of the importance of an X-ray service but also the need for a properly organised training programme. Barclay was a prodigious worker and during this period ran the whole of the Infirmary's X-ray service single-handed.

In 1916 he tried to raise funds to establish a Chair in Radiology, but monies were not forthcoming. He then approached the University of Cambridge to consider the setting up of a structured course leading to a Diploma in Radiology. The University, ever cautious about the financial implications, required Barclay's personal guarantee against loss before agreeing to establish this unique systematic training programme in 1920. Manchester Royal Infirmary, recognising not only the first class department Barclay had established but also the increasing status of radiology in the medical world, appointed him to the honorary staff on 30 September 1918. This appointment was not without opposition from some of the physicians who would have preferred one of their number to be titular head. It was, however, a significant step in the advancement of radiology, giving Barclay full clinical responsibilities, enabling him with the backing of colleagues and the lay Board to work for a new and more adequate department. On 18 November 1912 Sir Humphrey Rolleston, President of the Roentgen Society with Sir William Cobbett in the Chair, opened a new X-ray Department at the Infirmary. This Department, a great tribute to Barclay, was considered to be the best in the country at the time.

It was during these formative years in Manchester that Barclay gained international recognition. He was a great traveller and made many radiological contacts throughout the world, particularly in the United States and Australasia. The British Institute of Radiology owes much to Barclay, who was President of the Roentgen Society in 1924 and worked together with Robert Knox and Stanley Melville to bring about the amalgamation of the Institute and the Roentgen Society. He was also instrumental in arranging the first International Congress of Radiology held in London in 1925. Barclay's memory is honoured by the British Institute of Radiology in its two prestigious annual awards, the Barclay Prize and the Barclay Medal.

In 1928 at the height of his professional standing Barclay left Manchester to go to Cambridge to organise the teaching of the now well established Diploma in Medical Radiology. This he did at considerable financial sacrifice meeting the expenses of the new department and the course out of his own pocket. Here began his interests in the mechanisms of swallowing and in direct cine-roentgenography. His classic book on the digestive tract appeared in 1933 and was re-published in 1936. He was replaced in Manchester by Edward Wing Twining (1887-1939) who was to become the first and one of the most significant British neuroradiologists. In 1937 at the age of 61 Barclay was invited to join the Nuffield Institute of Medical Research at Oxford. Here with great energy he re-entered the field of research first collaborating with Franklin, Barcroft and Barron on studies of the foetal circulation. He explored with the aid of cine-roentgenography the problems of the ductus arteriosus, demonstrated the workings of the foetal circulation and solved the 300 year old controversy surrounding the changes that occur when the adult circulation is established. This work was published in book form in 1944. Research followed on the vascularisation of the kidney with original observations on hitherto unknown vascular shunts. These investigations with Trueta and others were published in *Studies of the Renal Circulation*, an important survey with far-reaching implications. In collaboration with Bentley he sought and found similar shunt mechanisms in the gastric wall. Out of this work came important papers on micro-arteriography. This new outlook on physiology was termed 'Barclay's Physiology'.

The second world war interrupted his scientific work. In his capacity as Adviser in Radiology to the Ministry of Health, Barclay assumed responsibility for the organisation and supervision of all the radiological services in the enormous Emergency Hospital Scheme, with beds in all parts of England. During the first year he personally visited every hospital in the Scheme and his role in correlating the needs of the civil and military services throughout the war years cannot be overestimated.

Barclay received many honours from many parts of the world, but particularly prized the Honorary DSc awarded by both Oxford and Manchester Universities. He gave many memorial lectures and occupied many national and international positions of honour. Much of his success he attributed to his wife and life long companion, Mary, whom he married in 1906. He had outstanding mechanical gifts which he used to great advantage, not only in radiology, but also in the service of his sporting Bentley. His outside interests were wide and varied, from fishing to classical music. 'Barclay of Manchester', as he was known to countless friends and colleagues throughout the world, died at his home in Oxford on 26 April 1949, at the age of 72. His life in and for radiology was long and valuable. Many of his contributions were seminal and he was instrumental in establishing diagnostic radiology as a responsible clinical discipline. He extended medical knowledge by the application of technology and yet never lost sight of human understanding 'as the first essential of medical service'.

II

7.13 EVELYN DAVISON TELFORD, 1876–1961
    MA, MSc, FRCS


Professor Evelyn Davison Telford was born in Middlesborough in 1876
and so he always claimed to be a Yorkshireman. His father was an
engineer who came from Middlesborough to work on the Liverpool
Overhead Railway when Evelyn was ten years of age. He was sent to the
Manchester Grammar School where he worked industriously and became
Secretary of the Soccer Club.

From Manchester Grammar School he obtained an open exhibition to
Gonville and Caius College, Cambridge later becoming a Foundation
Scholar and Special Prizeman of that College. In 1896 he was head of
the list in the Second MB, and took a First in the Natural Sciences
Tripos. He was again head of the list in the Final MB, BS in 1899
having pursued his clinical studies at the old Manchester Royal
Infirmary in Piccadilly. In 1901 he was house surgeon to Sir William
Thorburn at Manchester Royal Infirmary, later becoming surgical
registrar, surgical tutor, and resident surgical officer. He acquired
his FRCS in 1903 and was later appointed as surgeon to the Royal
Manchester Childrens' Hospital and assistant surgeon at Salford Royal
Hospital. In 1908 his application (accompanied by lavish testimonials
from no fewer than eight referees!) for the post of assistant surgeon
at Manchester Royal Infirmary was successful: he was the first surgeon
to open up S2 Unit at the New Infirmary in Oxford Road.

Telford's interest in the surgery of children and in orthopaedic
surgery led him to work at the Swinton Residential School, the
Lancastrian School and Abergele Sanatorium in North Wales where
children with rickets and bone tuberculosis were treated. His great
humanity and sympathy with patients is revealed in his monograph *The
Problem of the Crippled Child* published about that time.

In 1922 Telford was appointed to the Chair of Systematic Surgery. He worked in conjunction with J S B Stopford: this partnership pioneered research in the anatomy, pathology and surgery of the autonomic system. On Saturday mornings they investigated the effect of cervico-thoracic ganglionectomy in Raynaud's disease, acrocyanosis, hyperidrosis, cardiospasm and scleroderma. Lumbar ganglionectomy was tried in thromboangiitis obliterans, poliomyelitis, Hirschsprung's disease and constipation. Their numerous and beautifully written papers in impeccable English were published in the *British Journal of Surgery*, the *Lancet* and the *Journal of Anatomy*.

In hospital one remembers his unhurried gait, his imperturbability and his memorable '9.20' lectures distinctly delivered in a slow measured precise voice. They were models of conciseness, clarity and lucidity. Telford's punctuality was proverbial. As an operator he was neat, bloodless, unhurried and conservative; as a teacher superb.

In private life Telford loved his garden and was an authority on auriculas. He and his wife Sarah loved walking in the Yorkshire Dales, the Derbyshire hills and the mountains of North Wales – indeed it was to Prestatyn that he retired, though he returned to Manchester Royal Infirmary to help while younger surgeons were at the war.

In his house at Prestatyn he had a notable collection of English watercolours and of mezzotints, on which he was an authority. He enjoyed his retirement in North Wales until his death in 1961 at the age of eighty-four. His wife Sarah died on 20 August 1961 very soon after he did, and under the terms of her will (which was almost identical with that of her husband) the Manchester Medical Society became the residual beneficiary. As has been indicated in chapter 6 the considerable legacy which passed in due course to the Society's trustees has stabilised the Society's financial position, and the Telford Memorial Lecture has been one of the highlights of the annual programme which has kept alive the memory of this great man.

WWW

7.14 EDWARD FALKNER HILL, 1877-1974

MRCS, LRCP, DPH, MD, FFARCS, Hon FFARCS

Among the distinguished anaesthetists who have been part of the Manchester school since it was founded by Alexander Wilson in the last century, none has a greater claim to be recognised than Dr Edward Falkner Hill, who during the 97 years of his life spanned more of the 150 years which are at present being celebrated than any other anaesthetist in this area. Dr Falkner Hill was born in Wellington in 1877, was six years a scholar at Sidcot School and spent seven years in residence in Dalton Hall while he was a medical undergraduate in the Victoria University of Manchester. He graduated in 1900, served as house surgeon in Manchester Royal Infirmary and thereafter went into general practice. His main interest was anaesthesia, and in 1909 he became assistant anaesthetist to Manchester Royal Infirmary. Subsequently he became one of its visiting anaesthetists. Owing to the exigencies of the second world war he remained in this post until 1947 when he was 70 years old. He eventually became senior anaesthetist and University lecturer in anaesthesia.

Dr Falkner Hill published many papers during his career and it is perhaps germane to our present interest that one of these was concerned with 'The evolution of anaesthesia in Manchester, 1900 to 1945'; it appeared in the *British Journal of Anaesthesia* in 1947. He had two main spheres of interest in his speciality. That which led to the greatest number of papers was spinal anaesthesia, about which he wrote extensively in the years between 1930 and 1951, publishing twelve papers on this subject over this period. At one stage of his career he was the preferred anaesthetist to some of the most eminent surgeons in Manchester, notably Burgess, McAlpine and Milligan. The retirement (or death) of these three surgeons within a month or two of

each other, left Falkner Hill underemployed. This gave him the
opportunity to study the problems of spinal anaesthesia in the
experimental animal. This work became the basis of an MD thesis
concerned with the 'Blood Pressure Changes during Spinal Anaesthesia',
a thesis which earned a Gold Medal. His other interest was in
'Automatic Anaesthesia'. He designed and developed the first draw-over
vapouriser for ether and chloroform, an apparatus which provided for a
limited amount of rebreathing in addition. With this apparatus, once
anaesthesia had been established its depth was determined by the tidal
volume of respiration. The alveolar concentration of the drug, and
therefore its concentration in the arterial blood, was the resultant
of a balance between the rate of uptake of the drug on the one hand
and the rapidity of its redistribution to the tissues of the body on
the other. If anaesthesia became unduly deep the tidal volume
diminished. Less anaesthetic was taken into the lungs. The processes
of redistribution however continued so that the blood concentration
level of the anaesthetic agent was reduced and the depth of the
anaesthesia diminished. If on the other hand, anaesthesia was
insufficient, the patient would respond to stimulation by increase in
depth of respiration. The result was the indrawing of larger volumes
of anaesthetic vapour and appropriate deepening of anaesthesia. His
pioneer work in this field has unfortunately not received the
recognition which was his due, mainly because he himself did not write
very much on the subject. Indeed it was not until uptake and
distribution of anaesthetic agents was studied in detail in the 1950s,
especially in relation to halothane, that the importance of Dr Falkner
Hill's work became apparent.

Dr Falkner Hill's connections with the Manchester Medical Society
were numerous. He was elected to its membership in the year 1902 and
was Vice-President from 1939 to 1943. When in 1945 the anaesthetists
in the Manchester area formed themselves into the Manchester and
District Society of Anaesthetists he was the obvious choice as its
first President. Like the other Manchester anaesthetists he became a
member of the Section of Anaesthetics of the Medical Society when it
was formed and in 1959 he was its President. The subject of his
Presidential address, not inappropriately, was '50 years of
anaesthesia'.

Dr Falkner Hill was a foundation Fellow of the Faculty of

Anaesthetists of the Royal College of Surgeons and was elected as an
Honorary Fellow in 1961. The *British Journal of Anaesthesia* owes a
tremendous debt to him. He was a member of the governing body of this
organisation for many years, and in 1959 he was made the joint editor
of the Journal, sharing the responsibility with Dr Cecil Gray of
Liverpool, and he served in this capacity until 1964. Thereafter he
was chairman of the board and after relinquishing this office he
continued to proof-read for the Journal. Indeed, he served the Journal
in one capacity or another until a year before he died.

Dr Falkner Hill had many gifts. He was good company with a warmth
of heart and sometimes a puckish sense of humour. He was above all a
man of strong character and high principle with an excellent brain. He
was a member of the Society of Friends, and like so many of them, was
a conscientious objector during the 1914-18 War: this stand cost him
dearly, for surgeons who might have availed themselves of his services
during the years from 1914 onwards did not do so because of his known
objector's principles. He was a keen sportsman in his day, though his
later years were marred by disability: it was however typical of him
that when his hip joints became too creaky to allow him to continue to
play golf he still went out to his golf club to putt. He had a keen
interest in motor cars and many in Manchester will remember the
'yellow-peril' - the name given to an old Vauxhall which he drove for
many years. In 1903 he married Agnes Thomson who was joined to him in
60 years of happy married life, terminating in her death in 1963. Mrs
Hill was profoundly interested and active in social work in the
Manchester area, and Dr Hill, though very busy professionally, none
the less took an interest in her work and helped her. Her death eleven
years before his was a great loss to him. Even in his later years,
however, his constancy of purpose and his personal faith sustained him
when life proved difficult. When he died in 1974 Manchester
anaesthesia lost its grand old man.

ARH

7.15 CATHERINE CHISHOLM, 1878-1952
     CBE, BA, MD, FRCP


Dr Catherine Chisholm, Manchester University's first woman graduate in medicine, and the only woman to have held the office of President of the Manchester Medical Society during the first 150 years of its existence, was born on 2 January 1878. She was the daughter of a general practitioner in Radcliffe and was educated initially at a private school. Although she wished to do medicine, she first studied arts at Manchester University (then Owens College) and graduated BA in 1898. This undergraduate career was distinguished and she gained the Bishop Lee New Testament Greek Prize.

After considerable effort she was accepted as one of the first two women medical students by the University and graduated in 1904. Her acceptance was not without considerable opposition from the medical staff and one or two of the tutors had declared they would resign before they taught women students. It was felt inappropriate for them to be instructed by any other than the Dean (Professor Young) and the senior demonstrator. They had a dissecting room to themselves: reminiscing on this, Dr Chisholm in 1949 commented that the room contained a delightful blackboard for drawing, four pegs on which to hang their overalls, a row of wash basins, and a looking glass - but unfortunately no toilets were available for the women students. This small dissecting room served them for lunch room, common room and dissection room for two years, and only later did they join the rest of the class for further instruction.

The life of women medical students at that time was vastly different from University life today. Men and women students did not walk to college together unless they were old family friends. No woman was on Christian name terms with her male fellow students and only intimacy justified it between women. The women students had to sit on the front rows and some of the men were so scared of talking to the women that knowledge of special lectures and arrangements never reached the girls. When she and her colleague, Miss Corbett, started their clinical course, men were just beginning to wear white coats: this however was not obligatory for women and Miss Chisholm decided that whilst she wore a 'clean washable blouse and a long serge skirt fringed with "brush braid" the important thing was to substitute a white pique skirt renewed at least weekly'. When the students progressed to clinical classes, she was allowed in most wards in the Infirmary but was banned from male surgical outpatients and expected to 'fade out' when cases involving the scrotum were examined. Indeed fifty years later, male patients continued to have this special protection from examination by female students, who also were not allowed in the special diseases clinic.

Catherine Chisholm was a distinguished student, gaining Class 1 certificates in forensic medicine, pathology, obstetrics and surgery, but she had a much broader field of interest, for she became Secretary, later Vice-Chairman and then Chairman of the Manchester University Women's Union. After graduation in 1904 she was unable to obtain a post in Manchester and had to go south for employment. She was first appointed a junior resident medical officer at the Battersea branch of Clapham Maternity Hospital, later a senior house surgeon at the same hospital and by 1906 was the resident medical officer at the Eldwick Sanatorium in Bingley, Yorkshire.

In 1906 she decided to enter general practice in Manchester and was responsible for providing a considerable proportion of the medical care in that part of the slum area of the city lying close to the University. She built up a large practice consisting mainly of women and children and during this time developed an interest in their welfare which was to last throughout the whole of her life. In 1908 she was appointed the Medical Officer to Manchester High School for Girls and many of her publications reflect her interest in the welfare of the girls, particularly with respect to their growth and physical development. She was an enthusiastic advocate of exercise and its beneficial effect on dysmenorrhoea, writing and obtaining her MD with commendation on this subject in 1912.

In 1912 she applied for the post of physician to children at St

Mary's Hospital for Women and Children but was unsuccessful. She felt that her application had failed because of her sex and from reading the correspondence in the Manchester Medical School *Students' Gazette* at about this time, she may well have been right. Partly because of this refusal she turned her attention to the founding of a hospital which would have a staff of women doctors. Together with her women colleagues and some prominent lay women such as Margaret Ashton and Lady Simon, she drew up plans for a small hospital of twelve cots. This hospital was opened in 1914 and has since then grown into a much larger hospital - the Duchess of York Hospital for Babies.

Her interest in paediatrics continued and she was appointed the same year as consultant physician for children at Manchester Northern Hospital and as paediatrician to Hope Hospital at Salford. During the ensuing years she developed an interest in the problems of nutrition in babies and her paper on breast milk feeding[1] is a classic in the practical care of babies. She also studied rickets in children aged less than two years, especially in the slum and suburb areas of Manchester, carrying out her investigations over two years in order to observe the seasonal incidence of the condition. Inner city children, she found, were more likely to develop rickets than the others; in the inner city however the incidence of 6.2 per cent in good homes contrasted markedly with 19.4 per cent in bad homes. Similar figures for the suburbs were 3.4 per cent and 25 per cent. She also observed that the second child in a family had a better chance of escaping rickets than the first or subsequent children. She felt that this was due to better mother craft with the second child; with successive child bearing however the mother became overwhelmed so that the standard of her care for the later infants deteriorated. The University recognised her services to infant and child welfare and she was appointed lecturer in children's diseases and vaccination in 1923.

Her interests were not confined purely to clinical medicine and after graduation she continued to be practically involved in the welfare of students and later women graduates. She was a founder member of the Medical Womens Federation and later became its President. She was also a member of the British Paediatric Association, Chairman of the Manchester Division of the British Medical Association 1938-39, President of the Manchester Medical Society 1943 and President of the Manchester Paediatric Club 1950. Her services to women and children were recognised by the award of a CBE in 1935 and of a Fellowship of the Royal College of Physicians in 1949. However, the honour which pleased her most was the naming of one of the wards for premature babies at the Duchess of York Hospital after her.

She was a likeable woman, was extremely fond of the colour green and she also had the trait of forgetfulness, leaving innumerable spectacles and stethoscopes in her trail. Her interest in medicine continued after her retirement in 1950 until her death in 1952.

AMH

## 7.16 SIR WILLIAM FLETCHER SHAW, 1878–1961

### MD, FRCP, FRCOG, Hon LLD, Hon MMSA, FACS

William Fletcher Shaw was one of the most distinguished gynaecologists of the Manchester School. His contribution to our speciality is almost of the order of that of some of the giants, such as Charles Clay, but it is as much in his work in the founding of the Royal College of Obstetricians and Gynaecologists as in his clinical work that his eminence is to be found.

He was born on the 13 April 1878 in Clayton, Manchester. His father was David Shaw an industrial chemist who ran away from school in Scotland at the age of 14 years. His mother was Zilliah, daughter of William Fletcher a woollen manufacturer of Littleborough in Lancashire. As a boy, Shaw was a pupil of Manchester Grammar School from where he went to Owens College, Manchester. In his final year Owens became the Victoria University of Manchester and it was from here that he graduated in 1903. William Brockbank in his book on the honorary medical staff of the Manchester Royal Infirmary recounts how Shaw had the unusual experience of going by horse-drawn tram to the University to hear the final results of the MB, and going by electric tram on the following day to graduate. While an undergraduate he became president of the Medical Students Debating Society and he grew a magnificent handlebar moustache. A picture taken of him in 1905 reveals it in all its glory. Because of this he was nicknamed 'Hairy Bill' and this pseudonym was to be his for the rest of his days. I recall as an undergraduate and a student of his wondering idly how he had got the name – for he was clean-shaven in later life. During his time as an undergraduate his rather smooth manner was noted by an anonymous fellow student who composed an alphabetical series of couplets which claimed to represent the characteristics of some of his

13. A pencil drawing of the old medical school in Coupland Street as it would have been known to many of those whose lives are recorded in chapter 7. Note the horse-drawn tram. Sir William Fletcher Shaw is said to have travelled to the medical school by horse-drawn tram to get the results of his final MB in 1903, and to have gone by electric tram the following day to graduate. See biography 7.16.

fellow students. Shaw's reads,

U is the unction with which Fletcher Shaw
I imagine addresses his mother in law.

Although this sounds a little cool, to those who knew him it depicts
accurately his manner in later life. It led to his critics noting his
lack of warmth and his rather Olympian manner when dealing with his
juniors.

After graduating he became house surgeon to the Accident Room at
Manchester Royal Infirmary and then full house surgeon to Professor
G A Wright. His third post was that of RMO at St Mary's Hospital, and
this was the hospital to which he was attached for the rest of his
working life. Nine months after this he also became senior resident at
St Mary's and resident assistant obstetric surgeon. The obstetric
service of St Mary's in those days was, of course, at Whitworth Street
and it undertook 4500 deliveries annually, which is approximately the
same number which the modern St Mary's Hospital undertakes. He held
this post for 3½ years. The chief who had the greatest effect on him
was Archibald Donald who was one of the pioneers of the
internationally famous Manchester operation for genital prolapse. This
was then an extremely common disease, not only in the North West of
England but throughout most of the world. His next post was that of
doctor in charge of the pathology laboratory at St Mary's Hospital.
There was at that time no regular appointed pathologist. It was a
mixed job as it also involved duties as assistant to the out-patients
department. His post in the pathology laboratory was of great
importance to his development and many of the papers he wrote in later
years had a strong pathological foundation to them. By the time he
applied for the post of assistant gynaecological surgeon to the Royal
Infirmary in 1912 he had written 32 papers, many of them dealing with
chronic metritis and he wrote in great detail about its pathological
basis. It is easy now to be rather dismissive about these papers
because, of course, they were written long before the days of
understanding the endocrine basis of much of the disease he believed
to be inflammatory. However, in re-reading them they do show an
astonishing insight into uterine pathology and many of his papers bear
some excellent illustrations. In the same year he was elected honorary
gynaecologist to the Christie Hospital. Nineteen hundred and twelve
was also an important year to him as in that year he became  assistant

14. A reading room in the main University building as it would have been known to generations of students during the late 19th century.

15. One of the laboratories at the University of the same period.

lecturer in obstetrics and gynaecology in the University of Manchester and his work with the University lasted throughout the rest of his professional life.

Two years after his appointment the first world war began. Shaw did not go to war but he lived in St Mary's Hospital two weeks out of every four, alternating with Dr Clifford. They coped almost single handed with the massive amount of emergency work which the hospital undertook. It is probable that this clinical experience formed the basis of the whole of his future career. In particular during the war he looked after the patients of his former chief, Archibald Donald, who had gone to France in 1914. In the first two years of the first world war he also became gynaecologist to Withington Hospital and again most of the work he did during that time was single handed. This ceased in 1916 when the whole of Withington Hospital was taken over by the military.

The variety of topics on which he wrote was enormous. Apart from his writings on chronic metritis and endometritis (which had earned him an MD with gold medal in 1906), there are papers on chorea gravidarum, uterine fibroids, Wertheim hysterectomy and even vaginal hysterectomy, which was an operation little practised in those times. In 1919 he was elected as a member of the Gynaecological Visiting Society. This is a society of senior gynaecologists from teaching hospitals throughout the Kingdom. Its members are limited to 30 and its meetings are held regularly throughout the country. The penalty for failure to attend more than three consecutive meetings is expulsion. As a member of this Society, Shaw met most of his contempories and senior colleagues during this time. The most fateful of these meetings was with Blair Bell who was Professor of Obstetrics and Gynaecology in Liverpool University. Shaw records how in 1924 he had discussed with Blair Bell the possible founding of a College of Obstetricians and Gynaecologists. He also tells how the original idea came from Sir William Japp Sinclair who occupied the chair of obstetrics and gynaecology in our University until his death in 1912. Shaw had been one of his junior residents. The years from 1924 to 1929 were the most fruitful which Shaw ever had. Due to his enthusiasm and drive and the persuasive powers which he could exert on many of his colleagues, the College of Obstetricians and Gynaecologists was founded in 1929. Its first premises were in Queen Anne Street, London in a house owned by William Blair Bell. Blair Bell became the first president and Shaw was the first honorary secretary of the College. Nine years later in 1938 he was elected to the presidency of the College and he was the longest serving president in its history as he filled this post for five years until 1943. He was also the first president of the College, by now the Royal College of Obstetricians and Gynaecologists, to receive the honour of Knighthood while holding office. As the College became nationally and internationally established it became obvious that the small premises in Queen Anne Street were not going to be able to house its activities for very much longer. A different group of gynaecologists, therefore, undertook to persuade wealthy industrialists, such as Lord Nuffield and Sir Simon Marks, to make their contribution to a new and extended College in Regent's Park. This magnificent new building was opened by Her Majesty the Queen in 1960. At the beginning of this venture Shaw had his doubts but he ultimately became very enthusiastic about it and the official portrait of the opening of the College by Her Majesty shows Shaw in his College robes standing near the front row of those assembled looking rather quizzical about the whole business. At the entrance of the College there is a dual plaque commemorating the founding of the College and the work which William Blair Bell and William Fletcher Shaw did.

He had a happy home life and had three sons by his first wife who pre-deceased him. One son, David, became a gynaecologist and another, William, was killed in the second world war. Shaw founded the William Meredith Fletcher Shaw Memorial Lecture, still given annually in his memory at the College. In 1939 Shaw re-married. His second wife was Mabel Mary Stevenson; unhappily she died in 1947. There were no children of the second marriage. He retired from the chair in 1943 but still remained very active in obstetrics and gynaecology. During his years as president and as a member of the Council of the College he had travelled widely in the United States and elsewhere, and had made a host of international friends. These he kept up with. He was interested in the training of young gynaecologists and was always ready to suggest and advise. However, his manner was rather austere and remote and some found him slightly forbidding and difficult to know. During much of Shaw's time at the University there were two professors of obstetrics and gynaecology, the other being Daniel

Dougal who was six years Shaw's junior. Dougal was also a man of considerable professional stature but unhappily the personalities of Shaw and Dougal were not always compatible. Dissension arose from time to time, very often about trivia which I think made both Shaw and Dougal very unhappy, but they did not resolve their differences readily or easily.

As a student of Shaw and later a house surgeon when he still had strong connections with St Mary's, I can still recall him with great clarity. He had an enormous memory for distant events but he had a frightening capacity and inability to identify people and faces, and the stories are legion of his confusing the identities of various members of staff. He had great difficulty in recalling the names of his house surgeons and he solved this by a master stroke. In his later years he called them all 'Potter'. It was quite usual to be 'phoned in one's room at night at St Mary's by Sir William and when he asked to speak to Potter the form was to put down the telephone with a clatter, pick it up again and say, 'Potter here, Sir'. This removed a great deal of misunderstanding in the mind of Sir William if not in those of his house surgeons.

He remained active almost until the end of his life. He died in 1962 at the age of 83 in the month of November. Until June he was well and active and his terminal illness was mercifully short. His memorial is his work with the Royal College of Obstetricians and Gynaecologists and the very large role he played in its establishment. Also he trained a generation of gynaecological surgeons in a meticulous and methodical kind of way. He remains a giant in the history of British obstetrics and gynaecology.

RWB

7.17 SIR GEOFFREY JEFFERSON, 1886-1961
     CBE, FRCP, FRCS, FRS


Geoffrey Jefferson was born in County Durham on 10 April 1886, the son
of Dr A J Jefferson who became a well known general practitioner and
surgeon in Rochdale. He was educated at the Manchester Grammar School
where he 'cordially detested' some of his teachers and at Manchester
University, from where he qualified, taking the London degree with
honours and distinction in surgery in 1909, and having won most of the
available prizes and medals on the way. After holding resident
appointments at the Infirmary and elsewhere, and winning his
Mastership in Surgery with a gold medal, he went out to British
Columbia 'because there appeared to be no opening in Manchester for a
young and ambitious man with limited means'. He was developing a
surgical practice when the war broke out and he was invited by Sir
Herbert Waterhouse to go out to Russia to help in the Anglo-Russian
Hospital in St Petersburg. He returned to England in 1917 and was sent
as a surgical specialist to the 14th General Hospital in France, where
he formed a department for the treatment of gun-shot wounds of the
head and had an excellent opportunity of studying and treating acute
head injuries.

     After the armistice he was appointed to the honorary surgical staff
of Salford Royal Hospital and visiting surgeon to the Ministry of
Pensions Hospital at Grangethorpe, where he had charge of gun-shot
wounds of the head and spine, and thus was able to continue his
observations on the effects of injury of the nervous system and make a
study of traumatic epilepsy. This naturally led in 1924 to a visit to
America where he worked in Harvey Cushing's clinic in Boston and
visited other neurosurgical clinics in that country, Scandinavia and
Russia.   He was appointed honorary neurological surgeon to the

Infirmary in 1926. His application lists original observations on the anatomy of the nervous system, on the localisation of cerebral tumours and on perfecting methods of operative approach as well as on injuries to the nervous system and on a number of general surgical subjects. Twenty-two papers in all are recorded, ten of them neurosurgical. These were his achievements at the age of 40.

In 1939 the University created a special chair of neurosurgery for him. Knighted in 1950 and elected an FRS in 1947, perhaps his greatest attainment, he brought great distinction to our University and School of Medicine and to British neurosurgery. He was awarded countless honours at home and abroad.

Sir Geoffrey was one of the greatest medical personalities of his time and although his life's work was devoted to neurosurgery, a specialty which he himself did much to create, he combined the meticulous skill of the surgeon with the care and insight of a physician and the wisdom of a philosopher. His knowledge was based on researches in anatomy and neurology of his own designing and above all he was an original thinker of rare quality. It was therefore very proper that he should be elected a Fellow of the Royal College of Physicians in 1947.

He continued all his life to write papers based on his original observations and vast experience. Many of these and some of his philosophical writings were collected in a volume entitled *Collected Papers* published in 1960.

At the time of his appointment to the Infirmary he was provided with a small neurosurgical department but the opportunities provided were scanty and the hospital beds too few and there is no doubt that he had an uphill struggle in those days. In 1933 he was invited to join the surgical staff of the National Hospital, Queen Square, London. He visited Queen Square once a fortnight and operated there, but he remained based on Manchester. Finally in 1950 a fully equipped neurosurgical unit was opened at the Infirmary a year before his retirement.

During the second world war he was consultant neurosurgical adviser to the Ministries of Health and Pensions and secured the establishment throughout the country of neurosurgical centres, his visits being an inspiration to all those who worked there. He was much in demand as a lecturer in this country and abroad, especially in the United States and Canada. He received many honorary degrees and was elected an honorary fellow of many foreign medical societies.

No account of Jefferson's achievements, remarkable though they were, can give any picture of the man as he really was - a man who influenced everyone with whom he came in contact and who had friends all over the world, all of whom remember him with the deepest affection. It was legendary that Jeff (as he was always called) took no heed of the passage of time and would frequently be one, two, three or even more hours late for an appointment or a ward round or a party or anything else. Although this could be exasperating at times he was invariably forgiven for his presence was so worth while. He seemed to bring with him some sort of an aura of a great, benign, friendly personality, never pompous, never aloof or unapproachable. Many are the stories told of his unpunctuality, not as an eccentricity but because it was an essential part of his nature and contributed much to his greatness. In the diagnosis and in the surgical treatment of neurological disease it must be a great gift to have a personality which can completely shut out all the demands of the day except the work immediately in hand and be completely oblivious of being two hours late for an appointment. More important still he always had time to contemplate, to talk and to think and thus register for future use the experiences of the day while they were fresh in his mind. He was late because his attention had been called to something that interested him and he couldn't be weaned away from it until he had thought about it and discussed it. And having arrived two hours late he was not in a hurry and had infinite leisure for the next encounter.

He spoke in the same calm leisurely way in which he did his work. Everyone listened to him because he never said anything that wasn't worth hearing and he never said it as anyone else would have said it. He had an extraordinary genius for giving a verbal picture of a person with the greatest economy of phrase. Speaking of an austere man he once said 'No one would empty a country pub more quickly. They'd just slink away'.

He never had any doubts about his own ability but it was calm assurance and never conceit. He never lost his sense of humour, delighting in the most absurd stories, the creases of his waistcoat rippling up and down with his laughter.

He became the doyen of neurosurgery. His acute clear philosophical mind enabled him to assess properly the value of things. He made great contributions to the clinical aspects of neurology which profoundly influenced the safety of neurosurgical operations. Thus his observations on tumours of the frontal lobe of the brain enabled him to assure neurosurgeons how much of that lobe could be safely removed. He preached all over the world that clinical study was the sheet anchor and the gadgets must be kept in their place.

Lord Platt has recorded that he was a wonderful patient, not because he was ever likely to do as he was told, or because he would ever give a wholly truthful account of his symptoms, but because to visit him and steer him through a serious illness was a great experience. His quaint ways of expression and his human understanding remained with him to the end. Once during one of his worst illnesses, he said 'Robert, I feel petulant, peevish and easily upset. I think they have transfused me with women's blood'. On the last day of his life and after a night of cardiac pain he greeted Sir Robert with these words 'I always feel I ought to think up something to cheer up my physician, but this morning I must confess I find it pretty difficult'. He died on 29 January 1961 in his seventy-fifth year. It will be years before our Medical School will see his like again.

His wife Gertrude, a wonderful companion for him, died a fortnight later. She combined a seriousness of purpose with great natural charm and shared Geoffrey's imperturbability. She did her best often against overwhelming odds to protect him from taking on too much, especially in the latter years when his health was so much in danger. There were three children. Their two sons followed him in his profession, Michael as a neurologist and Anthony as a neurosurgeon.

WB

7.18 JOHN SEBASTIAN BACH STOPFORD,
     LORD STOPFORD OF FALLOWFIELD, 1888-1961
     KBE, MD, ScD, DSc, LLD, FRCP, FRCS, FRS

John Sebastian Bach Stopford (known to friends as 'Jock' and friends, enemies and students alike as 'Stoppie') was a man of his time and place. Physically small, he was an intellectual giant amongst his contemporaries, many of whom were men of international repute when the University of Manchester was in its academic hey day.

He was born on 25 January 1888 in Hindley Green, Lancashire, the son of Thomas Rinck Stopford, a coal mining engineer, and Mary Tyrer (née Johnson) the daughter of a coal merchant of Rivington, Lancashire. Whether his parents nurtured a hope that their new-born son would become a famous musician is not formally recorded; it is clear that they themselves were versed in music and their choice of their son's name was an indication of their culture. They certainly were not unambitious for their son - who, however, never showed any musical talent. After attending a local school, Stopford gained entrance to Liverpool College, but his main schooling came from Manchester Grammar School to which he travelled daily by train and tram from his home in Wigan, an achievement which suggests a degree of reliance on public transport which might be difficult to emulate today - even though the tram has been replaced by a more flexible vehicle. Over the years his daily journeys brought him into contact with many people of his own, and different, age groups and it may be that one particular young woman influenced his career significantly. Whilst he was a schoolboy, showing an aptitude for medicine by incompetence in mathematics, he travelled daily with Catherine Chisholm; she was a medical student and became the first woman medical graduate, in 1904, of the recently chartered University of Manchester. How much she

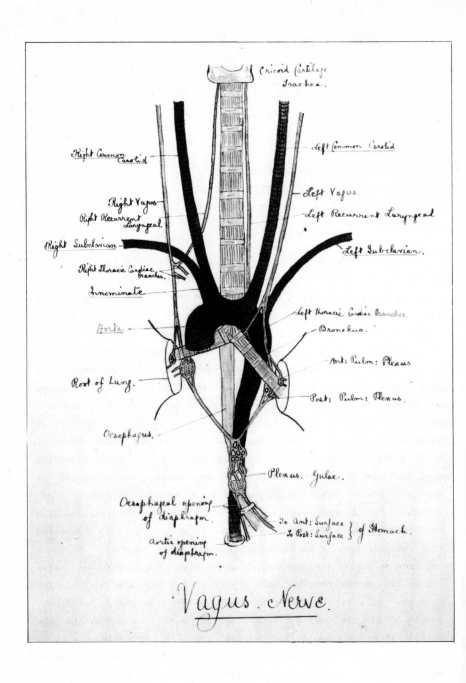

16. One of the anatomical drawings from the notebook of John Sebastian Bach Stopford showing the meticulous attention to detail which he gave to his work as a student.

attracted Stopford to medicine, or whether he had already determined that his future lay in medicine, is less certain than the fact that she helped him considerably with his homework and tutored him specifically in mathematics.

In due course Stopford entered the medical school and, after a brilliant undergraduate career, qualified in 1911 with second class honours, collecting the Dumville Surgical Prize and the Bradley Memorial Scholarship on the way. The quality of his work can still be seen in the meticulous notebooks on anatomy and histology which are, from time to time, displayed in the foyer of the new Medical School which bears his name. His first postgraduate clinical experience was gained in Rochdale Infirmary as a house officer, but he quickly returned to the 'Centre' and became assistant medical officer in Manchester Royal Infirmary shortly afterwards.

Within a year or so he had abandoned clinical medicine and moved into the University as a demonstrator in Anatomy where his fundamental work on the blood supply of the brain stem earned him a Doctorate of Medicine with gold medal in 1915. But his interest and possible future in the clinical sphere must have persisted since he was awarded the Tom Jones Memorial Scholarship in Surgery in 1913. Even so, the influence of the then Professor, Grafton Elliot Smith and the Lecturer Wingate Todd, outweighed any other and he became a confirmed anatomist, accepting a lectureship in 1915. He specialised in the anatomy of the nervous system, and the presence of many servicemen with wounds of central or peripheral portions of this system offered opportunities for study and he published many papers, some with an up-and-coming young orthopaedic surgeon, Harry Platt. He studied sensation in a physiological way, and even brought his medically qualified wife, Lily (née Allan, of Blackburn), whom he married in September 1916, into some of the arguments over 'protopathic' and 'epicritic' sensation which were then at their peak.

It was only three years later when Professor Elliot Smith moved to London that Stopford's early excellence in research was recognised and his unique ability to teach led him to the Chair at the early age of thirty. It was unusual in those days for the single-chaired department to be headed by a locally grown staff member and it was only because of a vigorous campaign conducted by leading members of other 'uni-sellar' departments and by the vociferous demands of his

students, that he was appointed to this high academic office. As head
of department, he ran a tight ship, keeping control of the
purse-strings and yet encouraging the young up-and-coming members of
staff to engage in research and to develop their powers of exposition.
Many followed his example of visiting the wards of the Royal Infirmary
and other hospitals where he worked in close association with the
surgical giants, Jefferson, Morley, Harry Platt - and Telford with
whom he worked on the anatomy (and physiology) of the autonomic
nervous system. His importance to the hospital was recognised and he
was appointed 'Honorary Advisory Anatomist' in 1923, remaining in post
until 1945: this preclinical-clinical link was unique and might have
presaged closer collaboration between the two major curricular
sub-divisions if his future had been different.

His national stature had been recognised early; he was made an MBE
in 1920. As his work continued and his academic prowess grew, so were
his administrative skills recognised resulting in his appointment as
Dean of the Medical School in 1923-7 and again 1931-3. Even so, his
research was not impeded by the chores of his office work and he was
elected Fellow of the Royal Society in 1927, an accolade which he
sincerely cherished. In his second stint as Dean, during which he
found additional time to be President of this Society (1931-2), the
term of office of Sir Walter Moberly as Vice-Chancellor was drawing to
a close and he was again the local man who was selected for this
highest of academic posts. Many felt that this was a great blow to
Anatomy and that his loss to teaching and research in the lecture
theatre and laboratory was too high a price to pay for an
administrator. Even he seemed to have doubts and is quoted as saying:-

> It is a joy to me to work in this place and I can assure you it is
> easy for me to give my best; I am only afraid that my best may not
> be good enough.

But the future was to show that the price paid for his leadership in
the wider University was small indeed - and he need not have worried!
His academic medical connections were maintained, however, perhaps a
little tenuously, as he was appointed to the Chair of Experimental
Neurology which he retained until retirement.

Continuing the medical thread of his career, he became the
Vice-Chairman of the Goodenough Committee (1942-4) which made
far-reaching recommendations about medical education including one

which indicated that the proportion of women admitted to medical
schools should be about 25 per cent - a great increase from the time
of Catherine Chisholm.

But perhaps his most significant contribution to his first
profession occurred in 1947. By that time Stopford had gained
experience in the management of hospitals by his membership and
chairmanship of the Manchester, Salford and Stretford Joint Hospitals
Advisory Board between 1935 and its dissolution on the vesting day of
the National Health Service in 1948. It was no surprise, therefore,
that he accepted the invitation to take the chair of the Manchester
Regional Hospital Board, and to join the Board of Governors of the
United Manchester Hospitals in 1947-8. These positions gave Stopford
significant influence over the development of the National Health
Service in his native area and it became clear that his presence on
both major administrative bodies, the former concerned more with
service and the latter emphasising teaching and research, produced a
balance which was mutually beneficial.

His contribution to and experience and knowledge of matters of
health led him to the Chair of the National Selection Committee for
Hospital Administrative Officers (Ministry of Health) from 1956 to
1960. Stopford influenced the profession at large by his membership of
the General Medical Council particularly by chairmanship of its
business activities. He served on many of its other committees during
his membership from 1927-43 playing important roles on the Examination
(which he chaired), Executive and Penal Cases Committees, more
specifically by his Vice-Chairmanship of the Managing Trustees of the
Nuffield Foundation between 1943 and 1961 when latterly he presided
over its Fellowship and Rheumatism Committees.

In the University's relationship with the City of Manchester, his
influence was as great as is ever likely to be reached. His
Trusteeship and Chairmanship of the Council (1937-61) of the John
Rylands Library (which was an independent institution) probably
influenced its transfer to the University a decade or so later. His
contributions to City life are too numerous to list, but one must be
mentioned, for paradoxically, he was Chairman of the Royal Manchester
College of Music between 1935 and 1956. In that latter year the wealth
of his work for the City of Manchester was rewarded by his being
elected an Honorary Freeman of the City, the highest honour the City

could bestow. Men such as Stopford cannot avoid spreading their influence widely; his other great achievements were in diverse areas of interest ranging from the Committee of Vice-Chancellors and Principals, of which he became not only Chairman, but also acknowledged sage and chief inspiration. It was immediately after the war in 1945 that the reconstruction of the country was of fundamental importance. By 1948, working with a driving Chairman of Council Lord Simon of Wythenshawe, and a team of loyal and visionary staff, he had published the plan for the development of the University. There were those who felt the plan was too ambitious, but, some twenty-five years later, the University as we know it was virtually complete - built to Stopford's blue-print. This experience helped him to assist in the start and development of Keele University of which he was a member of the Court of Governors. His charisma spread abroad too; membership of the British Elective Committee of the Commonwealth Fund was one area, chairmanship of the Universities' Bureau of the British Empire was another, as was membership of the Committee on Higher Agricultural Education.

There were personal rewards too; Dublin recognised his work by awarding a Doctorate of Science, honoris causa, in 1937 followed by Leeds in 1939 and Cambridge in 1951. In that year his Alma Mater awarded an honorary LL D as did Liverpool in 1953; Durham followed with a DCL in 1957. The two existing Royal Colleges recognised him with Fellowships, the Physicians in 1942 and, strangely late, the Surgeons in 1955, and during this period of recognition he was made a knight in 1941. The Manchester College of Science and Technology made him an Honorary Fellow in 1960.

Well-earned retirement came in 1956 and 'Stoppie', now his universal pseudonym, moved out of his native Lancashire, as Professor Emeritus, to live in Westmorland; but when he received his Life Peerage in 1958 not only did he select 'Fallowfield' as his barony, but he expressed his intention of continuing his work in education and medicine in the House of Lords. However, the long years of high-pressured work took their toll and his health prevented his attendance in the House other than for his Introduction. He died on 6 March 1961; Lady Stopford and his son, Tom, survived him.

John Sebastian Bach Stopford was a Lancashire man 'out of the top drawer' as Lancashire men say of those whom they respect; he always exhibited his pride in his origins and devoted his energies to bringing higher education of ultimate quality to his people – particularly those who joined his university. He lived with great men from whom our University derived its foundations and understanding of excellence; he attracted others and found ways of assisting their progress. If you did not know the man, visit the Whitworth Hall where his portrait hangs; there he remains. The bright and shrewd eyes, the interrogating expression with a faintly benevolent smile and the attitude of the shoulders all betoken 'Stoppie' – our most famous member.

FBB

7.19 JOHN CRIGHTON BRAMWELL, 1889-1976
    MA, MD, FRCP


John Crighton Bramwell came from a long line of distinguished doctors. His greatgrandfather, grandfather, father, brother and son were all doctors. His father, Sir Byron Bramwell, and his brother, Professor Edwin Bramwell, were both in their day Presidents of the Royal College of Physicians of Edinburgh. Born in Edinburgh in 1889, he went up to Trinity College, Cambridge, in 1907 as an exhibitioner, and graduated with first class honours in the natural sciences tripos. He then spent an extra year with Keith Lucas working on the physiology of muscle and nerve. He came to Manchester University and the Royal Infirmary in 1911 to do his clinical work, but volunteered for the Army in 1914, before he had qualified, and had to be given special leave in 1915 to come back to Manchester to qualify MB in 1915. He had further service abroad in the Army, and when he left the Forces he became house physician to Professor George Murray and subsequently was registrar in medicine for four years. During this period he worked with Professor A V Hill (later a Nobel Prize Winner) on pulse wave velocity and established the ECG Department at Manchester Royal Infirmary which was the forerunner of the University Department of Cardiology, and obtained his MD with gold medal and his MRCP. In 1923, as one of the earliest Rockefeller Fellows, he went to the United States, where he studied under Professor Erlanger (another Nobel Prize winner) at Washington University, St Louis and then toured other centres to see how teaching and research were developing in the United States.

On his return to England in 1924 he continued his academic work in the Department of Physiology with research grants from the Medical Research Council and the Royal Society, and at the same time he did some private practice. In 1926 he was elected physician at the Royal

Infirmary and the list of his sponsors is a remarkable one, with many distinguished physicians both in Britain and the USA supporting him. During the interwar years he still continued with academic activity, and no year passed without at least one or more publications from his pen. In particular he worked on gallop rhythm and on heart disease in pregnancy, and produced some remarkably fine papers on these subjects as well as other cardiac problems. This academic activity was recognised by his appointment as Professor of Systematic Medicine in 1940 and in 1946 as Professor of Cardiology - an appointment which he held until he retired in 1954.

As a cardiologist he was the first to be elected to the Cardiac Club which had been started by fifteen people in 1922. He was Secretary of the Club from 1928 to 1932 and Chairman of the Meetings in 1931, 1936, 1937 and 1955. In 1936 he presided over the meeting to change the organisation to the British Cardiac Society and was made an honorary member of this Society in 1956. In that year a volume of the *British Heart Journal* was dedicated to him and he was elected an honorary member of the Society.

He became a Fellow of the Royal College of Physicians in 1929 and served that organisation for three years as a member of the Council, as the Senior Censor, as a member of the Scientific Committee and as an examiner. He was also external examiner in Medicine at various times for the Universities of Cambridge, Aberdeen, Sheffield, Edinburgh and St Andrews. He was elected to the Physiological Society at an early stage and was soon a member of the Association of Physicians and was President of that Association 1955-6, when he was elected an Honorary Member. He was an editor and eventually Senior Editor of the *Quarterly Journal of Medicine*.

Locally, he was at one time a member of the Manchester Literary and Philosophical Society and was a keen supporter of our own Medical Society. He was Secretary of the old Medical Society from 1926-8. As President of the Section of Medicine for 1950-1 he read a paper for his presidential address on 'Recent Advances in Cardiology'. He was President of the re-constituted Society from 1952-3 and his presidential address in October 1952 was on 'Heart Disease in Pregnancy'.

He wrote a number of books, some on heart disease in pregnancy; I think the best was the book with Dr King entitled *Principles and*

*Practice in Cardiology.* A clearer account of the subject could be found nowhere. He delivered many named lectures, the Lumleian in 1937 at the Royal College of Physicians, the Gibson to the Royal College of Physicians at Edinburgh, the Finlayson to the Royal College of Physicians and Surgeons in Glasgow, the Ramsden to the Manchester Literary and Philosophical Society, the Carey-Coombes lecture in Bristol, the John Hey at Liverpool and the Harvean to the Royal College of Physicians in London. 'Practice, Teaching and Research' was the title of the latter which he delivered in October, 1956. In it, he pointed out that there was no sharp division between the scientist and the clinician, and the good teacher should have the spirit of an investigator. The specialist was a generalist with an added knowledge of his particular speciality, and he stressed the unity of medicine. Throughout his medical life he devoted himself to these ideals in his clinical and academic activity.

What sort of man was he? Tall, distinguished, he had a commanding presence. He was perhaps shy and a little austere, and as a young man, and one of his juniors, I felt a little over-awed in his presence, yet I am told he could be extremely kind and considerate to his juniors. I am not sure that he understood the problems of ordinary working men – in many ways he was an aristocrat. His hobbies were fishing and gardening and in early retirement he could indulge in these to the full from his home in the Lake District. His contributions to Manchester medicine, raising the standard of clinical and scientific research at Manchester Royal Infirmary, were very great indeed. He was a nationally and internationally known figure, and those of us who knew him and worked under him at Manchester Royal Infirmary are grateful for the experience and the knowledge gained.

SO

7.20 JAMES RALSTON KENNEDY PATERSON, 1897-1981
    CBE, MC, MD, FRCS, FRCR


The Christie Hospital and Holt Radium Institute, along with its
Paterson Laboratories, is the largest complex of its kind in the
United Kingdom at the present time. It is a regional organisation for
cancer treatment and research, serving a population approaching five
millions. And it is a lasting memorial to Ralston Paterson who, more
than any other single person, was responsible for its development and
its international reputation.

    Ralston Paterson, known by his friends and colleagues throughout
the world as RP, was born in Edinburgh on 21 May 1897, the elder son
of the Reverend David Paterson. RP was educated at George Heriot's
School in Edinburgh and served during the First World War as an
officer in the Argyll and Sutherland Highlanders. While in the
front-line trenches he observed that enemy hand-grenades had
delayed-action fuses. He promptly picked them up and threw them back
from whence they had come and his brave example was then followed by
the soldiers under his command. For this outstanding bravery Ralston
Paterson was awarded the Military Cross. After the war RP returned to
Edinburgh and to a distinguished undergraduate career in Medicine. He
graduated MB ChB, with honours, in 1923, acquired the FRCS (Ed) in
1926, and the MD, with commendation, in 1927. His interest in
radiology began with his DMRE of Cambridge in 1924, followed in 1926
by a Fellowship at the Mayo Clinic which he greatly valued throughout
his life. He also spent some time in the University of Chicago
Clinics, in Toronto, and also in South Africa. He became the Acting
Director of the Radiological Department in Edinburgh Royal Infirmary
in 1930.

    RP's real life began, however, when he was appointed the first

Director of Radiotherapy at the Christie Hospital and Holt Radium Institute in 1931. This was when the old Christie Cancer Hospital and the Holt Radium Institute were combined under one roof, a symbiosis which rapidly grew in stature under RP's dynamic personality. The first 10 to 15 years, spanning the second world war, were the truly formative years of the Manchester school of radiotherapy. Like so many men of distinction RP had the knack of attracting first class disciples around him and with RP's stimulus many fundamental developments in clinical radiotherapy were established. With the physicist H M Parker, RP devised the Paterson-Parker Rules for radium therapy, a reliable guide to safe dosimetry which is still the essential basis for radium therapy in spite of many attempts to modify, revise and extrapolate. With Margaret Tod, for many years his Deputy, and with yet another first class physicist, W J Meredith, RP catalysed, as it were, the Manchester method for treating cancer of the uterine cervix. In this context he also explored and developed the concept of optimum dosage, extending and confirming this principle for cancers in other anatomical sites. During these exciting years there also emerged the sophisticated beam-direction treatment associated with the name of J L Dobbie, and so taken for granted in these days of isocentric mountings, megavoltage X-ray machines and computerised treatment planning. During these years it must indeed have been an intellectually stimulating experience to work in RP's department surrounded by people like Tod, Dobbie, Fulton, Mitchell, McWhirter, Parker, Meredith, Edith Paterson and Walter Dale – and a host of others, not to mention the many distinguished visitors from far afield who came to see what was afoot in Manchester.

Looking back on the six or seven years before the second world war – a remarkably short period of time – it seems that everything RP did proved to be a model of its kind. Already he had seen the need both to establish a well and fully equipped radiotherapy centre, and to set up a network of peripheral consultation and follow-up clinics throughout the entire region, providing a unique service for a very large population. This principle was enshrined in the 1939 Cancer Act and later in the National Health Service Act of 1948. It has also been copied in other countries and in many of these after RP had been invited by the relevant governments to visit and advise. His insistence on evaluation had led to the appointment of Marion Russell as a statistician in 1936 and detailed statistical analyses were published in 1939, followed by second and third Statistical Reports in 1946 and 1950. Such analyses would not have been possible without adequate medical records and here again RP, ably supported by Elsie Royle (later Mrs Royle-Mansell), created a superb Department of Medical Records, essential for evaluation but equally essential for maintaining reliable contact with patients. The need for a comprehensive mould room was another of RP's creations, to provide precision-made surface applicators and beam-direction shells. These were the indispensible prerequisites to high quality and reliable treatment which are now taken for granted in radiotherapy departments around the world.

The end of the war released RP from the many wartime constraints and he rapidly strove to expand the hospital and its range of radiotherapy equipment, and still his imaginative drive continued. With junior and senior staff gathered together on a memorable evening in 1947 RP listened patiently to various ideas for further research and development, and then himself suggested a randomised clinical trial to test the efficacy of radiation therapy for breast cancer. All were taken by surprise, were appalled, then intrigued, and finally convinced that here was a novel and statistically valid approach to improvements in cancer therapy. The first of many such clinical trials followed: such trials are not only now taken for granted but are considered de rigeur by most oncologists and other clinicians as well. RP also recognised that if earlier diagnosis is important, the education of the public is as necessary as educating the medical profession itself. Thus he was the architect of what is now the Manchester Regional Committee for Cancer Education. And once again he insisted on the need to measure and evaluate the impact of public education, and it was this that attracted world attention and professional support.

In 1953 Ralston Paterson was appointed Honorary Director of the Medical Research Council's Betatron Research Unit and, typically, he established an integrated study of the relative biological efficiency of megavoltage radiation. This study ranged from radiation chemistry, tissue culture and various animal models in the laboratory, to a variety of human reactions in the clinics at the Christie Hospital. This was yet another fundamental contribution to clinical radiotherapy

and to radiobiology, and RP presented all of these important data in
the form of a comprehensive symposium at the British Institute of
Radiology in December 1956.

Having been President of the British Association of Radiotherapists
in 1938/39, Ralston Paterson was one of the founders of the Faculty of
Radiologists and was its President from 1943 to 1946. In 1949 he was
awarded the CBE and the following year he was the president of the
first post-war International Radiological Congress, held in London. In
1948 he was appointed a Fellow of the Royal College of Surgeons of
England, honoris causa; in 1961 he was awarded the Gold Medal in
Therapeutics of the Society of Apothecaries; and in 1966 he was
awarded the Gold Medal of the Faculty of Radiologists for his
outstanding contributions to radiotherapy. He served on the Grand
Council and the Scientific Committee of the British Empire Cancer
Campaign (now the Cancer Research Campaign), on various Medical
Research Council and government committees, and internationally was
much involved in the International Union Against Cancer (in which he
was Vice-President for the British Commonwealth), in UNESCO, in WHO,
and was Vice-Chairman of the International Organisation of Medical
Science. He was by temperament a true internationalist and was a great
ambassador for British radiotherapy and indeed for Britain. The many
national and international honours that underlined Ralston Paterson's
high calibre, the fame and prestige which he brought to Manchester and
its Christie Hospital were all in sharp contrast to the response of
Manchester University. It was not until two years before he retired
that the University offered him a professorial chair (unpaid!) and it
is typical of RP that he accepted this title graciously. Though he
certainly never said so himself, many of his close colleagues felt
that this belated university recognition of his international
reputation was accepted by RP because it was for the good of the
hospital in whose interests he had laboured so long and so hard.

After retiring in 1962, although he maintained a burning interest
in the affairs of *his* hospital, he became busily engaged for nearly
twenty years in creating a first-class sheep and cattle farm near
Moffatt in southern Scotland. Having displayed so much organisational
flair in the field of medicine, it was a common joke amongst his
medical colleagues that on his farm RP would make sure that his ewes
would lamb, his cows would calve and his hens would lay according to a

pre-arranged plan - and profitably so! RP enjoyed the joke. Ralston Paterson was the first to admit that music - so beloved by his wife Edith - held nothing for him. But he had a wide field of intellectual vision. He was much concerned by the socio-economic problems of his time and was a life-long socialist. He welcomed the inception of the National Health Service in 1948 but was often saddened, indeed enraged, by its bureaucratic slowness to satisfy his urgent demands on behalf of the hospital and its patients. Those who worked closely with RP were aware of his kindness, of his eager support for new ideas, of his understanding and tolerance of youthful enthusiasms that might go wrong from time to time. He demanded high standards and hard work from his staff but never higher nor harder than his own. He led by example and as a consequence was rewarded by important contributions from his colleagues. Physically Ralston Paterson was a big man, about six feet two inches in height, and indeed looked rather more like the farmer he became than the academic he was. In spite of his size he was a gentle man and with his large cared-for hands his surgical dexterity and precision were a joy to see. Like so many successful leaders, not only in the medical field, RP had remarkable stamina, both physical and intellectual. When arguing in all sorts of committee, he not only presented his case with persuasive logic but, when he thought it necessary, he would pursue his argument until everyone else on the committee was too exhausted for further resistance.

The Christie Hospital and Holt Radium Institute, and its associated Paterson Laboratories continue to expand physically, technologically and scientifically. But the foundations were undoubtedly laid and well developed by Ralston Paterson. Emeritus Professor Ralston Paterson died in 1981 at the age of 84. So long as the Christie Hospital exists his name and his work will be remembered.

ECE

7.21 VICTOR FRANCIS LAMBERT, 1899-1981
    MD, ChM, FRCS(E), FRCS


Victor Francis Lambert was born in the neighbourhood of Bolton on 12
August 1899. He was educated at Bolton Grammar School and Manchester
University from where he qualified in 1923. On leaving school during
the 1914-18 war he volunteered for service with the Inns of Court
Officers Training Corps, later taking a commission in the Royal
Artillery and serving from 1917-19. On demobilisation he commenced his
medical studies at Manchester University and graduated in December
1923.

    After qualifying, his first hospital appointment in 1924 was as
house surgeon to Sir William Milligan at the Royal Infirmary. Sir
William had founded the Ear Nose and Throat Department at the Royal
Infirmary around the turn of the century. Sir William was a man of
outstanding ability and had developed both a national and
international reputation in his speciality. A year or so later he
again was house surgeon to Sir William at the Manchester Ear Hospital.
Victor was greatly influenced by Milligan's teaching and outstanding
ability and this experience laid the foundation of his education in
the speciality and attracted him to pursue a career in otolaryngology.

    In the late 1920's he had a period of post graduate study working
as clinical tutor under the direction of Dr J S Fraser in the Ear and
Throat Department of the Edinburgh Royal Infirmary. It was during this
time that he obtained the Fellowship of the Royal College of Surgeons
of Edinburgh.

    On returning to Manchester he was appointed assistant surgical
officer in the Ear Nose and Throat Department at the Royal Infirmary.
During this period he was appointed honorary aural surgeon to the
Victoria Memorial Jewish Hospital. He found this a particularly happy

appointment and it gave him the opportunity to build up an excellent department. At this early stage he impressed his colleagues by his clinical and technical skill, ability and judgement and his kindness and consideration to patients under his care. With staff and students alike he won respect and affection for he was a gifted teacher and had great personal charm. It was at this time in 1932 that he obtained the Mastership in Surgery (ChM) of the Manchester University and it is interesting to note that he was the first person to receive this higher qualification for work in a surgical speciality.

Although busily occupied with his clinical commitments he found time to pursue his research. He continued to investigate fundamental problems in the morphological field and also to elucidate the intricate anatomy of the bones forming the base of the skull and their associated nerves and vessels. This research was done with colleagues in the Anatomy department at Manchester University and some excellent combined papers were published. In this work he was greatly encouraged and supported by Lord Stopford and later by Professor Wood Jones and they both regarded Victor as an excellent anatomist and investigator of wide outlook and knowledge. Resulting from his excellent work some years later in 1939 he was elected a member of the Anatomical Society of Great Britain.

In 1934 he was appointed honorary laryngologist to the Christie Cancer Hospital and Holt Radium Institute. This post presented an opportunity for him to pursue investigations into the diagnosis and management of malignant neoplasms of the upper respiratory tract and as time passed he built up a national reputation in this field. It was also during this period that he developed an interest in children with hearing problems and was appointed honorary consultant otologist to the Department of the Education of the Deaf, Manchester University. He always maintained a close association with the University and it was during the mid-thirties that he was appointed tutor and lecturer in Otology and became closely involved with the teaching of medical students.

In 1939 he was appointed consultant otolaryngologist to Manchester Royal Infirmary and he held this post until his retirement in 1964. It was in the following year 1940 that he was awarded the Doctorate of Medicine (MD) of Manchester University.

During the war years 1939-45 he was unable to serve in the Forces as he was medically unfit but during this time he continued his heavy clinical commitments both at the Christie Hospital and the Royal Infirmary.

In 1947 he was promoted to Professor of Otolaryngology at Manchester University: this was the first academic chair in the specialty of otolaryngology in a University in Great Britain. He held the Chair until his retirement in 1964. During this time he built up a teaching unit of international status. He was very keenly interested and eminently successful in the training of his juniors. He had wide vision and following visits to North America he developed contacts with world wide famous colleagues which enabled some of his registrars to supplement their training by working in centres of excellence over there. It can be seen that Victor Lambert was a man of great intellect along with a very high academic achievement. He made many contributions to medical literature both in journals and in text books. His outstanding ability was recognised by the award of lectureships by learned Societies, Universities and Colleges. In 1949 the Royal College of Surgeons of England honoured him by conferring the 'Ad Eundem' Fellowship upon him. Also during this period he was a member of the Court of Examiners of the Royal Colleges of Surgeons of England and Edinburgh. In 1959 he was invited to present the Semon Lecture in Laryngology by the University of London. Later he was a Guest Lecturer to the Canadian Medical Society in Vancouver, British Columbia in 1963. Also during the same year he was awarded the Walter Jobson Horne Prize by the British Medical Association in recognition of distinguished work in the science and practice of laryngology and otology particularly in reference to general medicine. The following year 1964 he gave the Watson Williams Memorial Lecture at the University of Bristol.

In 1950 he was elected President of the North of England Otolaryngological Society. Before the 1939-45 war he was elected a Fellow of the Royal Society of Medicine and a member of the Sections of Laryngology and Otology and regularly attended their meetings in London to which he made many contributions. In 1954 he was elected President of the Section of Laryngology and some years later was made an Honorary Member of the Section. In 1955 he was President of the Section of Surgery of the Manchester Medical Society. From 1960 to 1964 he was President of the British Association of Otolaryngologists.

When the First British Academic Conference in Otolaryngology was held at the Royal College of Surgeons, London in 1963 he was chosen to be the Chairman of the General Committee. In 1963 he was elected President of the Manchester Medical Society.

I would now like to describe Professor Lambert as a colleague. I had the good fortune to be a trainee in his Department immediately after the war. I found him a most kind, considerate and helpful chief. He was greatly skilled as a surgeon and was an outstanding clinician with very wide knowledge and clinical background. He was a stimulating teacher and ever ready to encourage and help his juniors in every way. He was a man of great charm and warm personality and had the great gift to develop excellent relationships with all around him and this resulted in a very happy department.

Professor Lambert always had a great interest in music and singing and for many years he was honorary laryngologist to the Royal Manchester College of Music. He was also a director of the English Sewing Cotton Company and he served as Chairman of the Richard Arkwright Education Scholarship awarded to students in the textile industry. He was invited by Manchester University to represent them as a governor at his old school in Bolton and during that time he was elected president of the Old Boltonian's Association. It was always a great joy for him to visit the town of his birth and these appointments presented the opportunity for him to do so. In his relaxation he was keenly interested in all forms of games, particularly golf, rugby and association football.

Following his retirement in 1964 he remained a keen member of various societies and attended the meetings but as time passed due to ill health this was not possible. Even so he still continued to take a great interest and was always ready to hear about the meetings and discussions that took place and how his old friends were.

He died on 8 June 1981 in his eighty second year, after a period of increasing ill-health. In 1929 he married Myra Farnworth who died in 1950 and they had a son who is a member of the Benedictine Order, Downside Abbey and a daughter who has four sons, one of whom graduated in medicine and another is a medical student - both at his old University. In 1954 he married Margaret Norris and they had one daughter.

KH

7.22 ROBERT PLATT, LORD PLATT OF GRINDLEFORD, 1900–1978

    MD, MSc, LLD, FRCP


As he says himself in his informal autobiography entitled *Private and Controversial*, Robert Platt 'avoided a good deal of mental arithmetic by being born in 1900'. He came of an interesting family, connected with both music and the stage, and addicted to travel. Music was to remain for him a life-long interest, but for the stage and travel he substituted medicine. Like many others who have distinguished themselves in later life, he confessed to varied distractions during his time in Sheffield as a medical student, including practising the piano and cello for four hours a day. He devoted only the necessary minimum of effort to subjects which did not interest him; but in medicine and in pathology he won gold medals, whose authenticity he tested by Archimedes' principle! The preclinical subjects did not capture his attention, but when he entered the wards, he knew that he 'was destined to be a physician, and delighted at the prospect'. His attitude to medicine was greatly influenced by Hall, Barnes and Naish: and he early developed a great capacity for empathy with patients, and a flair in communicating with them. He dissociated himself from the view that 'medical students should be trained to cultivate emotional detachment as if it were a virtue'.

In 1918, he was commissioned in the Infantry, but was prevented from going to France by an attack of the prevailing influenza. Nevertheless, he qualified in 1921, and entered with enthusiasm on the practice of medicine, combining clinical work with responsibility for clinical biochemistry. In 1933, he became a physician on the staff in Sheffield, and soon built up a very busy part-time practice. He told many stories of the busy life which he led in those days, and to some extent he may have been more fulfilled at that time of this life   than later on when more visibly eminent and successful, and a doyen of academic medicine. In revealing phrases, he said he was 'very uncertain as to whether I really wanted to become an academic doctor'; and, after the event, 'Although this gave me both opportunity and satisfaction, I no longer quite felt myself a real doctor'. However, the transition from consulting practice to a university chair was not immediate, because of intervening distinguished medical service in the war of 1939-45. After a period in Chester, there came overseas service in North Africa, Italy, and India. As consulting physician to Southern Army, he attained the rank of Brigadier. He made regular journeys from Bangalore, where he was based, to Poona, where the Board was held which decided whether officers were qualified to be invalided home. On one of these journeys, he met a talkative young officer who explained to him how he was going to hoodwink the Board. Robert Platt's experience both of war-damaged Naples and of undernourished India engendered strong socialist convictions, which remained with him, even though he felt that as a representative of medicine in the House of Lords he should sit as a cross-bencher. His socialism was perhaps a factor in determining him to apply for a full-time chair, rather than return to private practice.

In 1945, although full-time chairs had been established in the London medical schools for some time, they were practically unknown outside London, the clinical teaching being carried on by part-time teachers, some of whom might hold personal chairs. The Goodenough Commission, although recognising that this method could provide a sound practical training, were concerned that it did not give sufficient stimulus to research, even though part-time teachers had made considerable research contributions. Manchester was one of the first medical schools in England to advertise a full-time chair, and they were indeed fortunate to receive an application from Robert Platt, and wise to appoint him. His experience of private practice in Sheffield certainly made it easier for him to come to terms with the part-time colleagues who did most of the teaching. He was, of course already a gifted teacher, with a quite notable gift for getting to the heart of any matter. And he had already developed his main specialist interest in renal disease, having published in 1934 the monograph 'Nephritis and Allied Diseases'. His Sheffield experience as a clinical biochemist equipped him to study the important chemical distortions which arise in patients with renal failure.

It is a necessary condition for the success of an academic unit that its head should be respected as a clinician; and it was here that Robert Platt's experience and flair was so valuable in earning the unqualified respect of his colleagues. He was particularly good with younger colleagues, and formed a dining club for registrars and lecturers; these informal contacts he very clearly enjoyed for their own sake, but they were also valuable as providing part of the basis for influencing future appointments. His first loyalty was always to his patients, and he did many things for them outside the line of strict duty, such as persuading the hospital authorities to provide hairdressing facilities in the wards, at any rate for the ladies. His great reputation among clinical colleagues was not gained at the expense of neglecting the research potential of his own unit. Not only did he continue his own work on renal disease, but he built up a research team in whose work he took an active and informed interest. In the Lumleian Lecture given to the Royal College of Physicians in 1952, he developed the 'intact nephron hypothesis', which suggests that although nephrons are of course lost in the course of progressive kidney disease, nevertheless those which remain function remarkably normally, given that they are exposed each of them to a greater than normal load of solute requiring excretion. Another of his great interests at this period was hypertension, which he regarded as largely an inherited disease, with a dominant gene which did not always find expression. This view led to a prolonged debate with George Pickering, who championed a multi-factorial heredity analogous to that which influences height and weight. The two champions perhaps proved more indefatigable than many of their readers, and in a way both were right, Pickering scientifically and Platt pragmatically. At the end of the day, in a *Lancet* obituary, Pickering recalled the controversy thus:-

> The argument was continued in your columns for some years, but always with tolerance and humour. It greatly increased my affection and respect, already high, for Robert. He was indeed an adversary with whom it was a pleasure to engage in battle. I grieve for him.

Robert Platt of course played a notable part in the more general affairs of the Faculty of Medicine, and of the University. He was President of the Section of Medicine of the Manchester Medical Society in 1955-56; and of the Society in 1962-63. On the first occasion, his

Address on 'Life (biological and biographical)' brought out his
interest in heredity. On the second occasion, he tackled, in a more
philosophic vein, 'Reflections on ageing and death'. It was on that
occasion that he indicated with perhaps atypical circumspection a view
which he was later to state much more openly. Speaking of belief in an
after-life he said 'I can only say that there are some who find such
beliefs out of line with man's present knowledge of his place in the
biological world'. And he revealed a sympathy with those who are
'content to believe that life is something which happens but once, and
that death is the end of it'. He left a letter to the President of his
College, which included this sentence 'Just in case the College wanted
to arrange a Memorial Service for me, I would like it to be clear that
I do not want one, as I am not a man of religion, as is well known'.
In the event, we were able to fulfil his positive suggestion, that he
might be commemorated with music, and in this his second wife was able
to recruit players who had made music with him. At this point, it is
appropriate to mention his own devotion to cello playing, and his
Chairmanship of the Manchester Chamber Concerts Society from 1952 to
1965.

His success in Manchester, and also of course his involvement in
the Association of Physicians and in the Royal College of Physicians,
made it inevitable that he would be in great demand for national
commitments. He became a member of the Medical Research Council, and
in 1964 he succeeded his friend and colleague Sir Geoffrey Jefferson
as Chairman of the Clinical Research Board. Within the College, he
served as an examiner and on the Council; and in 1957 he was elected
President, an office which he occupied with great distinction for the
next five years. He resigned from the full-time chair in Manchester,
but continued on a part-time basis, to the great benefit of the
Manchester Royal Infirmary and of the University. Under his
leadership, the post-graduate activity of the College expanded
remarkably, and the College for practically the first time became more
than a place of occasional resort, but rather a place frequented on
many occasions by gatherings both of its own and of other bodies. This
greatly increased activity required its counterpart in more extensive
accommodation; and it was in Robert Platt's tenure of the Presidency
that the vital decisions were taken to move the College from Pall Mall
to Regent's Park, to make it a spacious modern building, and to

entrust the task to Sir Denys Lasdun. It was under his guidance too that the College published its first Report on *Smoking and Health*, based on the work of a Committee set up in 1959, 'to report on the question of smoking and atmospheric pollution in relation to carcinoma of the lung and other diseases'. This interest continued, with his Presidency of Action on Smoking and Health (ASH).

He moved from Manchester to Cambridge in 1965, on what I suppose has to be called technical retirement, though the reality was vastly different. He was chairman of the Merit Award Committee, which involved travel throughout England and Wales, and of course many difficult decisions. He studied and reported on hospital staffing, and produced, as Rock Carling Lecturer, a monograph, *Patient and Doctor*, for the Nuffield Provincial Hospitals Trust. In 1967, he was created a life peer, with the title 'Lord Platt of Grindleford' - a recollection of the Derbyshire village where his parents had kept school. He greatly enjoyed both the responsibility and the social aspects of the House of Lords; and he continued, along with his second wife, to play a full part in music and in affairs, until his death after a short illness following a fractured femur in 1978.

I think that his own gifts, and those which he gave to the world, can best be summed up in two statements from obituary notices in the *Lancet*, which I have, properly or improperly, rescued from the anonymity of initials - I think Robert would have done the same.

The first, from George Pickering:-

Robert Platt was unique in being a great physician with a deep interest in and devotion to medicine as a service to the sick, a scientist who advanced medical fact and thought, and a practical philosopher who campaigned for a better world based on knowledge, understanding, and human kindness.

The second, from George Godber:-

He has been one of the great personalities of British medicine over the past half century, and still a human, approachable and friendly man. He could show firm authority, yet he never failed to give full weight to, and ensure a just hearing for, the views of others. He thought it right to state the strong beliefs he held on some controversial subjects, but he never sought to force them on others. He became a widely respected public figure. In any medical generation there are a few who are recognised by a wider public not merely as great figures in their profession, but as men and women of stature in the world beyond it, and able to take the broader view. Robert was such a one and for that, as well as for the man, we will miss him deeply.

DAKB

7.23 JOHN LANCELOT BURN, 1902-73

   MD, DHy, DPH


By his farsightedness and reforming enthusiasm, Dr J.L. Burn wrote
a memorable chapter in the history of public health. Indeed, his
achievements helped to change the whole tone of the term 'public
health', for he was, in fact, one of the first 'community
physicians'.(1)

Lance Burn was the youngest member of a small non-medical
Northumbrian family. What first excited his interest in pursuing a
career in medicine is surrounded in mystery. He had left school at the
age of fourteen years convinced that the most able teachers had been
drafted into the armed services. Initially employed as a clerk in a
Tyneside shipping office, he was guided and supported by his devoted
uncle Rowland Lishman who encouraged him to enter the medical
profession some seven or eight years after leaving school. During this
intervening period he established himself as a competent musician and
a gifted pianist.   His entrance into the University of Durham Medical
School in 1924 followed his successful surmounting within the short
space of three months of the hurdle posed by the necessity of gaining
a pass in Latin at matriculation level. In 1930, as a final year
student, he wrote an essay entitled 'Some modern attempts on the
treatment and prevention of Pulmonary Tuberculosis' which was
subsequently published in the University Medical Gazette. This essay
was a comprehensive account of the problems posed by tuberculosis in
the early part of this present century and focussed attention on such
wide ranging aspects as the role of surgery in its treatment and the
psyche in its cause! Lance Burn was awarded the University of Durham's
Medical Society prize for this contribution to the medical literature.
The penalty for his success was his later election to the post of
secretary of the Society! He graduated MB, BS, in 1931 and proceeded

17. The sun struggles to force its way through the smog over a street in Salford in the early 1950s. The drive to improve housing conditions, and after 1956 to implement the Clean Air Act, was a major preoccupation of medical officers of health like Dr J L Burn. (See biography 7.23.)

to MD in 1933. In the following year he obtained the Diploma in Public Health and Bachelor of Hygiene.  His first appointment in public health was in Hebburn, and in 1935 he moved to Plymouth as assistant MOH.  In 1937 he was appointed Medical Officer of Health in Barnsley and after a three year spell he moved to his final appointment in Salford where he spent most of his professional life.

At the time of his arrival in Salford in June 1941 the infant mortality rate was 84 per thousand live births and less than 5 per cent of the childhood population were immunised against diphtheria. Enemy air raids had inflicted considerable structural damage to the city's hospitals.  Substandard housing and air pollution were major problems contributing to the high morbidity and mortality from chronic respiratory disorders.  During the war years, Burn addressed himself to these problems and Salford witnessed the results of many of the innovations of its MOH.  The immunisation rate soared.  Salford became one of the first towns to introduce passive immunisation for measles, BCG vaccination and the widespread use of penicillin.  Although the fall in the infant mortality rate 'more than paralleled' the national decline, there was still cause for concern.  Burn continually re-emphasised the importance of providing the children of Salford with their basic health needs, namely physical and psychological nutrition and warmth, protection from adverse factors in the environment and having access to readily available sound professional advice.  To this end he organised a domiciliary consultation service whereby the Health Department paid the fees of hospital based paediatricians when they visited sick children at home at the invitation of the family doctor.

Realising that the quality of mothering was the basis of infant mortality and morbidity, he endeavoured to provide more support to vulnerable 'problem' families. The introduction of the 'home help' service, the formation of a 'club' for parents of handicapped children and the establishment of a hostel in Kersal for children with diabetes were a few examples of numerous schemes promoted by the Health Department in Salford.

Lance Burn seemed to have an insatiable appetite for work. The first edition of his book *Recent Advances in Public Health* was published in 1947 and was followed twelve years later by an almost completely re-written and redesigned second edition.  In the early chapters, he emphasised the importance of team work.  He drew an analogy with a football team with the family doctor as the 'spearhead' and delegating the role of central defender ('sweeper') to the MOH. He appreciated the value of co-operation between the family doctor, branches of the National Health Service, voluntary organisations and the public. This text illustrated his conviction that the promotion of health depended on much more than mere prevention of disease.

The London 'smog' of 1952 and the associated high morbidity and mortality from chronic bronchitis served to bring home the importance of curbing the degree of air pollution in our inner city areas. Burn was a member of the Beaver Committee on Air Pollution and in the following twenty years he became the architect of the first smokeless industrial city in Europe. This drive to protect the community from avoidable and adverse hazards in the environment resulted in Salford receiving the 'Arnold Marsh' award by the National Society for Clean Air in what proved to be the last year of Burn's life. Although he displayed initiative and a crusading spirit, he was very much aware of some deficiencies and voids in his argument. He acknowledged the formidably difficult problem of disentangling and identifying the relative significance of the many aetiological factors in chronic bronchitis operating in a complex combination. Throughout his fight for cleaner air he always preferred to use persuasion and health education based on obtaining the most reliable technical advice that was available. The need to resort to legal enforcement in his campaign was taken infrequently and reluctantly.

During the 1950s Burn was appointed Lecturer in the Department of Social and Preventive Medicine at the University of Manchester. One of the results of this link between teaching, practice and research was the setting up of the Salford Psychiatric Case Register. This record linkage scheme was designed to collect demographic, diagnostic and service use data on every resident of the County Borough of Salford who used either the hospital or the local authority mental health services. The system has survived all the upheavals of the 1970s (Social Services, Health and Local Government reorganisations and boundary changes), and continues to this day to accumulate a considerable volume of data on the epidemiology of mental health in Salford. Dr H L Freeman has commented,

> This imaginative and unique arrangement resulted in a research programme which has continued ever since. It is now the longest running enterprise of its kind anywhere in the world.

One early and disturbing finding of this extensive survey was the apparent lack of co-ordination and integration between the health and the social services. The resultant discontinuities were to some extent ameliorated by the establishment in 1955 of the Salford Health Services Council under which an attempt was made through voluntary co-operation to integrate and co-ordinate the work of family doctors, hospital staff and the Local Authority services.

Lance Burn had an absorbing interest in preventive medicine. He pioneered many schemes aimed at the early detection of disease through regular free health 'check-ups'. In the mid-1960s he was approached by Dr George Komrower, Director of Willink Laboratories at the Royal Manchester Children's Hospital to take part in a screening programme for several inborn errors of metabolism including phenylketonuria. This project involved the health visiting service being responsible for the collection of heel-prick blood samples early in the neonatal period, and the management and follow up of diagnosed cases. In his early years in Salford Lance Burn was fervently interested in the problem of hearing impairment - particularly in children. He worked alongside the Ewings in the Department of Audiology, at the University of Manchester and stimulated Mary Sheridan's interest in the detection and management of deaf children. This subject formed the basis for his thesis submitted to the University of Durham for the degree of Doctor of Hygiene. In this thesis he attempted to prove the beneficial effects of Vitamin A in hearing impaired children. Approximately ten years after the completion of this work he gave an address to the North Western Branch of the Society of Medical Officers of Health.[2] In this address, entitled 'Causes of Failure in Medico-Social Experiments', he was self critical and registered his disappointment at the methods and results of several research programmes upon which he had embarked. In this same analysis he refers to and supports Bowlby's work on the effects of maternal separation on the welfare of children and questions the benefit of rehousing families for what may be termed 'mental health' reasons. He initiated health education campaigns following his 'health check-ups' and screening programmes and later organised many anti-addiction groups. He became president of the National Society of Non-Smokers.

In 1963 Lance Burn spent three months in India at the invitation of the World Health Organization. Most of this time was spent in

Bangalore advising the authorities on several wide ranging schemes to improve environmental hygiene and promote programmes of health education.

In the 'eventide' of his professional career his enthusiasm for innovating new schemes never flagged. In conjunction with the consultant obstetric staff at Hope Hospital and the Salford family doctors, Burn was instrumental in the development of the General Practitioner (short stay) Maternity Unit. This unit comprised a four bedded wing attached to the Maternity Unit and it was proposed to admit a selected group of mothers in labour, deliver them and transfer them home after approximately six hours. This scheme had several advantages. It enabled the mother to be transferred through to the hospital obstetric unit should unforeseen complications arise and allowed the family doctor and domiciliary midwife the continuity of care so much appreciated by many mothers. The husband was encouraged to stay throughout and the mother was away from her 'warm' home and family for only a short period. The success of this scheme depended on careful selection of mothers using generally agreed criteria.

Dr Burn's main ambition upon his retirement was to be able to enter general practice. Dr Tom Whitaker in Longsight invited him to join his well established practice, and he was delighted to take advantage of his opportunity. Although he admitted that he found the work of the family doctor difficult, many patients benefitted from his wise counsel.

Little has been mentioned about his family and home life. Five of his six children embarked on careers in nursing and medicine. He was a devoted father and his unfailing loyalty and support to his family reflected his concern for the community he served for over a quarter of a century. He died in harness on New Year's Day in 1973 just before going to visit some patients at their homes.

It is touching and fitting that shortly before his death he was still seeking, in nearby Longsight, the registration of Edwin Chadwick's - the first 'Officer of Health' - birth.(1)

JLB

7.24 SIR JOHN CHARNLEY, 1911-82

    CBE, DSc, FRCS, FRS


*Editor's note*: The following address was delivered by Sir Harry Platt at the thanksgiving service for Sir John Charnley held in Manchester Cathedral on Wednesday 15 September 1982

How are we to contemplate the life and work of the great man who still lives in our hearts and minds? Do we see him in isolation, the central figure in a recital of the events which give a picture of a career of outstanding distinction? I think not. For all men who achieve world-wide fame are part of a continuum. It was Isaac Newton who once said: 'I stand on the shoulders of those who have gone before'. In such a historical context the words from Ecclesiasticus come to our aid, 'Let us now praise famous men and the fathers who begat us'.

In a short space of time it will be 50 years since a great congregation assembled in the Anglican Cathedral in Liverpool, then uncompleted, to pay tribute to the life and work of Sir Robert Jones (1858-1933). To those of us who had been inspired by his leadership, and by the warmth of his humanity, it seemed to be the end of an era. Three years later, Lord Moynihan (1865-1936) died in Leeds. These two men, world figures in surgery, were united by ties of deep affection. Their combined leadership during the years of the Great War of 1914-18, and in the years which followed, had been paramount. Berkeley Moynihan, as a supreme master surgeon, represented the surgery of the body cavities. Robert Jones, by contrast, represented the surgery of the organs of locomotion; the diseases and injuries which led to crippling and deformity. Before Sir Robert's death in 1933, he had been justly acclaimed as the founding father of modern orthopaedic surgery, and as the greatest mender of the maimed in surgical history. The year 1935 was to be one of great significance. Another master surgeon, destined to be world-famous, was in the making. In that year the young John Charnley qualified after a brilliant undergraduate career in the medical school of the University of Manchester. He had entered the medical school armed with the liberal education of the 18th century Grammar School of his native town of Bury. There he had chosen science in his senior years. Not that classical sixth-formers were then unwelcome in British medical schools. Our own Geoffrey Jefferson (1886-1961) had entered medicine through that portal.

## The Post-graduate Years

John Charnley had only four years available for post-graduate experience before the outbreak of the second world war in 1939, but he used those years to great advantage. One year in physiological research into the problems of shock; and three years in resident hospital posts. As he had obtained the Fellowship Diploma of the English Royal College of Surgeons a year after qualification - at the earliest permissible age of twenty-five - he was eligible for a senior surgical resident post. For him, this was to be at the Salford Royal Hospital. These resident surgical officer posts were a characteristic of the major teaching (and some non-teaching) hospitals in the North of England. Their holders were not attached to any one chief, but were available to assist in difficult operations, and they were in full delegated charge of the emergency surgical practice of their hospitals. This experience was unique, both in acquiring diagnostic judgement, and in operative skills. The young men who after such experience, ultimately entered any one of the divisions of surgery - the so-called specialities - carried the hall-mark of the 'generalist' throughout their active surgical lives. This was especially true of John Charnley. His roots in the principles and unity of surgery were deep and lasting.

## The War Years, 1939-45

On the outbreak of the war John joined the RAMC as a surgical specialist. After the Dunkirk evacuation, in which he served on one of the rescue ships, he was posted to the Middle East. In 1940 he joined the staff of a base hospital in Cairo. There he had to deal with the battle injuries from the Desert Campaign, who had received primary surgical care in forward operating units fully equipped for modern wound treatment; antibiotics, shock treatment and blood transfusion. John's patients were predominantly limb injuries. He began to experience the famous dictum of Berkeley Moynihan, who after returning from a visit to France in 1915, said to Sir Alfred Keogh, the Director General of the Army Medical Service:- 'This is a war of orthopaedic surgery'. Curiously enough, during his days at Salford Royal, John had found the surgery of trauma relatively uninteresting. But his Cairo experiences determined that, for him, the surgery of the locomotor system would be his future life-work.

## The Post-War Years

On returning to England in 1945, temporary attachments were arranged for him at the Robert Jones and Agnes Hunt Hospital, Oswestry, and at the Biddulph Grange Orthopaedic Hospital. There and elsewhere, John worked closely with me for some five years. For me it was a period of great intellectual enjoyment. The maturity of his mind - on which others had commented - was a striking feature. The generation gap (of twenty-five years) between us soon disappeared, and gradually a lasting friendship developed. He was not naturally a gregarious man, although he enjoyed people and times of relaxation; there was, I sensed, a patina of dignified reserve. His first consultant appointment at Park Hospital was notable as the background from which came his earlier contributions of great originality: on the healing of fractures; the role of compression in arthrodesis of joints; and for a brief and brilliant intervention in the surgery of the intervertebral disc. The problems which had loomed large in the repertoire of Sir Robert Jones, and the surgeons of my own generation - tuberculosis of bones and joints, and the crippling aftermath of poliomyelitis - were disappearing fast. My own time at the Royal Infirmary was nearing its end, and I had already been joined by two brilliant young men - David Lloyd Griffiths and John himself. Surgery was changing, as it has always done throughout the ages. Transplantation of tissues - skin and bone - had a long heritage; but organ transplantation was coming into the picture. The new age of implants had begun - welcome news to the great number of the population whose hip joints had deteriorated; a cause of widespread suffering. The complete substitution of the damaged hip-joint by a prosthesis was to become John Charnley's life-work.

## The Wrightington Hospital Story

Wrightington Hospital had been designed and built by the Lancashire County Council for the treatment of patients affected by surgical tuberculosis. It was in some respects unique in providing accommodation for mixed cases - i.e. patients with lung tuberculosis who also had joint or spinal lesions. The rapid decline in the incidence of tuberculous bone and joint diseases which, by 1950, had become spectacular, posed the problem of Wrightington's future. This was the year that John Charnley decided to leave the Royal Infirmary - an act of courage and vision - to establish a special unit at Wrightington. He needed a special research unit, which soon was erected from a grant from the National Fund for Research into Crippling Diseases, and opened by Field Marshal Lord Harding, who had been a patient of John's in Cairo. A search for materials for the prosthesis taking shape in his mind, led John to contacts with industry, and to collaboration with distinguished engineers. Next came the environment of the operation of implantation - the ideal of a completely sterile theatre. At first, this was a makeshift design, but later came the purpose-built theatre and special theatre clothing for the surgeon. For the prosthesis, there were the problems of the endurance of the materials and their secure bonding within the human bone of the pelvis and femur. And so the Centre for Hip Joint Surgery at Wrightington became world famous - a surgical Mecca to which pilgrims from many countries made their way - some to watch, some to be trained. Every great commander needs an able chief of staff, and at Wrightington John Charnley found Keith Barnes. John himself became a world figure, overwhelmed at times by demands for his presence at meetings in all continents, and international honours were conferred on him in profusion. All this publicity was borne with characteristic modesty; and at times he seemed unaware that he was now a world figure. In Great Britain he achieved two summit distinctions; the

Fellowship of the Royal Society and Lister Orator. But, true to his modest personality, he valued the local honours which came to him - the freedom of Bury, and the Personal Chair in the University. Although the story of Wrightington has been his saga, it was inevitable that the Southern half of England would demand a centre for him; and this was found at Midhurst.

## His Last Year, 1981-2

His last year of activity was one of single-minded purpose - a perfectionist to the end - on fire with ideas relating to the design of his prosthesis and to the operative techniques involved. Circumstances brought us together again. Although the occasions were relatively brief encounters, the old rapport between us burned brightly. The first was the Harding Award ceremony in London in 1981, where it was my privilege to present him to the Prime Minister, who then spoke and handed him the symbol of the Award. In so doing, the Right Hon. Margaret Thatcher completely ignored her typescript. She obviously sensed that here was a very great man. The next occasion was the recent BBC North-West Television programme, the last of the season's Home-Ground series. For this, John and I had been separately 'researched' but came together for the 'take'. We also saw the broadcast together, as his devoted and accomplished wife had thoughtfully arranged for me to be transported to their house for the occasion. There in his garden I also saw the new laboratory, not yet equipped, which John had designed to enable him to continue research into some of the problems yet unsolved. The television programme was a historical vignette, covering a considerable span of the 20th century, beginning with pictures of Sir Robert Jones and ending with John; the two most famous master surgeons, the greatest menders of the maimed of the 20th century, seen and heard by millions. The film preserved in the archives of the BBC here in the North-West, will, I trust, be available to surgical generations yet to come.

## ENVOI

And now, our own John Charnley has become part of surgical history, and has taken his place in the gallery of the great master surgeons who have gone before. Was he also a great engineer, or a bio-engineer, if such a hybrid exists? There is a danger in the creation of analogical myths. Some biological mechanisms can be picturesquely described in engineering terminology, but design in engineering has its own basic philosophy. The Charnley prosthesis is in essence a biological design by a man who was also an artist. It is something which a Leonardo da Vinci might have envisaged. But today we are thinking about the man, the human person we knew and held in affection. He had so much more to give to the world of surgery, both in fundamental knowledge and to the relief of suffering. But it was not to be. That is the mystery of life, in which a Divinity doth shape our ends.

Thanks be to God for the life and work of John Charnley.

HP

APPENDIX 1

PRESIDENTS OF THE MANCHESTER MEDICAL SOCIETY

Past Presidents

| 1834 | JOHN HULL, MD |
|------|---------------|
| 1838 | JAMES LOMAX BARDSLEY, MD |
| 1843 | WILLIAM JAMES WILSON, FRCS |
| 1845 | JAMES LOMAX BARDSLEY, MD |
| 1848 | THOMAS RADFORD, MD |
| 1849 | THOMAS ASHTON, MD |

Office of President abolished October, 1850; the Treasurer
of the Society to be ex officio Chairman of its Meetings

1850-58 JOHN WINDSOR, FRCS, Treasurer
Office of President re-established January, 1859

| 1859 | JOHN WINDSOR, FRCS |
|------|---------------------|
| 1860 | SAMUEL CROMPTON, MRCS |
| 1861 | CHARLES CLAY, LRCS (Edin) |
| 1862 | LOUIS BORCHARDT, MD |
| 1863 | EDWARD LUND, FRCS |
| 1864 | DANIEL NOBLE, MD |
| 1865 | WILLIAM ROBERTS, MD |
| 1866 | THOMAS WINDSOR, MRCS |
| 1867 | HENRY BROWNE, MD |
| 1868 | THOMAS MELLOR, FRCS |
| 1869 | HENRY SIMPSON, MD |
| 1870 | JAMES OGDEN FLETCHER, MD |
| 1871 | JOHN THORBURN, MD |
| 1872 | JOHN GALT, FRCS |
| 1873 | DAVID LLOYD ROBERTS, MD, MRCP |
| 1874 | JOHN EDWARD MORGAN, MD, FRCP |
| 1876 | ARTHUR RANSOME, MD |
| 1878 | FREDERICK ASHTON HEATH, MRCS |
| 1880 | DAVID LITTLE, MD |
| 1881 | EDWARD LUND, FRCS |
| 1883 | DANIEL JOHN LEECH, MD, FRCP |
| 1885 | WALTER WHITEHEAD, FRCS (Edin) |
| 1886 | JAMES HARDIE, FRCS |
| 1888 | JULIUS DRESCHFELD, MD, FRCP |
| 1889 | JAMES ROSS, MD, FRCP |
| 1891 | THOMAS JONES, BS, FRCS |
| 1892 | ALFRED WILLIAM STOCKS, MRCS |
| 1893 | CHARLES EDWARD GLASCOTT, MD |
| 1894 | JOHN DIXON MANN, MD, FRCP |
| 1895 | FREDERICK ARMITAGE SOUTHAM, FRCS |
| 1896 | HENRY ASHBY, MD, FRCP |
| 1897 | GRAHAM STEELL, MD, FRCP |
| 1898 | GEORGE ARTHUR WRIGHT, MB, FRCS |
| 1899 | WILLIAM JAPP SINCLAIR, MD, MRCP |
| 1900 | THOMAS CARLETON RAILTON, MD, MRCP |
| 1901 | ALFRED HARRY YOUNG, MB, FRCS |

| | |
|---|---|
| 1902 | THOMAS HARRIS, MD, FRCP |
| 1903 | ABRAHAM MATTHEWSON EDGE, MD |
| 1904 | JUDSON SYKES BURY, MD, FRCP |
| 1905 | WILLIAM THORBURN, FRCS |
| 1906 | SAMUEL BUCKLEY, MD |
| 1907 | SIEGMUND MORITZ, MD, MRCP |
| 1908 | ARTHUR THOMAS WILKINSON, MD, FRCP |
| 1909 | WILLIAM COATES, CB, LRCP, MRCS |
| 1910 | EDWARD STANMORE BISHOP, FRCS |
| 1911 | ABRAHAM EMRYS JONES, MD |
| 1912 | ERNEST SEPTIMUS REYNOLDS, MD, FRCP |
| 1913 | JOSHUA JOHN COX, MD |
| 1914-18 | ARCHIBALD DONALD, MD, FRCP |
| 1919 | JOHN WILLIAM SMITH, FRCS |
| 1920 | ROBERT BRIGGS WILD, MD, FRCP |
| 1921 | THOMAS ASHTON GOODFELLOW, CBE, MD |
| 1922-23 | Sir WILLIAM MILLIGAN, MD |
| 1923-24 | EDWARD MANSFIELD BROCKBANK, MBE, MD, FRCP |
| 1924-25 | GEORGE REDMAYNE MURRARY, MD, FRCP, DCL |
| 1925-26 | ARTHUR HENRY BURGESS, MSc, FRCS |
| 1926-27 | ALFRED ALEXANDER MUMFORD, BSc, MD |
| 1927-28 | JOHN GRAY CLEGG, MD, BS, FRCS |
| 1928-29 | RICHARD WALTER MARSDEN, BSc, MD, MRCP |
| 1929-30 | ALBERT RAMSBOTTOM, MC, MD, FRCP |
| 1930-31 | JOHN HOWSON RAY, ChM, FRCS |
| 1931-32 | JOHN SEBASTIAN BACH STOPFORD, MBE, MD, FRS |
| 1932-33 | EVELYN DAVISON TELFORD, MA, MSc, FRCS |
| 1933-34 | CHARLES PAGET LAPAGE, MD, FRCP |
| 1934-35 | ERNEST BOSDIN LEECH, MA, MD, FRCP |
| 1935-36 | ARNOLD GREGORY, MRCS, LRCP |
| 1936-37 | GARNETT WRIGHT, FRCS |
| 1937-38 | WILLIAM FLETCHER SHAW, MD, FRCP, FRCOG |
| 1938-39 | HENRY STANLEY RAPER, CBE, MD, DSc, FRS |
| 1939-43 | THOMAS HERBERT OLIVER, MA, MD, FRCP |
| 1943-44 | CATHERINE CHISHOLM, CBE, BA, MD |
| 1944-45 | FREDERIC WOOD JONES, MB, DSc, FRCS, FRS |
| 1945-46 | WILSON HAROLD HEY, FRCS |
| 1946-47 | DANIEL DOUGAL, MC, MD, FRCOG |
| 1947-48 | JOHN MORLEY, ChM, FRCS |
| 1948-49 | GEOFFREY JEFFERSON, MS, FRCS, FRS |
| 1949-50 | ARTHUR HILLYARD HOLMES, MD, FRCP |

The Society was reconstituted in 1950

---

| | |
|---|---|
| 1950-51 | WILSON HAROLD HEY, FRCS |
| 1951-52 | Sir WILLIAM FLETCHER SHAW, MD, FRCP, FRCOG |
| 1952-53 | JOHN CRIGHTON BRAMWELL, MA, MD, FRCP |
| 1953-54 | JOHN MORLEY, ChM, FRCS |
| 1954-55 | HUGH PATRICK FAY, MB, ChB |
| 1955-56 | WILLIAM BROCKBANK, MD, FRCP |
| 1956-57 | JOHN FREDERICK WILKINSON, MD, MSc, DSc, PhD, FRCP, FRSC |
| 1957-58 | ROBERT LEECH NEWELL, MD, FRCS, LRCP |
| 1958-59 | FERGUS ROBERT FERGUSON, MD, FRCP |
| 1959-60 | CHARLES ERNEST SYKES, TD, FFA, RCS |

| | |
|---|---|
| 1960-61 | WALTER SCHLAPP, MB, ChB, MSc, PhD. |
| 1961-62 | HARRY TEESDALE SIMMONS, MD, FRCS |
| 1962-63 | Lord PLATT, MSc, MD, FRCP |
| 1963-64 | VICTOR FRANCIS LAMBERT, MD, FRCS, ChM |
| 1964-65 | GEORGE ARCHIBALD GRANT MITCHELL, OBE, TD, MB, ChM, DSc |
| 1965-66 | ERIC DUFF GRAY, MA, MD, DMRE, FFR |
| 1966-67 | RONALD EPEY LANE, CBE, MD, FRCP |
| 1967-68 | DENIS SMITH POOLE WILSON, BA, MCh, FRCS, FRCSI |
| 1968-69 | ALAN HOWARD HILTON, LDS, FLS |
| 1969-70 | ARTHUR MORGAN JONES, MSc, FRCP |
| 1970-71 | ALEXANDER COLIN PATTON CAMPBELL, MSc, FRCP, FRC Path |
| 1971-72 | WILLIAM FRANCIS NICHOLSON, MBE, MA, MD, FRCS |
| 1972-73 | MARTIN CYRIL GORDON ISRAELS, MSc, MD, FRCP |
| 1973-74 | ARON HOLZEL, MD, FRCP |
| 1974-75 | THOMAS MOORE, MD, FRCS |
| 1975-76 | HENRY TAYLOR HOWAT, CBE, MD, FRCP |
| 1976-77 | PATRICK SARSFIELD BYRNE, CBE, MSc, FRCGP |
| 1977-78 | AMBROSE JOLLEYS, MD, FRCS |
| 1978-79 | ANDREW RENNIE HUNTER, MD, DA, FFARCS, FRFPS, FRCS |
| 1979-80 | SAMUEL OLEESKY, FRCP, MD |
| 1980-81 | ALAN HADFIELD GOWENLOCK, MSc, PhD, FRC Path, FRSC |
| 1981-82 | NORTHAGE JOHN DE VILLE MATHER, MA, MB, ChB, DPM, FR Psych |
| 1982-83 | JOSEPH REGINALD MOORE, OBE, MDS, MSc, FDSRCS |
| 1983-84 | RHYS TUDOR WILLIAMS, MB, BChir, FRCP |

## Anniversary President

| | |
|---|---|
| 1984-85 | SYDNEY WILLIAM STANBURY, MD, FRCP |

APPENDIX 2

FURTHER BIOGRAPHICAL NOTES

This appendix contains brief details of the careers of the office holders of the Society and of other eminent individuals connected with the Society. The Manchester Medical Schools are for the sake of brevity referred to by their street names. Some information about them will be found in the biographies of Joseph Jordan (7.1) and Thomas Turner (7.2) and in the note on George Southam. Most abbreviations are standard but (Manc.) has been used instead of (Vict.) to indicate a degree conferred by the Victoria University now usually known as Manchester University.

TD = Territorial Decoration

DL = Deputy Lieutenant of the County Palatine of Lancaster.

ASHBY, Henry,    MB(Lond.1874),    MD(Gold Medal 1878),    MRCS(1873),    FRCP
(1846-1908)            (1890, M 1883)
President 1896         Lecturer on diseases of children from 1881.  Best
                      remembered for his textbook *Diseases of Children
                      Medical & Surgical* (co-author G A Wright q.v.)
                      which ran to five editions.

ASHTON, Thomas, MD(Leiden 1832), L(M)RCP(1841)
(1800-1883)            Clerk to the Manchester Royal Infirmary from
Treasurer 1842-49      1820. In private practice as a surgeon from 1825.
President 1849         Well known in literary and scientific circles.

BAKER, Stephen Leonard,    PhD(Lond.1931), MSc(Manc.1935),    MRCS(1913),
(1888-1978)            LRCP(1913), DPH(1918)
                      Procter Professor of pathology and pathological
                      anatomy from 1931 to 1950 when he described
                      fibrogenesis imperfecta ossium. Became in 1951
                      the first incumbent of the first Chair of
                      rheumatology (osteopathology) to be endowed in
                      the world.

BARCLAY, Alfred Ernest,    OBE(1918),    MA(Cantab.1904), MB, BCh(Cantab.
(1876-1949)            1904), MD(1912), MRCS(1904),    FRCP(1941, M 1935,
                      L 1904), DMRE(Cantab.1921)
                      See Biography 7.12.

BARDSLEY, Sir James Lomax, Kt(1831), MD(Edin.1823), FRCP(1831), JP, DL
(1801-1876)            The youngest physician to be elected to the
President 1839-43      honorary staff of Manchester Royal Infirmary in
          1845-48      1823. Thesis on rabies. Introduced emetine to
                      treat dysentery. Lectured at Pine Street on
                      physics, materia medica and medical botany.

BARTON, Samuel, FRCS(by elec.1844, M 1811), JP
(1790-1871)            In 1815, became second surgeon to the Eye
Treasurer 1841         Hospital. Advocated excision of an injured eye to
                      prevent the occurrence of sympathetic ophthalmia
                      in the other.

BISHOP, Edward Stanmore, FRCS(1884, M 1871)
(1848-1912)            Won the Turner Scholarship for three successive
President 1910         years at Pine Street and became a general
                      practitioner in Ardwick. Was appointed honorary
                      surgeon at Ancoats Hospital and specialised first
                      in abdominal surgery and then in gynaecology. Did
                      much to make Ancoats a leading hospital and
                      possessed a considerable European reputation.

BLACKLEY, Charles Harrison, MD(Brux.1874), MRCS(1858)
(1820-1900)            General practitioner in Manchester who may be
                      regarded as a founding father of immunology
                      since, a sufferer himself, he demonstrated the
                      association of pollen with hay fever and
                      published a classic work on the subject entitled
                      *Experimental researches on the causes and nature
                      of catarrhus aestivus* (hay fever).

BORCHARDT, Louis, MD(Berlin 1838)
(1813-1883)            Born in Brandenburg,  he organised medical relief
President 1862         for a Silesian  typhus  epidemic in 1845.   As a
Treasurer 1863-65      political agitator in 1848, he was imprisoned for
                       two years.   Came to  England and in  1853 became
                       honorary physician to the Central Dispensary  for
                       Children  and was  mainly responsible for   the
                       provision  of  the  first  in-patient  Children's
                       Hospital in Manchester (c1854).

BOYD, Alexander    Michael,  MB,BS(Lond.1929),  FRCS(1931,  M  1929),
(1905-1973)        LRCP(1929)
                   Interested in vascular disease, he was  appointed
                   as the first full-time  Professor  of  surgery at
                   Manchester in 1946.   A popular lecturer,  he was
                   also a brilliant bedside tutor.His eccentricities
                   became legend although some were the consequences
                   of  the  ankylosing  spondylitis  from  which  he
                   suffered.

BRAID, James, L(M)RCS(Edin.1815)
(1795-1860)        The  first  surgeon  in England to perform tendon
                   shortening  for  paralytic  talipes.   Usually
                   remembered for his establishment of a  scientific
                   basis  for  hypnosis  which term he introduced to
                   replace the unscientific word mesmerism.

BRAMWELL, John Crighton,  BA(1st cl.Hons.Cantab.1910),  MA(1921),  MB,
(1889-1976)        ChB(Manc.1915),  MD(Gold Medal 1923),  FRCP(1929,
Secretary 1926-28  M 1921), FRCP(Hon.Edin.1960)
President 1952     See Biography 7.19.

BRENTNALL, Edward Stanley, MB, ChB(Manc.1913), FRCS(Edin.1918)
(1889-1976)        Won  a  classical  scholarship  to  University.
Treasurer 1930-35  Orthopaedic surgeon at Ancoats Hospital.

BROCKBANK, Edward Mansfield, MBE(1919),  MB, ChB(Manc.1890), MD(1893),
(1866-1959)        FRCP(1902, M 1894)
President 1923     Born  in  Australia, was  the  first  Manchester
                   graduate to become a member of the  Royal College
                   of Physicians. In 1903 became the first editor of
                   the  Medical  Chronicle.   His  textbook on heart
                   disease ran  to  six  editions  but  he  is best
                   remembered  as a  local  medical  historian who
                   served  as  Chairman of  the  University  Library
                   Committee (1930-51),  having been responsible for
                   the negotiations to merge the  Society's  Library
                   with that of the University.

BROOKE, Henry Ambrose Grundy, BA(Lond.1874), MB(Lond.1880), MRCS(1880)
(1854-1919)        A dermatologist of renown in  North West England.
                   Described  the  rare  congenital  epithelioma
                   adenoides cysticum (Brooke's disease)  in  1892.
                   Was  the  first  joint  editor  of  the  *British
                   Journal of Dermatology* founded in 1888.

BROWNBILL, Thomas Frederick George, FRCS(1852, M 1837), LSA(1834)
(1812-1863)          In 1847, became consulting surgeon to the Salford
Secretary 1841-43    and Pendleton Royal Hospital and was surgeon to
                     the Salford Union Workhouse. Was also Chairman of
                     the Sanitary Nuisance Committee of Salford
                     Corporation.

BROWNE, Henry, BA(Glas.1839), MA(1840), MD(Lond.1848), MRCS(1844)
(1818-1901)          Appointed in 1846 physician to the Chorlton-on-
President 1867        Medlock Dispensary. Elected physician to
                     Manchester Royal Infirmary, the fever wards and
                     Lunatic Hospital in 1878. Lectured at Pine Street
                     on forensic medicine and later on medicine.
                     Remembered also for his idiosyncratic *Triglot
                     Dictionary of Scriptural Representative Words*.

BRYCE, Alexander Graham, MB, ChB(Manc.1912), MD(1913), FRCS(1923), DPH
(1890-1968)          (1915)
Secretary 1928-30    A pioneer of thoracic surgery in the North West,
                     he studied with Chevalier Jackson.    In 1932
                     devised an operation for partial pneumonectomy.

BUCKLEY, Samuel, MB(Lond.1880), MD(1885), FRCS(1873, M 1868), MRCP
(1847-1910)          (1894), BSc(Hon.Manc.1904)
President 1906       Resident medical officer to the medical and fever
                     wards of the Manchester Royal Infirmary from
                     1870-2. Subsequently honorary physician to the
                     Manchester Northern Hospital for Women and
                     Children.

BURGESS, Arthur Henry, BSc(Manc.1892), MSc(1895), MB, ChB(1896), FRCS
(1874-1948)          (1899, M 1896), FACS(1911), DL
President 1925       In 1903, recorded the first case of skin grafting
                     for laryngeal stenosis. Introduced the concept of
                     surgical asepsis first to Crumpsall Hospital and
                     then to the Manchester Royal Infirmary. Became a
                     famous abdominal surgeon, convincing his
                     colleagues of the value of appendicectomy at a
                     meeting of the Manchester Medical Society.
                     President of the British Medical Association's
                     meeting at Manchester in 1929. Later took an
                     interest in electrosurgery and diathermy. Elected
                     to the Chair of clinical surgery in 1921.

BURN, John Lancelot, MB, BS(Durh.1931), MD(1933), BHy(Durh.1933), DHy
(1902-1973)          (1944), DPH(Durh.1933)
                     See Biography 7.23.

BURY, Judson Sykes, BSc(Manc.1904), MB(Lond.1877), MD(1879), MRCS
(1852-1944)          (1877)
President 1904       Honorary physician at Manchester Royal Infirmary
                     from 1899. Main interest neurology. A popular
                     lucid lecturer. Elected in 1911 to the Chair of
                     clinical medicine but retired the following year.

BYRNE, Patrick Sarsfield, CBE(1975, OBE 1966), MSc(Manc.1976), MB, ChB
(1913–1980)             (L'pool 1936), FRCGP(1967)
President 1976          Became the first incumbent of the Chair of
                        general practice in 1972. Played an important
                        part in the foundation of the College of General
                        Practitioners and was its President during
                        1973–6.

CATLOW, Joseph Peel,    LRCS(Edin.1826), LSA(1819)
(1798–1861)             This cousin of Sir Robert Peel succeeded to Dr
Secretary 1834–38       Bardsley's practice circa 1834. His devotion to
                        mesmerism and aesthetic medicine forced his early
                        retirement. He was the first (joint) Secretary of
                        the Society.

CHARNLEY, Sir John,     DSc(Manc.1964), MB, ChB(Manc.1935), FRCS(1936),
(1911–1982)             FRS(1975), MD(Hon.L'pool 1976), Kt(1977)
                        See Biography 7.24.

CHISHOLM, Catherine,    CBE(1935), BA(Manc.1898), MB, ChB(Manc.1904), MD
(1878–1952)             (1912), FRCP(Hon.1949)
President 1943          See Biography 7.15.

CLAY, Charles, LRCP(ext.1842), LRCS(Edin.1823)
(1801–1893)             A pupil of Jordan.Practised in Ashton-under-Lyne,
President 1861          moving to Manchester 1839. By 1847, he was
                        medical officer to the Lying In Hospital and
                        Lecturer on medical jurisprudence and on diseases
                        of women and children. Became senior medical
                        officer at St Mary's and Lecturer on principles
                        and practice of midwifery in 1859. First in
                        England to remove an ovarian cyst successfully,
                        he also performed the first technically
                        successful hysterectomy but the patient died two
                        weeks later.

CLEGG, John Gray,       MB, BS(Lond.1893), MD(1894), MB, ChB(Manc.1893),
(1869–1941)             FRCS(1894), M 1891), LRCP(1891)
President 1927          An ophthalmologist who pioneered the treatment of
                        glaucoma and retinal detachment. Founded the
                        North of England Ophthalmological Society.
                        Prepared (with Alexander Wilson q.v.) a
                        descriptive catalogue of the contents of the
                        Pathology Museum. In 1933 he moved to London.

COATES, Sir William,    KCB(1930), CB(Civil 1905, Mil.1918), CBE(1920),
(1860–1962)             VD, TD, FRCS(1922, M 1881), LRCP & CM(Edin.1884),
Secretary 1894–98       DL
President 1909          See Biography 7.9.

COX, Henry Talbot,      MA, MB, BChir(Cantab.1934), MD(1940), FRCS(Edin.
(1902–1984)             1933), MRCS(Eng.), LRCP(Lond.1926)
                        Surgeon at Withington and Wythenshawe Hospitals.
                        In September 1945 was the first in Europe to
                        perform adrenalectomy for metastatic cancer of
                        the prostate. Recognised during the 1950s the
                        role of fibrinolysis as a cause of the gastric

bleeding associated with peptic ulceration.
President of the Section of Surgery of the
Society in 1958.

COX, Joshua John, MB(Edin.1875), MD(1881), FRCS(Edin.1880), LRCP(Edin.
(c1857-1923)    1880)
President 1913    Practised in Eccles. Later became consulting
physician to the Northern and Dental Hospitals.
Was chief medical officer in charge of recruiting
during the first world war.

CROMPTON, Samuel, MD(St And.1862), MRCS(1839), LSA(1839)
(1817-1891)    Initially a general practitioner, this grandson
Secretary 1843    of the inventor of the spinning mule became a
    "    1856-58    physician to Salford Hospital and Dispensary.
President 1860    Surgeon to Henshaw's Blind Asylum. During his
term as Secretary, he saved the Society when it
was in low waters.

CULLINGWORTH, Charles James,    MD(Durh.1881),    MRCS(1865),    FRCP(1887,
(1841-1908)    M 1878), LSA(1866)
Secretary 1879-84    Qualified in Leeds. Private practice 1868.
Librarian 1872-78    Surgeon to St Mary's Hospital 1873. In 1877 he
catalogued Radford's (q.v.) Library. A lecturer
on medical jurisprudence from 1879 to 1885 when
he was elected to the Chair of obstetric medicine
which he occupied for three years before moving
to London. He spent much time cataloguing the
books of the Manchester Medical Society. He
founded the *Journal of Obstetrics and Gynaecology
of the British Empire*.Was the first gynaecologist
to give the Bradshaw Lecture at the Royal College
of Physicians.

DELEPINE, Auguste Sheridan,    BSc(Lausanne 1872),    MSc(Hon.Manc.1905),
(1855-1921)    MB, CM(1st cl.Hons.Edin.1882)
See Biography 7.8.

DONALD, Archibald, MA(Edin.1880), MB, CM(Edin.1883),    MD(1886),    MRCS
(1860-1937)    (1883),    FRCP(1915, M 1890), F(R)COG(1929, Hon.
President 1914-18    1934), DL
See Biography 7.10.

DORRINGTON, Thomas, MRCS(1839), LSA(1839)
(c1818-1850)    A surgeon to the Manchester and Salford Lying-In
Secretary 1843-45    Hospital. Joined the staff of St Mary's Hospital
in 1842. A lecturer in the principles and
practice of obstetrics at Chatham Street, he gave
the inaugural address when the school was opened.
His reputation was high by the time of his early
death.

DOUGAL, Daniel, MC, TD,  Croix de guerre, MB, ChB(Manc.1906),  MD(Gold
(1884-1948)    Medal 1913), F(R)COG(1929)
President 1946    On the honorary staff of the Northern Hospital
for Women and Children, also pathologist at St
Mary's Hospital. Joined the honorary staff of the

latter in 1919.Elected to the Chair of obstetrics
and gynaecology in 1927.

DRESCHFELD, Julius, BSc(Manc.1883), MD(Würtzburg 1867), FRCP(1883,
(1845-1907)     M(L) 1869)
President 1888   Born in Bavaria. Studied at the Royal School in
Manchester completing his training in Würtzburg
after serving as assistant surgeon in the
Bavarian army. Was the first to teach systematic
pathology and pathological histology and founded
probably the first pathological laboratory in
Great Britain. His unpublished work on rabies
antedated that of Pasteur and he was the first to
use eosin to stain animal tissues. Appointed in
1882 to the first Chair of pathology in the
country but his interest in clinical medicine
increased and he relinquished this chair to
become Professor of Medicine (also in Manchester)
in 1891.

EDGE, Abraham Matthewson, BSc(Manc.1882), MD(RUI 1873), MRCS(1872),
(c1851-1922)    MRCP(1878)
President 1903   Joined the staff of the Southern Hospital for
Women and Children and when this hospital
amalgamated with St Mary's Hospital, he joined
the honorary staff of the latter.

ELLIS, Reginald, MB, ChB(Manc.1924), MD(1929), FRCP(1943, M 1932)
(1898-1970)     Assisted John Crighton Bramwell (q.v.) to
Secretary 1936-47  research the cardio-vascular systems of the
Treasurer 1939-46  athletes at the American Olympics in 1928. His
membership was conferred with a communication
from the President for high achievement. A
general physician, with an interest in
cardiology he held honorary appointments at the
Northern and Ancoats Hospitals and also at
Withington Hospital.

FAIRBROTHER, Ronald Wilson, TD, DSc(Manc.1936), MB, ChB(Manc.1923), MD
(1902-1969)     (Comm.1928), FRCP(1941, M 1933), FC Path(1963)
Won the Dickinson Research Travelling Fellowship
in 1927. After working as a research fellow at
the Lister Institute, became a lecturer in
bacteriology at Manchester and was subsequently
appointed Director of the clinical pathology
laboratory at Manchester Royal Infirmary. His
textbook had been published in nine editions by
1962.

FAY, Hugh Patrick, MB, ChB(Manc.1922)
(1897-1974)     General practitioner. Chairman of the local
President 1954   Division of the British Medical Association. A
Justice of the Peace for nearly twenty years. A
papal knight of Pope Pius XII, an honour
conferred for his work with the Salford Catholic
Rescue Society.

FERGUSON, Fergus Robert, MB, ChB(Manc.1920), MD(Gold Medal 1924),    DPH
(1899-1974)            (1924), FRCP(1934, M 1929)
Secretary 1930-32      Graduated  before  his twenty-first birthday.    In
President 1958         1923  was  appointed  assistant  Lecturer  in
                       bacteriology.    Returning to clinical medicine in
                       1925 he became a neurologist interested in
                       migraine  and  myasthenia  gravis.    Was on the
                       consultant staff of Manchester Royal Infirmary.

FLETCHER, James Ogden, MD(St And.1858), FRCS(1862, M 1848),   LSA(1848)
(1824-1874)            General    practitioner,    appointed    medical
President 1870         superintendent  of  the  temporary  hospitals
                       established  'to combat the very  prevalent fever
                       of a low type'.    He (and his brother) lectured on
                       anatomy at Chatham Street. In 1865 he was surgeon
                       to the Manchester,  Sheffield and Lincoln Railway
                       Company, medical officer to the gaol  and  to the
                       police.

FOTHERGILL, William Edward, MA(Edin.1886), BSc(Edin.1888),  MB, CM(1st
(1865-1926)            cl.Hons Edin.1893), MD(Gold Medal 1897)
                       See Biography 7.11.

FRANKLIN, Isaac Abraham, MRCS(1835), LSA(1834)
(1813-1880)            Medical referee for the Norwich Union Association
Secretary 1844-46      Society (1849).  Twenty years later was appointed
                       surgeon to the Manchester Cholera Hospital.

GALT, John, FRCS(1858, M(L)1840), LFPS(Glas.1858), LM(1858), LSA(1858)
(1810-1878)            Medical officer of health and the medical officer
President 1872         for the Hurst and  Dukinfield  Union (Workhouse).
                       Was also a certifying factory  surgeon.   At the
                       time of his death, he was surgeon to the  Ashton-
                       under-Lyne District Infirmary.

GAMGEE, Arthur,   MD(Gold Medal Edin.1862),   FRCP(1896, M 1885),    FRCP
(1841-1909)            (Edin.1872, M 1871), FRS(1872)
                       Born in Florence. Elected in 1873 to be the first
                       incumbent of the Brackenbury Chair of Physiology,
                       one of the earliest to be endowed in the country.
                       His   main   research   interests   were   the
                       physiological changes occurring in the  body
                       during  disease.   At the age of thirty he was
                       elected a Fellow of the Royal Society. In 1885 he
                       left Manchester to live abroad.

GASKELL, Samuel, FRCS(1844, M 1832)
(1807-1886)            See Biography 7.4.

GIBSON, Robert, MB, ChB(Edin.1898), MD(1905)
(c1877-1939)           After practising in Hong Kong for four years,  he
Secretary 1920-24      entered general practice in Manchester in 1905.
                       Following  infection his  left  arm had  to be
                       amputated;  this  disability  led him to become a
                       dermatologist  and  honorary  physician  to  the
                       Manchester and Salford Skin Hospital.

GLASCOTT, Charles Edward, MB, CM(Edin.1868), MD(1871), FRCS(Edin.1886)
(1847-1918)            Born in Istanbul, after qualifying he came to
President 1893         Manchester as House Surgeon to the Royal Eye
Treasurer 1887-1900   Hospital. As an eye surgeon, he became eminent
                      through his writings and he also enjoyed a
                      reputation as a practical lecturer.

GOODFELLOW, Thomas Ashton, CBE(1920), BSc(Lond.1883), BSc(Manc.1904),
(1865-1937)           MB(Lond.1889), MD(1891), MRCS(1888), LRCP(1888)
President 1921        General practitioner, Didsbury, Manchester.
                      Served on the Medical Consultative Council
                      established by Lloyd George. In 1936 was
                      President of the Lancashire and Cheshire Division
                      of the BMA. Lectured to undergraduates on ethics
                      and conditions of medical practice.

GREGORY, Arnold, MRCS(1902), LRCP(1902)
(c1879-1947)          Qualified in Leeds. Came to Manchester as a
President 1935        general practitioner in 1906. Interested in
                      medical education and its application to general
                      practice, and was active in the British Medical
                      Association.

HARDIE, James, MD(Edin.1862), FRCS(1882, M 1882), LRCS(Edin.1862)
(1841-1909)           First practised in Harpurhey, Manchester where he
President 1886        became visiting surgeon to the Manchester Poor-
                      Law Township Hospital. He assisted in the
                      organisation of the new hospital at Crumpsall. In
                      1876 he joined the staff of the Manchester Royal
                      Infirmary. He served on the Council of the Royal
                      College of Surgeons in 1894. He was the first to
                      operate openly upon Dupuytren's contracture. He
                      also reconstructed the bridge of the nose from
                      the terminal phalanx and must be regarded as one
                      of the earliest plastic surgeons.

HARRIS, Thomas, MB(Lond.1882), MD(1883), MRCS(1881), FRCP(1893,M 1886)
(1859-1906)           After studying in Manchester, Dublin and
President 1902        Würtzburg, became physician in charge of the
                      Throat Department at Manchester Royal Infirmary.
                      Lectured at Owens College on diseases of the
                      respiratory system having previously been
                      lecturer in pathology.

HARTLEY, James Blair, MB, BS(Durh.1924), MD(1945), DMRE(Cantab.1929),
(1901-1969)           FFR(1939)
                      Responsible for the development of obstetric
                      radiology and was known for his work on the
                      detection of foetal abnormalities. He is
                      commemorated with Eric Duff Gray by the founding
                      of the annual Gray Hartley Lectures.

HEATH, Frederick Ashton, MRCS(1852), LSA(1852)
(1830-1899)           Became a surgeon, joining the honorary staff of
President 1878        Manchester Royal Infirmary as successor to Joseph
Treasurer 1880        Jordan (q.v.). He lectured on descriptive anatomy
                      at the Royal School.

HEATH, William Ravenscroft, MRCS(1858), LSA(1858)
(    -1896)            Appointed in 1869 to the staff of the Southern
Secretary 1868-71     Hospital for Diseases of Children and the
                      Manchester Institute for Diseases of the Ear.

HEY, Wilson Harold, MB, ChB(Manc.1905), FRCS(1908, M 1905), LRCP(1905)
(1882-1956)           A Chevalier de Légion d'Honneur. Best remembered
Secretary 1919        for his method of prostatectomy. Interested in
President 1945        mountain rescue, he provoked prosecution in order
    "    1950         that rescue teams might be supplied with
                      morphine: the law was subsequently changed to
                      allow this.

HILL, Archibald Vivian,  CH(1946),    OBE(Mil.1918),    BA(1st cl.Hons
(1886-1977)           Cantab.1909), ScD(1920), FRS(1918)
                      Was awarded the Nobel Prize in 1922 for work he
                      did on the physiology of muscle while in
                      Manchester. Elected to the Chair of physiology in
                      1920 he stayed in Manchester for three years.

HILL, Edward Falkner,  MB, ChB(Manc.1900), MD(Gold Medal 1934), DPH
(1877-1974)           (Manc.1920), MRCS(1900), LRCP(1900), FFA RCS
                      (1948, Hon.1961)
                      See biography 7.14.

HOLLAND, Philip Henry, MRCS(1833)
(    -1893)           Succeeded John Walker (q.v.) as Secretary.
Secretary 1835-38     General practitioner who moved to London, and by
                      1855 had become Inspector of Burial Grounds.

HOLMES, Arthur Hillyard,  MB,  ChB(2nd cl.Hons Manc.1911),   MD(1914),
(1889-1954)           FRCP(1936, M 1921)
Secretary 1924-26     General physician with an interest in chest
President 1949        diseases at Manchester Royal Infirmary. He became
                      Warden of Lister House, a residence for clinical
                      medical students, after his own house was bombed
                      in the second world war.

HOLZEL, Aron,  MD(Prague 1933),  FRCP(1970, M 1965),  FRCP(Edin.1969, M
(1909-1978)           1964), DCH(1947)
President 1973        Paediatrician at Booth Hall Hospital. Remembered
                      for his work on enzyme deficiencies following
                      infantile gastroenteritis. Became Professor of
                      child health in 1971.

HULL, John, MD(Leiden 1792), MRCS(1784), LRCP(Extra 1806, full 1819)
(1761-1843)           After practising in Blackburn, he came to
President 1834-38     Manchester in 1796. Returning after obtaining his
                      degree in Holland, he became known as an
                      obstetrician and the post of physician at the
                      Lying-In Hospital was created for him. A
                      classical scholar and modern linguist, also a
                      very distinguished botanist. He was Secretary to
                      the Literary and Philosophical Society in
                      addition to being chosen to be the first
                      President of the Manchester Medical Society.

ISRAELS, Martin Cyril Gordon, MSc(Manc.1929),  MB,  ChB(Manc.1932),  MD
(1906-1979)            (1935), FRCP(1949, M 1939)
President 1972         After holding the  Lady Tata Research Scholarship
                       from  1933  to  1936,  continued  his  career  in
                       haematology  and  in 1938 was appointed Foulerton
                       Research Fellow of the Royal Society.  After war-
                       service  in  the  Royal Air Force,  became Deputy
                       Director  of  clinical  haematology at Manchester
                       Royal Infirmary.   Elected the first Professor of
                       clinical  haematology  in  Manchester  in  1971.
                       Remembered for his beautifully produced *Atlas of
                       Bone Marrow Cytology*.

JEFFERSON, Sir Geoffrey, Kt(1950),  CBE(1943),  MB, BS(Lond.1909),  MS
(1886-1961)            (1913),      FRCS(1911, M 1909),      FRCP(Hon.1947,
President 1948         L 1909), FRS(1947)
                       See Biography 7.17.

JEFFERSON, Gertrude, Lady, MRCS(1912), LRCP(1912), DPM(1937)
(1885-1961)            Wife of  Sir Geoffrey Jefferson.   Canadian  by
                       birth, she pioneered the family  welfare  service
                       for  the  detection  of  mental ill health in the
                       community. This was a unique organisation run  by
                       the Public Health Department of  the  Corporation
                       of Manchester.

JONES, Abraham Emrys, MB, CM(Edin.1875), MD(1877), LM(Edin.1875), MRCS
(1852-1925)            (1876)
President 1911         Studied  in  Glasgow  and  came  to Manchester as
                       resident medical officer at the Hulme Dispensary.
                       Later honorary assistant surgeon at the Royal Eye
                       Hospital. His address on the disposal of the dead
                       led  to  the  formation  of  the  Manchester
                       Crematorium Society and  the  erection  of  the
                       Crematorium.

JONES, Arthur Morgan,  BSc(Manc.1934),  MSc(1935),  MB, ChB(Hons Manc.
(1910-1979)            1938), FRCP(1948, M 1942)
President 1969         After qualifying he won no fewer than three major
                       post-graduate awards.  Specialised in  cardiology
                       and  was  on  the  staff  of  Manchester  Royal
                       Infirmary.

JONES, Frederic Wood,  BSc(Lond.1903),  DSc(1910),  MB, BS(Lond.1904),
(1879-1954)            FRCS(Hon.1930, M 1904), LRCP(1904),  FRACS(1935),
President 1944         FRS(1925)
                       Came to Manchester to occupy his fifth  chair  of
                       anatomy.  A  brilliant  anatomist,  interested in
                       comparative anatomy, and an able lecturer, he did
                       not stay long in the city but moved to London  to
                       restore  the  war  damaged  Hunterian  Museum and
                       occupy his sixth chair.

JONES, Thomas, MB(Lond.1872), BS(1879), FRCS(1875, M 1870),  LSA(1872)
(1848-1900)            In  1872 was appointed resident surgical officer
President 1891         to  Manchester Royal Infirmary.   Was  one of the
                       first  to  practise  solely  as  a  consulting and

operative surgeon. In 1874 was the first surgeon
to be appointed to the children's Hospital where
he rapidly established a large surgical unit.
Appointed Professor of systematic surgery, 1892.
Died within a few months of his arrival in South
Africa to join the Welsh Hospital serving there.

JORDAN, Joseph, FRCS(1843, M 1826; one of the original 300 Fellows)
(1787-1873)              See Biography 7.1.

KAY-SHUTTLEWORTH, Sir James Phillips, Bt(1849), MD(Edin.1827)
(1804-1877)              Practised for a short time in Ancoats but became
                         more interested in social reform. In 1831,
                         described the cotton-workers disease now
                         believed to be byssinosis. Was awarded the
                         Fothergillian Gold Medal of the Royal Humane
                         Society for a publication on asphyxia. Was a
                         member of the original Council of the Manchester
                         Medical Society.

KER, Henry Whitfield, MRCS(1832), LSA(1833)
(    -c1858)             Described in the 1847 Medical Directory as the
Secretary 1840           Medical Officer to the Manchester Union, formerly
                         Surgeon to the Ardwick and Ancoats Dispensary. In
                         1855 there is no occupation listed (perhaps
                         indicating retirement) and there is no entry for
                         1859. (In some years his name is spelt Kerr.)

LAMBERT, Victor Francis, MB, ChB(Manc.1923), MD(1940), ChM(1932), FRCS
(1899-1981)              (1949), FRCS(Edin.1927)
President 1963           See Biography 7.21.

LAPAGE, Charles Paget, MB, ChB(Manc.1902), MD(Commend.1905), FRCP
(1879-1947)              (1922,M 1908)
President 1933           Awarded the Ashby Memorial Scholarship in
                         Diseases of Children. Paediatrician at the
                         Manchester Children's Hospital. A keen
                         mountaineer, he climbed all peaks in England over
                         2,500 feet at the age of sixty-five.

LEDWARD, Ralph Worthington, MD(St And.1860), MRCS(1846), LSA(1859)
(1822-1892)              Little appears to have been recorded about this
Secretary 1853-56        secretary except that he was senior surgeon to
                         the Ardwick and Ancoats Dispensary and
                         subsequently was surgeon to St Michael's
                         Manchester Union.

LEECH, Daniel John, MB(Lond.1868), MD(1876), MRCS(1861), FRCP(1882, M
(1840-1900)              1875), LSA(1861)
President 1883           Said to have been a descendant of John the Leech,
                         doctor to Edward III. Physician who lectured on
                         materia medica and therapeutics at Owens and was
                         elected Professor in 1881. He attempted to
                         substitute the science of pharmacology for the
                         art of historical therapeutics. He was partially
                         responsible for the foundation of the Manchester

and Salford Hospital for Skin Diseases and the Cancer Hospital.

LEECH, Ernest Bosdin, BA(Cantab.1897), MA(c1903), MA(Hon.Manc.1937),
(1875-1950)          MB, BCh(Cantab.1903), MD(1907), DPH(Manc.1905),
Secretary 1911-18    MRCS(1901), FRCP(1919, M 1905, L 1901)
President 1934       Nephew of Professor D J Leech. Physician,
                     Manchester Royal Infirmary. Interested in
                     digestive diseases and pharmacology. He spent
                     much time improving the library and was
                     responsible for the creation of the biographical
                     files which form a valuable part of the
                     Manchester Medical Collection. He was president
                     in the centenary year of the Society.

LITTLE, David, MD(Edin.1861), FRCS(Edin.1891), L & LM(Edin.1861)
(1840-1902)          In 1863, appointed house surgeon and secretary to
Treasurer 1879       the Eye Hospital which received the Royal
President 1880       Accolade during his four years' tenure before he
Treasurer 1882-86    was appointed to the honorary staff. He succeeded
                     Thomas Windsor (q.v.) as lecturer in
                     ophthalmology. A careful, expert surgeon, he was
                     renowned for his treatment of cataracts and
                     glaucoma.

LIVERSEDGE, Laurence Atkinson, BSc(Manc.1935), MD(Duke,1943), MB, ChB
(1915-1979)          (Manc.1944), FRCP(1962, M 1946)
                     After taking honours in French, entered the
                     Medical School, won a Rockefeller Scholarship to
                     Duke University in the USA and graduated there
                     before taking his English finals. Appointed
                     lecturer in neurology in 1950 and later became
                     the Director of the Department at the Manchester
                     Royal Infirmary.

LUND, Edward, FRCS(1863, M 1847), LSA(1847)
(1823-1898)          Came to Manchester in 1848 and two years later
Secretary 1850-53    was appointed dispensary surgeon to the Royal
President 1863       Infirmary and demonstrator of anatomy at Pine
Treasurer 1866-72    Street (in the year Chatham Street opened). A
President 1881       full surgeon at the Infirmary by 1868, he was one
                     of the first to recognise the value of Lister's
                     work in antisepsis. He played a major role in the
                     union of the Royal Medical School with Owens
                     College and became Professor of surgery, at first
                     jointly with George Southam (q.v.).

MACALPINE, James Barlow, DSc(Hon.Caus.Manc.1943), MB, ChB(Manc.1907),
(1882-1960)          FRCS(1910, M 1907), LRCP(1907)
                     Appointed to the honorary staff of Salford Royal
                     Hospital, he started a department of genito-
                     urinary surgery. He published in 1928 the first
                     series of occupational cancers of the urinary
                     tract in dye-workers. Was a founder member in
                     1945 of the British Association of Urological
                     Surgeons and four years later was the first

recipient   of   its   St Peter's   Medal   for
distinguished services to the specialty.

MACKENZIE, Sir James, Kt(1915), MB, CM(Edin.1878), MD(1892),   FRCP
(1853-1925)                (1913, M 1908), FRS(1915), LLD(Edin.1911)
                           See Biography 7.7.

MAITLAND, Hugh Bethune, MSc(Manc.1929), MB(Toronto 1916),   MD(Starr
(1895-1972)                Medal 1922), MRCS(1919), LRCP(1919)
                           A Canadian working at the Lister Institute he
                           demonstrated that vaccinia virus would grow in
                           living tissue cells. The Salk polio vaccine was
                           prepared in his culture medium. Was appointed
                           Professor of bacteriology and preventive medicine
                           in Manchester and became one of the country's
                           leading microbiologists by the age of 32.

MANN, John Dixon,    MD(St And.1880), MRCS(1862),  FRCP(1890, M 1880),
(1840-1912)          LKQCPI(1863), LSA(1862)
President 1894       Physician   to   Salford   Royal Hospital 1832.
                     Appointed lecturer in forensic medicine   and
                     toxicology in 1885 and promoted to a Chair in
                     1812. His text book ran to four editions. Awarded
                     the Swiney Prize in 1899.

MARSDEN, Richard Walter, BSc(Manc.1887), MB, ChB(Manc.1899), MD(1896),
(1868-1949)              DPH(Manc.1898), MRCS(1891),  FRCP(1921, M 1899,
Secretary 1906          L 1891)
Treasurer 1909-18       Appointed   medical   superintendent of Monsall
President 1928          Hospital in 1901, five years later he became
                        medical superintendent of Crumpsall Hospital.
                        General physician under whose leadership
                        Crumpsall Hospital gained a high reputation.
                        After retiring in 1933, he was recalled to take
                        charge of the Emergency Medical Service in the
                        second world war.

MELLOR, Thomas, FRCS(1852, M 1834), LSA(1830)
(c1808-1884)         Anatomical   demonstrator at Marsden Street in
President 1868       1838. Became surgeon to the Female Penitentiary
                     and to Henshaw's Blind Asylum.

MILLIGAN, Sir William, Kt(1914),  MB, CM(Hons Aberd.1886),  MD(Highest
(1864-1929)            Hons 1892), LLD(1927)
President 1922         Appointed assistant surgeon to the Manchester Ear
                       Hospital in 1890.  Two years later became the
                       first  Lecturer on diseases of the ear. A
                       brilliant surgeon, he pioneered the use of radium
                       and diathemy in his speciality.

MORGAN, John Edward, BA(Oxon.1852), MA(1860), BM(Oxon.1861), MD(1865),
(1828-1892)          FRCP(1868, M 1861)
President 1874       Physician in Salford. Lectured first in pathology
                     and   then in medicine at the Royal School.
                     Appointed to the honorary staff of Manchester
                     Royal Infirmary in 1867. Elected to the Chair of
                     medicine at Owens College in 1873.  He campaigned

successfully for the right of the University to confer medical degrees.He was largely responsible for the founding of the Nurse Training Institute in Manchester.

MORITZ, Siegmond, MSc(Hon.Manc.1908), MD(Würtzburg 1877), MRCP(1881, (c1854-1932)    M(L) 1842)
President 1907    Born in Berlin. Studied at Berlin, Leipzig and Würtzburg. Came to Manchester in 1878 and was resident medical officer at Manchester Royal Infirmary for ten years. Became lecturer in diseases of the throat and nose in 1904. Until 1923, he was medical officer at the Manchester Hospital for Consumption.

MORLEY, John, MB, ChB(1st cl.Hons Manc.1908), ChM(1911), FRCS(1911, M (1885-1974)    1911), LRCP(1911)
President 1947    Appointed honorary surgeon to Ancoats Hospital at
"    1953    the age of 26, and became lecturer in applied anatomy. In the first world war, he established a forward operating theatre on the Gallipoli beach and received the Croix de Chevalier, d'Honneur.Joined the honorary staff of Manchester Royal Infirmary in 1923 and was elected to the Chair of surgery in 1936.

MUMFORD, Alfred Alexander, BSc(Manc.1904), MB(Lond.1887), MD(1889), (c1863-1943)    MRCS(1885), LSA(1885)
President 1926    Entered general practice and in 1903 founded the Greengate Dispensary and School for Cripples. Became consulting surgeon to the Northern Hospital and medical officer to Manchester Grammar school where he studied the growth of healthy boys. Provided Bosdin Leech (q.v.) with much information for the Society's biographical files.

MURRAY, George Redmayne, BA(1st cl.Hons Cantab.1886), MA(1895), MB (1865-1939)    (Cantab.1889), MD(1896), MRCS(1888), FRCP(1898, M
President 1924    1891), DL
Went to Berlin and Paris before working with Horsley at University College, London where he suggested that extracts of ovine thyroid glands might be used to treat myxoedema and so may be regarded as the father of endocrinology. After teaching bacteriology at Newcastle when Heath Professor of comparative pathology, he was elected physician to Newcastle Royal Infirmary. Appointed to the Chair of medicine at Manchester in 1908, he achieved a reputation as the leading physician in the city.

NEWELL, Robert Leech, MB, ChB(Manc.1916), MD(1921), FRCS(1921), (1894-1969)    M 1916), LRCP(1916)
President 1957    Was responsible for the evacuation of the wounded after the Battle of Piave and was awarded the Croce di Guerra in 1918. Commanded the Prisoner

of War Hospital at Arquata.  Appointed first to the honorary staffs of the Northern Hospital and Stockport Infirmary and then of the Manchester Royal Infirmary in 1936, he became a consultant twelve years later.  He was largely responsible for the founding of the department of medical illustration.  From 1936 to 1948 he was secretary of the Manchester Joint Hospital Advisory Board (the first in the U.K. to co-ordinate work of different hospitals).  He became Chairman of the British Medical Association's Consultant and Specialist Committee.

NIVEN, James, MA(Cantab.1877), AM(Aberd.1870), LLD(1910), MB(Cantab. (1851-1925)        1880), BCh(Cantab.1889).
                      See Biography 7.6.

NOBLE, Daniel, AM(Hon.St And.1860), MD(St And.1853), FRCS(1852, M (1810-1885)        1833), FRCP(1859, M 1859), LSA(1833)
Secretary 1838   Became a general practitioner in Manchester in
Treasurer 1859   the year the Society was founded.  During the
President 1864   typhus epidemic of 1847, he was in charge of the
                      medical arrangements in the city.  Became medical
                      officer to the Manchester Union (Workhouse).
                      Wrote on hypnotism, psychology and physiology of
                      the nervous system and typhus. Was also President
                      of the Manchester Statistical Society.

OLIVER, Thomas Herbert, BA(Cantab.1909), MA(1913), MB, ChB(Manc.1912), (1887-1961)        MD(1919), FRCP(1931, M 1920)
President 1939-43  After the first world war, was appointed
                      assistant director of the clinical laboratory at
                      Manchester Royal Infirmary and lecturer in
                      medicine in 1921.  Joined the honorary staff of
                      the Infirmary in 1934 and was elected to the
                      Chair of clinical medicine five years later,
                      resigning in 1946 to occupy the Chair of
                      therapeutics.

OWEN, Simeon Holgate, MD(QUI 1872), MRCS(1869), MRCP(1888), LSA(1869) (1844-1909)        Medical officer of health for Moss Side.Assistant
Treasurer 1908    physician at Manchester Royal Infirmary and
                      physician to the Northern Hospital for Women and
                      Children.

PATERSON, James Ralston Kennedy, CBE(1949), MC(1917), MB, ChB(Hons (1897-1981)        Edin.1923), MD(Comm.1927), FRCS(1948), FRCS(Edin.
                      1926), DMRE(Cantab.1924), FFR 1938)
                      See Biography 7.20.

PLATT, John Edward, MB(Lond.1889), BS(Hons 1891), MS(1894), MD(1890), (1865-1910)        FRCS(1891, M 1888), LRCP(1888)
Secretary 1902-05  Joined the staff of Manchester Royal Infirmary
                      becoming a full surgeon in 1905.  Was a
                      demonstrator of anatomy and later lecturer in
                      practical surgery.  Was joint editor of the
                      *Medical Chronicle* but his greatest contribution

to the Manchester Medical Society was to re-catalogue the periodicals in the library.

PLATT, Robert, LORD PLATT OF GRINDLEFORD, Baron(Life Peer 1967),    Bt
(1900-1978)                 (1959), MSc(Manc.1949), MB, ChB(Sheff.1921),   MD
President 1962              (1923), FRCP(1935, M 1925)
                           See Biography 7.22

RADFORD, Thomas, MD(Heidelburg 1839),  FRCS(1852, M 1817),  FRCP(Edin.
(1793-1881)                (1839), LSA(1817)
Treasurer 1834-41          Joined the Manchester  and  Salford Lying-in
President 1841             Hospital as Surgeon, 1818.   Later moved to St
                          Mary's Hospital. Founded the Manchester School of
                          Medicine in 1825 and was lecturer  in  midwifery.
                          His lecture on caesarean section in 1854 was  the
                          first obstetric address to be  delivered  to  the
                          Provincial (now British) Medical Association.  He
                          and his wife were mainly instrumental in  raising
                          the money to build a new St Mary's Hospital  (now
                          the Hospital for Diseases of the Skin).   In  1853
                          he presented his library to  St Mary's;   it  was
                          transferred to the University in 1927 which named
                          the then undergraduate Reading Room after him.

RAILTON, Thomas Carleton,   BSc(Manc.1882),  MB(Hons Lond.1873),   MD
(1844-1922)                (1882), FRCS(1872, M 1869), MRCP(1888)
Secretary 1890-93          Surgeon to the  Hulme  Dispensary  and  medical
President 1900             officer of health for Chorlton,  later Withington
                          and then West Didsbury Districts.Became physician
                          to   the  Clinical  (later  known  as  Northern)
                          Hospital for  Women  and  Children.  He  wrote on
                          rickets,  conditions  required for healthy houses
                          and the early symptoms of infectious fevers.

RAMSBOTTOM, Albert, MC, MB, ChB(Manc.1901), MD(1906), DPH(1903),  FRCP
(1877-1951)                (1920 M 1908)
President 1929             Physician. Won  the  military cross when serving
                          with a field ambulance unit.  He  returned to the
                          Manchester  Royal  Infirmary and succeeded to the
                          Chair of clinical medicine in 1921.  He  was only
                          the second provincial Fellow to be elected Censor
                          of the Royal College of Physicians.

RANSOME, Arthur, BA(Cantab.1857), MA(1860), MB(Cantab.1858), MD(1869),
(1834-1922)                FRCP(1899 M 1895), LSA(1856), LM(Dubl.1853),  FRS
President 1876             (1884)
                           See Biography 7.5.

RAPER, Henry Stanley, CBE(1919), BSc(Leeds 1923), MSc(Manc.1924),  DSc
(1882-1951)                (Leeds 1910),  MB,  ChB(Leeds 1910),  FRCP(Hon.
President 1938             1938), FRIC(1918), FRS(1929)
                          Elected to the Brackenbury Chair of Physiology in
                          1923. Later acted as Pro-Vice-Chancellor of  the
                          University.Pioneer in the field of fat metabolism
                          and,  with Alfred Alexander Harper  and  Henry
                          Taylor Howat, discovered the  enzyme pancreozymin
                          (cholecystokinin).

RAY, John Howson, MB, ChB(Manc.1894), ChM(1896), FRCS(1896, M 1894),
(1870-1946)          LRCP(1894)
President 1930        First to be awarded the ChM degree from the
                     University. On the honorary staff of Salford
                     Royal Hospital. Subsequently appointed to the
                     honorary staff of the Manchester Royal Infirmary
                     but it is for his work with crippled children at
                     Pendlebury that he is best remembered.

RAYNER, Henry Herbert, MB, ChB(Manc.1901), FRCS(1907, M 1907)
(1879-1960)          Surgeon, Manchester Royal Infirmary. One of the
                     founder members in 1922 of the Manchester
                     Surgical Society.

REID, Henry, MD(Edin.1843), LRCS(Edin.1842)
(   -1868)           Senior surgeon to the Ardwick and Ancoats
Secretary 1846-50    Dispensary and a demonstrator of anatomy. His
                     thesis on the statistics of amputation won the
                     Inaugural Prize.

RENAUD, Frank, MD(Edin.1844), MRCS(1844), LSA(1844)
(1819-1904)          Of Huguenot stock. Appointed in 1845 honorary
Secretary 1845       physician to the Ardwick and Ancoats Dispensary.
                     Elected to the staff of Manchester Royal
                     Infirmary, 1848. Taught medical jurisprudence,
                     then pathology and morbid anatomy at Pine Street.
                     Was regarded as one of the most scientific
                     medical men in Manchester, writing histories of
                     the Infirmary and House of Recovery (the first
                     purpose built infectious diseases hospital in
                     England). In 1859, he catalogued the Infirmary
                     and Portico libraries.

REYNOLDS, Ernest Septimus, BSc(Manc.1904), MB(Lond.1884), MD(1885),
(1861-1926)          MRCS(1883), FRCP(1896, M 1888), LSA(1883), DL
Secretary 1899-1901  Appointed to the honorary staff of Ancoats
President 1912       Hospital, he later joined that of the Manchester
                     Royal Infirmary. He lectured on the tropical
                     diseases and was elevated to the Chair of
                     clinical medicine in 1912. Best remembered for
                     his detection of the arsenical adulteration of
                     local beer in 1900.

RITCHIE, Christopher Currie, MB, CM(Hons Edin.1867), MD(1869), LM
(1842-1873)          (Edin.1867)
Librarian 1871       He came to Manchester Royal Infirmary as a
Secretary 1872       resident assistant physician in 1869 and was
                     appointed honorary physician to the Hulme
                     Dispensary the following year. His early death
                     terminated a promising 'career of research'.

ROBERTON, John, LRCS(Edin.1817), LSA(1822)
(1797-1876)          See Biography 7.3.

ROBERTS, David Lloyd, MD(St And.1859), FRCP(1878), MRCS(1857), LSA
(1834-1920)          (1857)
President 1873       Entered general practice in 1857, subsequently

joining the honorary staff of St Mary's Hospital. This gynaecologist played a prominent role in the amalgamation of the Manchester Women's Hospitals. In 1898 he produced a new edition of *Religio Medici* by Thomas Browne. He left money for the endowment of Lloyd Roberts Lectures in Manchester and London.

ROBERTS, Sir William, Kt(1885),   BA(Highest Hons Lond.1851),   MB(Lond. (1830-1899)   1853), MD(1854), MRCS(1853),   FRCP(1865, M 1860), Secretary 1859-63   LSA(1853), FRS(1877) President 1865   Elected physician at Manchester Royal Infirmary at the age of 25.   From 1859 he lectured on pathology and on medicine four years later, and was elected Professor in 1873. One of the first to demonstrate that knowledge of physiology might aid the treatment of disease, he wrote on the renal tract and his research on the digestive system added liquor pancreaticus to the Pharmacopoeia. He moved to London in 1887.

ROGET, Peter Mark, MD(Edin.1798), FRCP(Hon.1831, L 1809, Censor 1834), (1779-1894)   FRS(1815) Of Anglo-Swiss parentage. Physician to Manchester Royal Infirmary from 1805-7. During this time he taught physiology and prepared the earliest known (1806) outline of anatomy and physiology lectures. The first draft of his *Thesaurus of English Words and Phrases* was prepared in Manchester but was not published until 1852. Following his return to London, he developed the slide-rule in 1814. As a result he was elected to the Royal Society, of which he was secretary from 1827 to 1849.

ROSS, James, MB, CM(Hons Aberd.1863), MD(1864), LLD(Aberd.1883),   FRCP (1837-1892)   1882, M 1876) President 1889   After practising in Lancashire, he was appointed pathologist to Manchester Royal Infirmary and physician to the Children's Department of the Southern Hospital in 1876. Two years later he was elected to the Infirmary's honorary staff and became Professor of medicine in 1887. A neurologist, he did valuable work on the mechanisms and pathways of referred pain from a diseased viscus.

SATTERTHWAITE, Michael, MD(Hons Edin.1837), DipRCS(Edin.1837) (1812-1861)   Physician, Manchester Royal Infirmary from 1844 Secretary 1840-43   to 1847 when he joined his future brother-in-law to run a boarding school for boys near Preston.

SAVATARD, Louis Charles Arthur, MSc(Hon.Manc.1945), LSA(1903) (1874-1962)   A dermatologist who served on the Home Office Committee on Mule-Spinners' Cancer, he was one of the few medical persons to have an honorary MSc conferred upon him by the University.

SCHLAPP, Walter, BSc(Edin.1922), PhD(1929), MB, ChB(Edin.1929)
(1898-1966)              After a year in the Pharmacology Department in
President 1960           1930 he moved to Physiology and was elected to
                         Brackenbury Chair in 1946. He was Dean of the
                         Medical Faculty twice and also of Music for some
                         years. From 1957 to 1961 he served as a Pro-Vice-
                         Chancellor of the University.

SHAW, Sir William Fletcher, Kt(1942), MB, ChB(Manc.1903), MD(Gold
(1878-1961)              Medal 1906), FRCP(1939), F(R)COG(1929)
President 1937           See Biography 7.16.
     "      1951

SIMMONS, Harry Teesdale, BSc(Manc.1926), MB, ChB(Manc.1924), ChM
(1903-1972)              (1935), MD(1939), MRCS(1928), LRCP(1928)
President 1961           Hunterian Professor at the Royal College of
                         Surgeons in 1935, working on the sympathetic
                         nervous system. Appointed consultant to
                         Manchester Royal Infirmary in 1947.

SIMPSON, Henry, MB(Lond.1859), MD(1861), MRCS(1851), LSA(1852)
(1829-1911)              Practised in Lymm from 1852 until 1864 when he
President 1869           moved to Manchester. Was the last to be elected
                         by subscribers' votes to the honorary staff of
                         Manchester Royal Infirmary in 1866. He said later
                         that canvassing the voters 'was a task from which
                         my soul revolted'.

SINCLAIR, Sir William Japp, MA(Aberd.1869), MB, CM(Hons Aberd.1873),
(1846-1912)              MD(1875), MRCP(1875)
                         Resident medical officer at St Mary's Hospital
                         and house surgeon to the Clinical (or Northern)
                         Hospital for Women and Children, he then became
                         honorary physician to the Southern Hospital
                         becoming the sole consultant after the death of
                         Sir John Thorburn. Elected to the Chair at Owens
                         in 1888. Played a prominent part in the
                         controversy over the Midwives Bill, later
                         becoming a member of the Central Midwives Board.
                         Was the chief promoter of the *Journal of
                         Obstetrics and Gynaecology of the British Empire.*

SMITH, James Lorrain, MA(Edin.1884), MB, CM(Edin.1889), MD(1893), FRS
(1862-1931)              (1909)
                         Was largely responsible for the foundation of the
                         Pathological Society of Great Britain which first
                         met in Manchester in 1906. Achieved international
                         recognition for his work on fatty degeneration
                         and (after his return to Edinburgh) the devising
                         of the antiseptic Eusol (Edinburgh University
                         Solution).

SMITH, John William, TD, MB, CM(1st cl.Hons Edin.1886), FRCS(1890, M
(1864-1926)              1886), DL
Treasurer 1901-07        After various appointments in Manchester he
President 1919           volunteered for the Boer War in 1900 and returned
                         to the honorary staff of Manchester Royal

Infirmary. He became Professor of systematic surgery in 1911 and three years later with Frederic Hibbert Westmacott (1867-1935) an ear, nose and throat surgeon, he was responsible for the mobilisation of the Second Western General Military Hospital which grew into a remarkable establishment of 18,000 beds in 170 hospitals scattered throughout the North West.

SOMERFORD, Alexander Robert, MB, ChB(Manc.1924), MD(1930)
(c1902-c1974)
Treasurer 1935-39

Won the Bradley Memorial Scholarship for surgery but trained as a dermatologist and syphilologist.

SOUTHAM, Frederick Armitage, BA(Oxon.1873),  MA(1877),  MB(Oxon.1877),
(1850-1927)
Secretary 1885-89
President 1895

MRCS(1876), LSA(1876)
Son of George Southam (q.v.). Trained in Surgery at Manchester Royal Infirmary. Appointed to the honorary staff in 1880, and to the Chair of clinical surgery in 1900.

SOUTHAM, George, FRCS(Elec.1853, M 1838), LSA(1836)
(1815-1876)

Taught by Jordan, after an early career in Salford, he went to Manchester Royal Infirmary as a dispensary surgeon, becoming an honorary full surgeon five years after he founded the Chatham Street School of Medicine in 1850. After the amalgamations (first with Pine Street and then Owens) he was Professor of surgery and Director of medical studies. He was on the council of the Royal College of Surgeons during 1873-6 and concurrently President of the Council of the British Medical Association.

STEELL, Graham, MB(Edin.1872), MD(Gold Medal 1877), FRCP(1889, M 1877)
(1851-1942)
President 1897

After leaving Edinburgh in 1878 he came to be regarded as the leading cardiologist (of his time) in the North of England. First described his eponymous murmur of pulmonary regurgitation at a meeting of the Society in 1888. Appointed to the Chair of clinical medicine in 1907.

STOCKS, Alfred William, MRCS(1854), LSA(1853)
(    -1910)
President 1892

Since he had won so many medals at Pine Street, it was agreed that a microscope should be presented to him instead of yet another medal. Appointed surgeon to the Salford and Pendleton Hospital and Dispensary in 1854. Became superintendent of dissection at the Royal School.

STOPFORD, John Sebastian Bach,    LORD STOPFORD OF FALLOWFIELD,    Baron
(1881-1961)
President 1931

(Life Peer 1958),  Kt(1941),   KBE(1955, M 1920), MB, ChB(Manc.1911),   MD(Gold Medal 1915),   FRCS (Hon.1955), FRS(1927)
See Biography 7.18.

SUTHERLAND, Donald McKay, MB, ChB(Manc.1917),  MD(1921),  FRCS(1921, M
(1893-1962)          1921)
Secretary 1932-34    After holding all the available house officer
                     posts in Manchester Royal Infirmary he trained as
                     a surgeon and was appointed to the honorary staff
                     in 1942.


SYKES, Charles Ernest, TD, MB, ChB(Manc.1927), FFA RCS(1948), DA(1935)
(1899-1978)          Appointed in 1929 honorary anaesthetist to the
Treasurer 1952-57    Jewish Hospital. Also worked at Ancoats, Park and
President 1959       the  Royal Eye Hospitals.   Was Chairman of
                     Convocation of the University of Manchester in
                     1938. Served in the artillery in the first world
                     war and became advisor in anaesthetics to Eastern
                     Command in India in the second.   Subsequently
                     appointed as a consultant at Withington and
                     Christie Hospitals.


TELFORD, Evelyn Davison,  BA(Cantab.1897),  MA(1902),  MSc(Manc.1929),
(1876-1961)          BCh(Cantab.1903), FRCS(1903, M 1900), LRCP(1900),
Secretary 1908-10    See Biography 7.13.
President 1932


THORBURN, John, MD(Edin.1855), LRCS(1855), LSA(1857)
(1834-1885)          Entered general practice in Manchester in  1858.
Secretary 1864-67    Subsequently succeeded to John Roberton's (q.v.)
President 1871       gynaecological    practice,    being    largely
Treasurer 1873-78    responsible for the foundation of the Southern
                     Hospital  for   Women   and   Children.    First
                     obstetrician to be elected to the honorary staff
                     of the Royal Infirmary.  Lecturer at Pine Street.
                     First Professor of obstetrics at Owens, 1876-85.


THORBURN, Sir William, KBE(1919), CB(1916), CMG(1919), BSc(Lond.1880),
(1861-1923)          MB(Lond.1884), MD(1885), FRCS(1886 M 1883), DL
President 1905       Determined the distribution of the spinal sensory
                     pathways and won the  Jacksonian  prize of  the
                     Royal College of Surgeons in 1890 for his work
                     correlating the level of spinal cord injury with
                     the resulting paralysis.   Joined the honorary
                     staff of Manchester Royal Infirmary in  1889 and
                     became a full surgeon in 1900, having been
                     Hunterian Professor of surgery and pathology at
                     the Royal College of Surgeons in 1894.  Knighted
                     for his services in the 1914-18 war. As president
                     he brought the Society's library into closer
                     association with the  University's  medical
                     library.


TOD, Margaret Christine, MB, ChB(Hons Edin.1924), FRCS(Edin.1927), FFR
(c1893-1953)         (1938), DR(1936)
                     The best student in her year, she trained to be a
                     surgeon but became interested in  radiotherapy.
                     Appointed Assistant Director of the Christie
                     Hospital and Holt Radium Institute in 1937.
                     Served on the Radium Commission in 1945. Awarded

the Roentgen Medal by the British Institute of Radiology in 1951.

TURNER, Thomas, FRCS(1843, M 1816; one of the original 300 founder
(1793-1873)            Fellows), LSA(1816)
                       See Biography 7.2.

TWINING, Edward Wing, MRCS(1913), LRCP(1913), MRCP(1938, L 1913), DMRE
(1887-1939)            (Cantab.1923)
                       A post in neuroradiology was specially created
                       for him at Manchester Royal Infirmary and he
                       joined the honorary staff in 1928. Awarded the
                       MRCP for his three-volume textbook of Radiology.
                       Appointed Hunterian Professor at the Royal
                       College of Surgeons in 1938.

TYLECOTE, Frank Edward, CBE(1956), MB, ChB(Manc.1902), MD(1904), DPH
(1879-1965)            (Manc.1906), FRCP(1923, M 1907), JP
Treasurer 1919-25      His MD thesis was on the pharmacology and
                       therapeutics of uranium. Joined the visiting
                       staff of Manchester Royal Infirmary in 1914.
                       Appointed Professor of medicine in 1929. He was
                       one of the earliest to connect cigarette smoking
                       with lung cancer. After he retired, he became an
                       Alderman of the City of Manchester in 1949.

WALKER, John, LFP&S(Glas.1829), LSA(1823)
(c1803-1847)           Assistant surgeon to the Eye Hospital and surgeon
Secretary 1834-35      to the Manchester Union (Workhouse). Published
    "     1838-40      a course of lectures on the eye in the *Lancet*
                       (1839-41). It was he who with Joseph Peel Catlow
                       (q.v.) canvassed the medical men in Manchester
                       about the formation of the Medical Society in
                       1834.

WARD, John Forbes, MB, ChB(Manc.1909), MD(1920), MRCS(1912), FRCP
(1886-1950)            (1938, M 1919)
Treasurer 1925-30      Paediatrician. Appointed a lecturer in the
                       subject in 1934 and held the post until his
                       death.

WHITE, Charles Powell, BA(Cantab.1889), MA(1897), MB, ChB(Cantab.
(1867-1930)            1896), MD(1900), FRCS(1896, M 1894), LRCP(1894)
Secretary's            The first holder of the Pilkington Research
Assistant 1911-18      Studentship. Appointed in 1915 a special
                       lecturer in pathology to continue his researches
                       on tumours. Subsequently became the Director of
                       the Helen Swindell's Cancer Research Laboratory.
                       Was also Treasurer of the Pathological Society.

WHITEHEAD, Walter, FRCS(Edin.1866), LSA(1864)
(1840-1913)            Honorary surgeon at St Mary's Hospital from 1867
Secretary 1874-78      until 1873 when he joined the Infirmary staff.
President 1884         Appointed lecturer in surgery in 1884, he
                       succeeded to the Chair eight years later. He
                       achieved an international reputation for his
                       operation of glossectomy. The Manchester and

Salford Hospital for Diseases of the Skin was separated from the Lock and Skin Hospital largely by his efforts. He was mainly responsible for the organisation of the British Medical Association Meeting at Manchester in 1902, over which he presided.

WILD, Robert Briggs, BSc(Manc.1883),   MSc(1889),   MB(Lond.1886),   MD
(1862-1941)             (1887), MRCS(1885), FRCP(1912, M 1898), LSA(1884)
President 1920          Most of his career was spent in the University Department of Pharmacology where he was elected to the Chair of materia medica and therapeutics in 1901. A leading Manchester dermatologist, he was also on the honorary staff of the Christie Cancer Pavilion and Home, and was especially interested in the action of analgesics.

WILKINSON, Arthur Thomas,  BA(Lond.1872),  BSc(Lond.1874),   BSc(Manc.
(1853-1945)              1882), MD(Lond.1880), MRCS(1876), FRCP(1907, M
President 1908          1888), LSA(1876)
                        Entered general practice in Stockport and Oldham. Also an anaesthetist at Manchester Royal Infirmary, he joined the honorary staff in 1892 as a physician and then specialised in diseases of the kidney.

WILKINSON, Matthew Alexander Eason, MD(Edin.1838), FRCP(1869)
(1813-1878             Physician to the Ardwick and Ancoats Dispensary, he was elected in 1844 to the honorary staff of Manchester Royal Infirmary.     Interested in infectious diseases, he was the only visiting physician to Monsall (fever) Hospital.  He gave the medical address (on scrofula) at the Provincial Medical and Surgical Association's Oxford meeting in 1852 and presided over the BMA meeting in Manchester in 1877.

WILLIAMSON, Richard Thomas, MB, BS(Lond.1885),  MD(1887),  MRCS(1884),
(1862-1937)             FRCP(1900, M 1890), LSA(1884)
                        Trained as a neurologist but did not become an honorary physician until he joined the staff at Ancoats in 1899 and at the Royal Infirmary three years later. Is credited with the introduction of the ophthalmoscope to Manchester.Was an authority on diabetes mellitus in the pre-insulin era.First lecturer in nervous diseases.  Observed that tumour cells were always present in the walls of cerebellar cysts.

WILSON, Alexander, FRCS(1890, M 1883), LRCP(1883), DL
(1860-1931)             Appointed to the newly created post of chloroformist at the Manchester Royal Infirmary in 1886. Worked as a general practitioner and at St Luke's Clinic. Twenty years later he was the first anaesthetist to join the Infirmary's honorary staff. In 1917 he took charge of the newly opened Venereal Diseases Department.

Commanded the 2nd Western General Hospital for a year and was appointed a Deputy Lieutenant of Lancashire after his war service.

WILSON, Sydney Rawson, BSc(1st cl.Hons Manc.1902), MSc(1903), MB, BS
(1882-1927)                (Lond.1905), MB, ChB(Hons Manc.1905), FRCS(Edin. 1910)
Was the first to show that mule spinners' cancer was an occupational disease. Subsequently he became the senior anaesthetist at Manchester Royal Infirmary and pioneered many new methods becoming one of the foremost authorities in the country. He is believed to have died during the course of an anaesthetic experiment.

WILSON, William James, FRCS(1843, M 1813; one of the original 300
(1792-1885)                Fellows)
President 1843             Was mainly instrumental in founding the Manchester Institute for Curing Diseases of the Eye where he worked for twelve years. Coincidentally he was on the staff of the Lying-In Hospital and remained a consulting surgeon there after he was elected to the honorary staff of Manchester Royal Infirmary in 1826. He presided over the 1854 Manchester meeting of the Provincial Medical and Surgical Association (later the BMA).

WINDSOR, John, FRCS(Hon.1844, M 1812)
(1787-1868)               Started to practise in Manchester in 1815 and
Treasurer 1849-58         became senior surgeon to the Eye Hospital. In
Ex Officio Chairman       1837, he lectured in medical jurisprudence,
of Meetings 1850-58       medical science and midwifery. He introduced the
President 1859            stethoscope to Manchester after visiting Laennec
Treasurer 1860-62         in Paris in 1822.

WINDSOR, Thomas, MRCS(1853), LSA(1854)
(1831-1910)               After qualifying he held several posts before
Secretary 1859            being appointed to the honorary staffs of the
President 1866            Royal Eye Hospital and Manchester Royal
Librarian 1858-83         Infirmary. Regarded as one of the best eye surgeons in the country, he was appointed lecturer on ophthalmology at Owens in 1874. As honorary librarian, he increased the collection fivefold during the quinquennium 1858-63 and continued to add to it during his extensive foreign travels. It was his idea to house the collection in the Medical School and he superintended its execution.

WRIGHT, Garnett, MB, ChB(Edin.1900), FRCS(1905, M 1905)
(1878-1945)               On the surgical staff at Ancoats Hospital he
President 1936            joined the staff at Salford Royal Hospital in 1910. Vice-president of the Section of Surgery at the British Medical Association Meeting in Manchester in 1929, his address was on thyroidectomy.

WRIGHT, George Arthur, BA(Oxon.1874),    MB(Oxon.1877),    FRCS(1878, M
(1851-1920)           1877), LSA(1877)
President 1898         Came to Manchester in 1880 to join the  staff  of
                      the Royal Infirmary and  in  1882  was  appointed
                      surgeon to the Children's Hospital at Pendlebury.
                      In  1900  he  was  appointed  to  the  Chair   of
                      systematic surgery.  First  surgeon  to  remove  a
                      dumb-bell neuroma from the spinal cord. His book
                      on diseases of the hip was a classic,  and he was
                      co-author  of   Henry  Ashby's  (q.v.)   book  on
                      diseases of children.  He played  a  considerable
                      role in the transfer of the Royal Infirmary  from
                      Piccadilly to Oxford Road and was responsible for
                      the provision of Lister House  as  a  hostel  for
                      medical students.


YOUNG, Alfred Harry, MB, CM(Edin.1876), FRCS(1880, M 1880)
(1852-1912)          Joined the Anatomy Department at Owens  in  1877.
President 1901       After working as registrar in pathology, medicine
                     and surgery, he became surgeon to  Salford  Royal
                     Hospital  in  1883.    Two  years  later  he  was
                     appointed to the Chair of Anatomy later  becoming
                     Dean and Pro-Vice-Chancellor. His research was on
                     the anatomy and development of blood vessels.

                                                                    AFT

APPENDIX 3

SOURCES AND REFERENCES

Note: Reference is made below, and in various places in this volume to the 'Manchester Medical Collection' or the 'Manchester Collection'. This unique collection includes: publications by and about medical men and women associated with Greater Manchester; their biographical details (the 'C' files); and information about many health service institutions, medical educational establishments and medical and other professional societies in the area. The Collection was initiated by Dr E Bosdin Leech (1875-1950) and is housed in the John Rylands University Library of Manchester (not on open access).

Chapter 1: The Manchester Medical Society, 1834-1950

Brockbank, E M: *A centenary history of the Manchester Medical Society with biographical notices of its first President, Secretaries and Honorary Librarian*, Manchester, Sherratt and Hughes, 1934.

Chapter 2: The Societies which merged in 1950

1. Minutes of the Manchester Surgical Society, 1922-50 (two volumes), in the Manchester Collection, ref.H2e.
2. Platt, Sir Harry, 1971, The story of the Manchester Surgical Society, *Manchester Medical Gazette*, *50*, 3, 5-10 and 4, 19-24.
3. The Pathological Society of Manchester, 1885-1950 and the Manchester Pathological Society, 1846-49. A considerable quantity of records running to 25 volumes is available in the Manchester Collection, ref.H2c and H21.
4. Dible, J H, 1957, *Journal of Pathology and Bacteriology*, *72*, 1-35.
5. Maitland, H B and Evans, D G, 1937, *Journal of Pathology and Bacteriology*, *45*, 715.
6. Minutes of The Manchester and District Society of Anaesthetists, 1946-50 (one volume), in the Manchester Collection.
7. The Manchester Odontological Society, 1885-1920: the printed *Transactions* of the Society for the period of its existence are available in the Manchester Collection, ref.H2z.
8. Laws of the Manchester Odontological Society, *Transactions*, 1890-1, Appendix.
9. The Manchester Odontological Society, *Transactions*, 1890-1, 2.

Chapter 3: The re-formation of the Society in 1950

Manchester Medical Society documents relating to amalgamation of the several Societies: Manchester Collection, ref.H2a xv.

Chapter 4: The formation of new Sections since 1950

1. Associated General Practitioners in Medicine of Manchester and its Neighbourhood, 1834, Manchester Collection, ref.H2p.
2. Povey, W.P., 1982, *Aspects of public health in Manchester and District in the late 18th and early 19th centuries: the rise and decline of the Manchester Board of Health, 1796-1815*, University of Manchester, thesis for the degree of Master of Science in the Faculty of Medicine.
3. North Western Association of Medical Officers of Health (from 1875) and North Western Branch of the Society of Medical Officers of Health (from 1888): Minutes available 1875-94, 1904-25, 1942-65 in the Manchester Collection, ref H2v.
4. Cunningham, C, *Victorian and Edwardian Town Halls*, London, Routledge & Kegan Paul, 1981.
5. North Western Branch of the Society of Community Medicine, Minutes 1973-6.

Chapters 5 and 6: Activities and developments since 1950

Manchester Medical Society: Published annual reports for each year; and unpublished Minutes of meetings of the Society, of its various Sections, and of the Council of the Society and of the Council of each of the Sections.

Biography 7.1: Jordan

To avoid repetition, unless otherwise indicated in the text, all quotations are from the 'Life of Joseph Jordan'.
1. Jordan, F W: *Life of Joseph Jordan, Surgeon, and an account of the rise and progress of Medical Schools in Manchester, with some particulars of the life of Dr Edward Stephens*. London: Sherratt and Hughes, 1904.
2. Brockbank, E M: *Sketches on the lives and work of the honorary medical staff of the Manchester Infirmary from its foundation in 1752 to 1830 when it became the Royal Infirmary*. (W Simmons, MRCS; pp.170-81). Manchester, Sherratt and Hughes, 1904.
3. Shepherd, J A: The evolution of the provincial medical schools in England. Tenth Henry Cohen History of Medicine Lecture, 4 November 1981. *Annual Report Liverpool Medical Institution*, 1982-3; 14-39.
4. Chaloner, W H: *The movement for the extension of Owens College Manchester 1863-73*. Manchester University Press, 1973; 19-20.
5. *Manchester Guardian*, 26 December 1835. (In this issue it is also recorded that the applicants for the post of Infirmary Surgeon were A M Heath, T Fawdington, J Jordan and J A Ransome and that the election would take place on 31 December 1835.)
6. Brockbank, W: The early history of the Manchester Medical School. *Manchester Medical Gazette*, 1968, *47*, No.3.
7. *Manchester Guardian*, 18 February 1927. Medical teaching under difficulties. How beginnings were made in Manchester.
8. Mitchell, G A G: 'Resurrection Days'. *Manchester Medical Gazette* 1948, *27*, 150-55.

9. *Manchester Guardian*, 21 February 1824.
10. *Lancaster Gazette*, 7 October 1826.
11. *Trial of John Eaton*, Sexton of St George's Chapel, Manchester.    J Pratt, 11 Bridge Street, Manchester. N.D. but probably 1827.
12. *Manchester Guardian*, 18 October 1834.
13. *Lancet*. Obituary notice, 31 May 1873.
14. Bellot, T: Galen *On the hand*; translated by Thomas Bellot and Joseph Jordan. Available in one of the bound volumes of articles, etc., collected by T Windsor and now in the John Rylands University Library. Main title page missing, but Library Catalogue gives place and date of publication as London, 1856.
15. Jordan, J: A case of obliteration of the aorta. *New England Medical Surgery Journal* 1830; pp 101-4.
16. *Manchester Guardian*, 2 April 1873.

## Biography 7.2: Turner

1. Turner, T: *Memoir by a Relative*. London: Simpkin Marshall and Co., 1875.
2. Wall, C: *A History of the Worshipful Society of Apothecaries of London*. Underwood, E A, Ed. Oxford University Press, 1963, 192-6.
3. Cope, Z: *The History of the Royal College of Surgeons of England*. London: Anthony Blond, 1959, 42-6.
4. Willcock, J W: *The Laws relating to the Medical Profession*. London: J and W T Clarke, 1830; ccxxxvi.
5. Copeman, W S C: *A History of the Worshipful Society of Apothecaries of London*: Pergamon Press, 1967; 58.
6. Royal College of Surgeons of Edinburgh: *Regulations to be Observed by Candidates*. Edinburgh, 1820; 7.
7. Society of Apothecaries *Annual Reports of the Court of Examiners*, 1816-18. Guildhall Library, M.S. 8239/1, London.
8. Brockbank, E M: *The Foundation of Provincial Medical Education in England*. Manchester University Press, 1936; 88.
9. Royal College of Surgeons of Edinburgh: *Minute and Letter Books*, 1825.
10. Royal College of Surgeons of London: *Minutes of the Court of Examiners*, 1826 and 1830; 34-5.
11. Jordan, F W: *Life of Joseph Jordan*. Manchester, Sherratt and Hughes, 1904; 43.
12. Manchester Royal Infirmary: *Minutes of the Board of Trustees*, 1835; 269.

## Biograohy 7.3: Roberton

1. Dictionary of National Biography, 1896, *48*, 373.
2. Carver, Anne: *John Roberton, surgeon, 1797-1876*. Gloucester, 1969.
3. Phillips, Miles H, 1938, The History of the Prevention of Puerperal Fever, *British Medical Journal*, *1*, 1-6.
4. *The English Independent*, 31 August 1876, 912.
5. Ashton, T S: *Economic and Social Investigations in Manchester, 1833-1933*. London, P S King & Son Ltd., 1934.
6. Young, J H, 1967, John Roberton (1797-1876), Obstetrician and Hospital Reformer, *Manchester Medical Gazette*, *42*, 2, 14-19.
7. King, Anthony, 1966, Revised Thoughts on the Origin of the Pavilion Principle in England, *Medical History*, *10*, 363.

Biography 7.4: Gaskell

Anon, 1886, The late Samuel Gaskell, Esq. (Occasional Notes of the Quarter). *Journal of Mental Science, 32,* 235-6.

Gaskell, S, 1859, On the want of better provision for the labouring and middle classes when attacked or threatened with insanity. *Journal of Mental Science, 6,* 321-7.

*Guest-Gornall, R G.* Unpublished manuscript in John Rylands Library, University of Manchester.

Hunter, R and Macalpine, I: *Three Hundred Years of Psychiatry.* London: Oxford University Press, 1963.

Notes and News, 1881, *Journal of Mental Science, 27,* 444-5.

Biography 7.5: Ransome

1. Obituaries in *Lancet,* 5 August 1922, 301-2, and *British Medical Journal,* 12 August 1922, 285-6.
2. Manchester Medical Society Roll of Members 1840-1898, under the year 1859, gives details of Ransome's offices and papers.
3. Power, Sir D'Arcy, 1930, *Plarr's Lives of the Fellows of the Royal College of Surgeons of England volume 2,* 212-214; Manchester Medical Society, Minutes of Council volume 1 1834-54, passim. Arthur Ransome's three sons also became doctors though not in Manchester: for their careers see *The Medical Directory* from the 1890s.
4. Ransome, Arthur, undated typescript autobiography: 'Some Great and Good Men and Women I have Known', 19-66, Manchester Collection.
5. Ransome, autobiography, 66-7, 75, 95; *The Medical Directory,* 1856 to 1922, passim; Brown, G H, 1955, *Munk's Roll of the Lives of the Fellows of the Royal College of Physicians of London, volume 4, 1826-1925,* 412-3.
6. Ransome, autobiography, 74-6, 103-4; Manchester Hospital for Consumption: Minutes from 1875, Manchester City Archives, and *Annual Reports* from 1875 with gaps, Manchester Local History Library, and Manchester Collection.
7. See obituaries and see Ransome, autobiography, 118-120. A list of Ransome's writings and copies of many of his works are held in the Manchester Collection.
8. Manchester and Salford Sanitary Association: *Annual Reports* 1853-1900, Minutes 1890-1924, Manchester City Archives. Ransome, Arthur, 1902, *History of the Sanitary Association;* Ransome, autobiography, 75-85.
9. Thompson, Joseph, 1886, *The Owens College, its Foundation and Growth,* 232, 631; Ransome, autobiography, 105-7, 109.

Biography 7.6: Niven

Borough of Oldham Reports of the Medical Officer of Health 1884-93.

City of Manchester Reports of the Medical Officer of Health 1894-1921, 1963-66 and 1973.

Annual Health Reports, Manchester and Salford Sanitary Association 1866-70.

Obituary for Dr James Niven, *Lancet,* 10 October 1925.

Obituary for Dr James Niven, *British Medical Journal,* 10 October and 17 October 1925.

James Niven: *Observations on the History of Public Health Effort*

*in Manchester 1894-1922*, published 1923.
W P Povey: *Aspects of Public Health in Manchester and District in the late Eighteenth and early Nineteenth Centuries - The Rise and Decline of the Manchester Board of Health 1796-1815*, unpublished MSc Thesis, University of Manchester 1982.
*Manchester Guardian*, 1 October 1925.
Sutton, C W: *Lancashire Authors Vol. II*, Manchester Local History Library, press article on appointment of Dr Niven, dated 2 February 1894.
Asa Briggs: *Victorian Cities*, Chapter 3, 1963.
Manchester City Council Proceedings, 1921-2.

## Biography 7.9: Coates

1. Kipling, Rudyard: Poem 'If'.

## Biography 7.12: Barclay

Obituary A E Barclay, *Acta Radiologica*, 1949, *32*, 1-10.
Obituary A E Barlcay, *American Journal of Roentgenology*, 1949, *62*, 119-25.
Obituary A E Barclay, *British Journal of Radiology*, 1949, *22*, 295-99.
Barclay, A E, 1948, Early days of radiology in Manchester, *Manchester University Medical School Gazette*, 115-21.
Barclay, A E, 1949, The old order changes, *British Journal of Radiology*, *22*, 300-308.
Brockbank, William: *The honorary medical staff of Manchester Royal Infirmary*, 1830-1948, 194-6, Manchester University Press, 1965.

## Biography 7.15: Chisholm

1. Chisholm, C, 1924, *Lancet*, *206*, 425-31.

## Biography 7.17: Jefferson

Sir Robert Platt, Bt.
D W C Northfield
Sir Harry Platt, Bt.
Library records
*British Medical Journal*, 1961, *I*, 365

## Biography 7.23: Burn

1. Brockington, Fraser. Obituary notice *Lancet*, 1973.
2. Burn, J L. Causes of failure in medico-social experiments. *Public Health*, 1955, *68*, 149-52.

## Appendix 2: Further biographical notes

The particulars given in this Appendix have been culled mainly from the following sources:
The biographical ('C') files of the Manchester Collection.
Brockbank, E M: *Honorary medical staff of the Manchester Infirmary, 1752-1830* Manchester, Sherratt and Hughes, 1904.

Brockbank, W: Manchester's place in the history of medicine in *Manchester and its Region*, 198-214 British Association, 1962.

*Dictionary of National Biography*: In many volumes including 1961-1970 Ed. Williams, E T and Nicholls, C S Oxford University Press, 1981.

*Graduate Registers* of the Universities of Cambridge, Durham, Edinburgh, Glasgow and Manchester.

*Medical Directories* and *Registers*.

Munk, William: *Roll of the Royal College of Physicians of London*; in five volumes, principally

   Volume 3, 1801 to 1825, Royal College of Physicians, 1878

   Volume 4, 1826 to 1925 Compiled Brown, G H, Royal College of Physicians, 1955

   Volume 5, Continued to 1965 Ed. Trail, Richard R, Royal College of Physicians, 1968

Power, Sir D'Arcy, Spencer, W G and Gask, G E: *Plarr's Lives of the Fellows of the Royal College of Surgeons of England*; in two volumes, 1843 to 1930 Royal College of Surgeons of England, 1930.

Power, Sir D'Arcy and Le Fanu, W R: *Lives of the Fellows of the Royal College of Surgeons of England*, 1930-1951 Royal College of Surgeons, 1953.

*Who was who*: in seven volumes, 1897 to 1980 Adam and Charles Black, London, 1920 to 1981.

INDEX